My Unkept Promise

BY
CURTIS MILLER

MEDITATIONS ON MY LIFE AS A MISSIONARY TO THE MIDDLE EAST

ISBN-13: 978-1-4796-1435-6 (Paperback)
ISBN-13: 978-1-4796-1436-3 (ePub)
Library of Congress Control Number: 2022906226

My Beloved Wife
Joy
and
My Beloved Daughter
Melody Jean Miller Drake

For
Inspiring Me
To Write
This Book

Table of Contents

Introduction

"God Moves in a Mysterious Way" is a Christian hymn, written in 1773 by the English poet William Cowper. His words have long been an inspiration to me:

God moves in a mysterious way His wonders to perform;
He plants His footsteps in the sea and rides upon the storm.
Deep in unfathomable mines of never- ailing skill
He treasures up His bright designs and works His sov'reign will.
Ye fearful saints, fresh courage take; the clouds ye so much dread
Are big with mercy and shall break in blessings on your head.

From my childhood I have felt God's guiding hand upon my shoulder, guiding me in the way He would have me go. I have endeavored to follow His leading in my life. In my mid-teen years, He inspired me to become a minister in the Seventh-day Adventist Church, and this became a reality upon my graduation from Walla Walla College in 1956 when I joined the Montana Conference as a pastor-teacher.

I was inspired to be a missionary by my heritage from my great-uncle, Clarence Rentfro, who was the first Seventh-day Adventist to take the Gospel to Portugal in 1904, and by my great-aunt, Bess Rentfro-Hankins, who with her husband, Winfred, were early missionaries in China.

The ten years I served in the Middle East Division of Seventh-day Adventists were the highlight of my ministry and my life. I will always treasure the six years of 1960–66 when I served in Turkey as President of the Turkish Mission, the year I was on furlough, 1966–67 and was able to attend Andrews University, and the three years I was Ministerial Director of the Middle East Division during which time I lived in Beirut, Lebanon, and ministered in the countries in that region.

Truly God moved in mysterious ways in my life. I thank Him for the many miracles He worked in my life of service to Him.

April 14, 2021
Lyle Curtis Miller

CHAPTER I

Turkey Calling

"Curtis Miller has a long-distance phone call, in the registrar's office," announced the secretary who stuck her head into the classroom. It was Monday, October 5, 1959; I was sitting in my very first class at the Seventh-day Adventist Theological Seminary in Berrien Springs, Michigan. Once on the phone, I heard my Montana Conference President, George Taylor, exclaim, "Curtis, you have just been appointed to mission service in Turkey!"

A tingle of amazement flashed down my spine. I was called to Turkey! How was it possible?

It all began the previous July, while I was leading the Junior Youth at the Montana Campmeeting. Pastor E. E. Roenfelt, a field secretary of the General Conference, was the Sabbath Morning speaker, one of his primary roles being a recruiter for mission service. His sermon that morning was full of thrilling stories from several mission fields. In closing his talk to the juniors, Roenfelt called upon them to dedicate their lives to Christian service, asking, "How many of you boys and girls would like to be a missionary someday?" Hands went up all over the room, and I remember distinctly Pastor Roenfelt turning to fasten his eyes upon me, as I sat behind him on the rostrum. Having dreamed of mission service since early boyhood, my hand, too, was raised.

After the Junior church service was over, Pastor Roenfelt approached me, and asked, "Now, brother Miller, did you truly mean it when you raised your hand?" I assured him that I did, indeed. He immediately handed me the necessary form to apply for mission service, as he said, "Fill this application form out and mail it to the General Conference Secretariat. We will contact you as soon as your application is processed."

Glancing at the forms, I inquired inquired of Pastor Roenfelt, "The Montana Conference is sponsoring me to obtain a graduate degree at the Seminary, beginning fall quarter of '59. If I submit these forms now, will it jeopardize my Seminary degree program?"

"How long will it take you to complete the degree," he queried?

"I will need four quarters," I replied.

"Then I will arrange for you to receive a mission appointment about a month prior to your graduation, which will give you time to arrange your affairs, visit family, and then you can proceed overseas."

As a fifth-generation Seventh-day Adventist, with several forebears who had pioneered the "Three Angel's Message" to several countries, the blood of missionaries flowed in my veins. Great-uncle Clarence Rentfro, along with his wife Mary (Haskell), was the first Adventist minister to Portugal, in 1904. Around that same time great aunt Bess, with her husband Winfred Hankins, sailed to China. A cousin, Joelle Rentfro, served as a medical doctor in India. The Rentfro and Hankins branch of my family grew up in the Sigourney, Iowa, area and then attended Union College in Nebraska, when the Seventh-day Adventist Church was young. They were involved with the early SDA youth motto: "This Gospel to All the World in This Generation." That "generation" was almost passed from the scene when I was born. My generation was now to pick up the "Gospel Trumpet," and I was motivated to blow that trumpet with all my might.

Many were the thrilling mission stories I heard about those faraway countries, from Uncle Clarence, and aunts Mary and Bess, and from my cousins, who were born or raised in Portugal, Brazil, or China. Add to this the blessings I received from attending Seventh-day Adventist schools, where as an elementary school student I was a member of the "JMV"—the Junior Missionary Volunteer Society. Each Wednesday morning we students conducted JMV meetings, as the school day began. At each meeting we repeated the JMV pledge, which included "I will go on God's errands." To me that meant I would be a missionary to foreign lands!

My generation was now to pick up the "Gospel Trumpet," and I was motivated to blow that trumpet with all my might.

My dream of mission service was almost dashed when Uncle Clarence preached in the small church in the small town of Orange, California. I was in my first grade of elementary school. Oh, yes, he did relate those thrilling mission stories amidst his sermon on the importance of preparing for the second coming of Christ, all of which raised my motivation to be a missionary. I was quick to shake hands with my uncle after the preaching service, but instead of grasping my hand, he placed his hand atop my head, saying to my parents, "Curtis will never grow up." I knew I was short for a boy my age, and I took his words to mean I would not "grow up" in height, a disastrous thought! But Uncle Clarence solemnly continued, "No, Curtis will not have a chance to grow up, because the Lord is coming soon." World War II had just commenced, motivating preachers of various denominations to declare, "The end of the world is upon us." I needed to be quick in doing my part to take the Gospel to all the world in "my generation."

An SDA colporteur spoke at my church, telling stories about how he witnessed for Christ as he sold SDA books door to door. "That is something I can do now," I told myself. The Adventist Book Center (often simply called the ABC) was right on the route I walked home from church school. I wasted no time going to there. Approaching the lady at the sales counter, I said, "I want to be a colporteur to help finish the Gospel work." I am ever thankful that lady did not laugh at a nine-year-old boy making such a request. She took me seriously and escorted me to the office of the man who directed colporteurs and he, too, took me seriously. He supplied me with a small stock of children's Bible story books, and I soon was going door to door as a bonafide colporteur minister. I didn't set a record in sales, but I felt great being a part of God's work! My commission on sales was another blessing for it provided partial funds for me to go to Youth Camp, the next summer.

Youth Camp was for kids 10–15 years old. Many of my 5th grade cohorts were going, for they were ten years old, but I was only nine because I entered first grade a year younger than the norm. Nonetheless, I filled out the camp application form, gathered my lifesavings, which consisted of the $3 in book sale commission and $2 saved from my weekly allowance of 25 cents. This left me $5 shy of the $10 camp fee for in those bygone years ten days at camp cost $10, so I sold my old second-hand bike for $5 and went to the Youth Director's office which was in the same building as the Adventist Book Center. I placed the application and all my money on the secretary's desk, saying, "I want to go to Junior Camp." Glancing at my application form, that required my date of birth, she said, "But you are only nine; you are too young."

I gulped in despair, but gathered courage to quickly say, "But I'm in the 5th grade, and many of my classmates are going. Please, please, let me go!"

"I can't give you permission," she replied, "but you can talk to the youth director; he will be the one who decides whether you can go to camp this year."

She led me into the office of Pastor William Loveless, Youth Director of the Southern California Conference of SDA. When I saw his name on his desk my heart plummeted for with a name like that—Loveless—I wondered if he would possibly give permission. I uttered a silent prayer as Pastor Loveless' secretary gave him my application and briefed him about my request! Pastor Loveless, God bless him, took time to listen to me, about my dream of mission service, about my right now being a colporteur minister.

Eliciting from me a commitment to "not get homesick" during camp and to do my camp duties which consisted of making my bed each morning, helping keep the cabin neat and clean, setting the tables at mealtime, and waking up promptly when the rising bugle was blown, he gave his permission. In my mind I changed the good pastor's name from Loveless to Lovemuch.

You can be certain I was a model camper at Camp Cedar Falls, in the Angeles National Forest in the San Bernardino Mountains. Cabins were inspected each day, and I never failed to ensure my bed and immediate area were immaculate. Points were given for inspection. Camp Cedar Falls, my first year at camp, had many cabins, with four sets of bunkbeds, where eight boys could sleep. But there were not sufficient cabins to house all the boys who wanted to attend, so a whole row of tents, also sleeping eight, were pitched and was captioned the "E Division." My tent never lost a single point during the ten-day camp. The E Division had the most points of all the divisions at Camp Cedar Falls. Pastor Loveless commended us to be known as "The Honored E Division," which meant our division, and my tent, had the honor or raising or lowering the flag more than any other division! My attending Youth Camp and Cedar Falls gave me the knowledge of how to fulfill the JMV Pledge to "Go on God's Errands."

Years later Pastor Loveless became the pastor of the Eugene, Oregon, district of churches, of which the church of my youth, at Junction City, Oregon, was a part. Elder Loveless remembered me, from my attending Camp Cedar Falls, the years of 1944–45. What I learned from that wonderful camp director, Pastor Loveless—I mean LoveMuch—served me well when I started the SDA youth camp in Turkey, in 1963, but that is another story that will be in another chapter of my autobiography.

While at camp I met many pastors and missionaries. Two were most memorable to me: Pastors Eric B. Hare, missionary to Burma, and Adlai Esteb, missionary to China. Both men held me spellbound by their mission stories around the evening campfires.

At that camp, Pastor Esteb taught a vocational honor class in rocks and minerals, which I took. It sparked my lifelong interest in collecting rocks. Esteb also gave me a geode, a hollow rock formation, which he cracked open for me; I was amazed by the quartz crystal formations inside. Several years later, when a boyhood neighbor, Chet Norris, was "rock hounding," he took me with him to a ranch in central Oregon to grub for moss and plume agate. He had a diamond saw to cut hard rocks, which I used and I was able to cut and polish a number of agates; years later, when I was in mission service, I stored my collection with my parents. My mother was teaching an eight-grade, one-room school at that time; to my dismay she used my rock collection to reward students for outstanding performance in reading!

Pastor Esteb crossed my path of life years later. He stopped by the mission field in Turkey, where I served and spent several days with the Miller family. He was pleased when I reminded him of his giving me the geode when I was nine years old. He was even more pleased to learn he was a part of inspiring me to mission service. He also imprinted in my memory that the Holy City, the New Jerusalem, is laid on twelve foundations of precious stones. He inspired me to determine that someday I will see those brilliant foundation stones with my own eyes, one for each of the twelve apostles. Like Abraham of old, I continue to "look for a city whose builder and maker is God."

When I was fourteen, I was appointed Missionary Volunteer Leader of the small Junction City, Oregon, Seventh-day Adventist Church, which position also made me a member of the church board at age fourteen. This boyhood church had much to do with molding me for mission service. It was during a Wednesday evening prayer meeting that the presiding elder gave opportunity for "a few to give a personal testimony." I remember standing to my feet, to declare simply, "I will go where HE wants me to go."

When I filled out those forms, applying for mission service, there was a question: Where would you like to serve as a missionary? I paused there, thinking, "Do I want to serve in

Brazil, following in the footsteps of Uncle Clarence; or would it be China, were Aunt Bess served?" Then I remembered Pastor Eric Hare and his thrilling stories of his Burma experience, "Should I volunteer for Burma?" Hare was the master storyteller from my junior camp experience. His stories from his mission service were full of suspense, holding the attention of children—and even adults—as they sat breathlessly on the edge of their seats. Hare was a primary mentor to me, for I still love to tell stories. One of his classic stories was about Peep Peep, a baby chick, and Old Mr. Hiss, a snake who pursued Peep Peep. In observing him and his mastery of vocal narrative, he became my inspiration in the art of storytelling. To this day I still love to tell stories, which is a prime purpose of my writing this book.

But, it's time to go back to the question, "What country should I choose for my field of mission service?" I pondered long and hard and was reminded of a story my cousin Beryl, daughter of Aunt Bess, told me about a happening with a baby chick when she was a small girl in China.

"I was born in Amoy Kulangsu, China," related Beryl, as she began her story. "We lived in the interior of China, where there were few non-Chinese. I remember times when we walked in the streets, the Chinese would shout at us, 'There go the foreign devils,' as they threw garbage at us. My sister Enid and I had no one to play with but ourselves. One of our hens hatched some chicks, which made me very happy, for Momma Bess let me choose one for my very own. My chicky was so soft and I loved to hold it against my cheek and hear it go 'peep, peep, peep.' For several days I played with my chicky. I made a nest in a small box, where it could sleep at night right by my own bed. I would hold ground grain in my hand and the chicky would eat right from it. Oh, I had fun with my chicky, until one tragic day." Beryl was silent for a few moments, as in her memory she relived the event.

"It was Momma Bess's day to do the ironing. She didn't have an electric iron, way back then. Instead she had a set of flat irons that she would heat on the wood-burning kitchen stove. She would use one iron until it became too cool, then she would set it back on the stove to get hot, and take another in her hand to continue ironing our clothes. That morning I was playing nearby, with my chicky. The chick was running around the floor, and sometimes even ran near Momma's feet, or under the ironing board.

"As Momma changed irons, she selected the largest one, that weighed about ten pounds. It was very, very hot when she picked it up. As she turned from the stove to the ironing board, hot iron in hand, my chicky ran between her feet. She stumbled as she avoided stepping on my chick, and dropped the iron. It came down, with a thud, landing right on top of my chicky. Momma let out a cry, as she picked up the iron. I saw my chicky was smashed flat.

"Momma stooped, picked up my chick as she said, 'O, Beryl, I'm afraid I've killed your chick when I dropped the iron on it.'

"I ran to Momma, took my chick, held it in both hands, put it against my cheek, but chicky did not make a single peep, but just laid limp in my hands.

"Still holding my chick in my hands, I ran sobbing to my own bed, where I knelt down on my knees, and prayed, 'Dear Jesus, please make my chicky well again, so I will have it to play with again.' And do you know, Curtis, as I was praying, and holding my chicky in both hands, I felt it wiggle a bit. I put my chicky against my cheek and heard a small 'peep.' I opened my hands and my chicky jumped out to the floor, where it ran around going 'peep, peep, peep' again. I was so happy Jesus answered my prayer."

Beryl's story held me in wonder, but I was also skeptical, so when I next saw Aunt Bess I asked her if Beryl's story was really true. "Curtis," she replied, "when I picked that chick up, it was very flat. The iron had been so hot it scorched the chick. I was quite certain the chick could not live. I followed Beryl into her room. I saw her kneel down, holding her chick in her hands. I heard her simple prayer to Jesus, and I do believe Beryl's prayer was heard. You know, Jesus loves to answer the prayers of little children."

I have never forgotten that story, for it was a lifelong lesson for me to go to God in prayer to answer my own needs. As I filled out the form to apply for overseas mission service, I thought of Uncle Clarence and Brazil. I remembered Beryl's story and wondered if I should write "Brazil" or "China" in the space asking where I wanted to serve. Then, remembering my boyhood testimony, "I will go where HE wants me to go," I wrote in the space, "Send me where no one else wants to go."

I heard her simple prayer to Jesus, and I do believe Beryl's prayer was heard. You know, Jesus loves to answer the prayers of little children.

Now, called from my first Seminary class, I held the phone to my ear, to hear Pastor Taylor, my Montana Conference President, informing me that I would be sent to Turkey. I remembered my church school studies in geography and history, so I was aware of Turkey's strategic location when it headed the Ottoman Empire. I remembered reading of the time when Napoleon sought to unite Europe under his rule. He sat on a barge in the middle of the Elbe River with Czar Nicholas of Russia as they met to divide much of Europe and Asia between them. The Czar demanded to have the Bosporus, that strait of water dividing Europe from Asia that led from the Black Sea to the Sea of Marmara, and thence to the Aegean and Mediterranean Seas. If Russia controlled the Bosporus, it would have an ice-free, all-weather route to the Middle East, North Africa, Southern Europe, and the vast Atlantic Ocean.

"Never!" exclaimed Napoleon, "He who holds the Bosporus holds the world." What I did not know about Turkey was that it was a mission attached to the recently formed Middle East Division of the General Conference of Seventh-day Adventists.

I marvel at the providences of God, how He brings a man and a country together, for it was the previous Friday afternoon, October

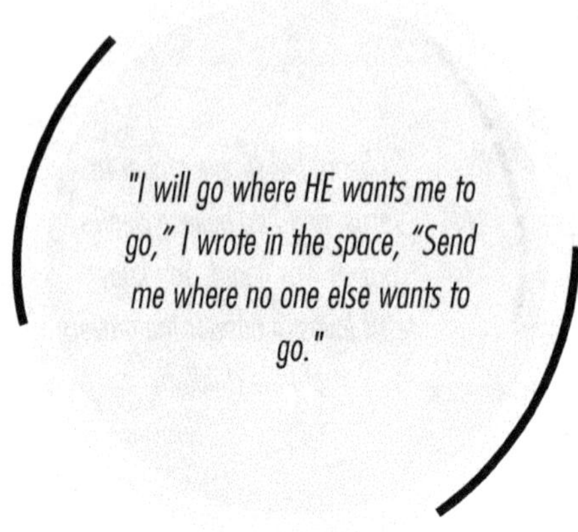

2, 1959, that my path of life crossed that of Pastor James Russell. When the Miller family left Montana, for Berrien Springs, Michigan, a couple weeks prior, we pulled a small U-Haul® Trailer behind our '59 Chevrolet Station Wagon which contained personal items we would need during our year at the Seminary. It also held a new Wurlitzer console piano.

When we arrived on campus the Garland Apartments were not ready for occupancy, so the Seminary hurriedly made arrangements for arriving students to be temporarily housed in a summer tourist camp on the banks of the nearby St. Joseph River. The cottages there were built only for warm, summer housing, for the windows and doors contained no glass, but only screens to allow fresh air to keep the cottages cool as possible during the hot and humid Michigan summers.

We had arrived in Berrien Springs, Michigan, in late September. By October summer was definitely over and the nights were growing chill and damp—which was not good for a piano in a cottage with no windows or heat. I decided to rent a house, for the sake of the piano. We found a very small, three-room house, at low cost. It was on that Friday, October 2, that I asked the gentleman in the cottage next to us if he could help me unload the piano at the house we had rented. The gentleman was James Russell.

As we unloaded the piano, I asked him where he was from. He informed me he was on furlough from Middle East College, in Beirut, Lebanon. I asked him what mission work was like in the Middle East. His story was one of miracles in an area of the world most difficult for Christian mission work.

James Russell briefly related to me an overview of his mission experience. "I, with my wife, Carolyn, and infant daughter, were being sent to serve in Africa. We sailed on the S.S. Zamzam, an Egyptian ship under orders from the British Admiralty, during the early months of WWII, prior to the U.S. entering that war. The Zam Zam was sunk by a German 'Pocket Battleship,' the Atlantis, for the battleship flew many varied flags as it preyed primarily on British ships in the South Atlantic.

Jim was Canadian and his wife, Carolyn, was a United States' citizen. They, with their baby daughter, who was listed on her mother's U.S. Passport, were sailing to an African country where they were to serve as missionaries. "When my family, along with all others on the stricken Zam Zam, abandoned ship, we were picked up by the Atlantis, which took us to a French Port under German control. I was interned in a German prisoner of war camp for the duration of WWII, while Carolyn and our daughter were returned to the neutral United States, where she served as Dean of Women at Atlantic Union College."

The Russell's were reunited after WWII and "then we were sent to work in Jerusalem," continued Jim. "We were there when Palestine was partitioned, in the late 1940s, between Israel and Trans-Jordan. During ensuing Arab-Israeli strife we had to evacuate Jerusalem and were transferred to the Egyptian SDA Mission, which we had to evacuate during the '56 Suez War. Still later, we were sent to Middle East College, in Beirut, from which we had to evacuate during the '67 Arab-Israeli War. It seems that wherever I go in mission service, war erupts and my family is forced to evacuate," concluded Jim.

My primary memory of what Jim related to me that October day, now so long ago, is that mission work in the Middle East Division was, and still is, fraught with danger of war, revolution, persecution, and is very challenging. Jim closed his conversation by saying, "You can labor for years and only baptize one or two persons; very few of them are Muslims; converts come mainly from the Christian sector of the population."

As we parted I remarked "I think the Middle East Division is the last place on earth I would want to serve."

As we moved into our small house, that Friday, I did not realize Turkey was a part of the Middle East Division, nor did I know that two days earlier, when at the weekly meeting of the General Conference Mission Committee, I had been appointed to serve in Turkey. Before I had said the Middle East was the last place I would want to serve, God had already called me to Turkey.

A few days later I met Pastor Hovik Saraffian, an Armenian from Iran, who was studying at the Seminary. When he found out I was called to Turkey, he solemnly shook his head, as he gravely intoned, "I feel sorry for you for you are going to the hardest place on earth." I later learned that I was called to Turkey because the General Conference could find no one else willing to go. I accepted the mission appointment, nonetheless.

At the time I accepted the call, I thought I would still be able to complete my year's graduate study at the Seminary, but it was not to be. The General Conference informed me that I was needed in Turkey immediately. The Miller's applied for U.S. Passports and began preparing to sail to Turkey "as soon as possible."

The May 19, 1960, Review & Herald published the following notice that the Miller Family had sailed for Turkey on April 8:

> *Mr. and Mrs. Lyle Curtis Miller and two children, of Berrien Springs, Michigan, sailed from New York City on the S.S. Hellas, April 8, going to Istanbul, Turkey. Prior to marriage Sister Miller's name was Phyllis Ann Edwards. She attended Walla Walla College, and has had experience as a church school teacher. Brother Miller is a graduate of Walla Walla College and also has taken work at Potomac University (Michigan campus). His experience has been as a church school teacher and pastor-evangelist in the Montana Conference. He has accepted appointment to Turkey as a teacher-evangelist.*

CHAPTER II

My Family Tree

I have a theory about life. I do not know if I originated it, or whether I learned it from sources and ways of which I am unaware. The theory is this: in order to know where I want to go, I need to know where I am at the present; in order to know where I am at the present, I need to know from whence I have come. Therefore, I will now address my ancestry, and I begin with the paternal side of my family.

My father was Lyle Monroe Miller, born February 17, 1908, in Canyon Creek, Lewis & Clark County, Montana; died in March, 1979, in my rural home on Wagon Road, near Colbert, north of Spokane, Washington. Lyle, my father, was the kindest man I have ever known. My mother was born November 12, 1913, in Missoula, Montana, and died in Colbert in March, 1984.

Lyle Monroe Miller and Cora Lynn Hiatt-Miller

My parents met at Mount Ellis Academy, located in Bozeman, Montana, where they were both students. After mother graduated from Mount Ellis Academy—the spring of '32—my parents married on September 18, 1932, at the home of mother's parents in Arlee, Montana.

After their marriage Lyle and Cora Lynn drove to Madison, Tennessee (about ten miles north of Nashville) to attend Madison College. Madison College was founded in 1904, under the visionary inspiration of Ellen White. This college was unique in offering a work/study program wherein a student could work for the college and earn their tuition and living expenses. A story entitled "Madison College, the College with a Built-in Pocket Book," appeared in the *Reader's Digest* magazine, telling how students could work at campus industries to earn their college education.

Lyle enrolled to become a nurse, while Cora Lynn studied to be an elementary school teacher. My father, to earn his way through Madison, worked as an orderly in Madison Sanitarium, where he cared for W. C. "Willy" White, son of Ellen G. White, one of the founders of the Seventh-day Adventist Church. Dad told me that Willy related to him many homespun stories about his mother's very interesting life. Shortly after beginning college Dad had acute appendicitis which resulted in surgery. The medical bill for the surgery and hospital stay quite depleted my parents' financial resources during the early years of the Great Depression triggered by the Wall Street Stock Market crash of 1929. Consequently, Mom and Dad got into their Model A jalopy and drove back to Arlee. They had barely any money to make that trip. When they arrived at the Mississippi River, it was all they could do to scrape together fifty cents to pay the toll to cross a bridge. For the rest of the trip they skimped on meals and rested in the Model A when they were tired. Finally, they arrived in Arlee—quite broke.

James was an engineer on the Great Northern Railroad for many years. After he retired, he moved to Spokane, Washington. I would like to be able to say James and Mary had a long and happy life together, but they did not. In the early 1930s Grandma Mary wanted their children to have an Adventist education, so she persuaded Grandpa James to move the family to Mount Ellis Academy, near Bozeman, Montana. My father, along with his mother and some siblings, joined the SDA Church, but James did not. It was during the Great Depression, and James could not find employment in the area; consequently, he wanted to return to Great Falls where he had worked for the railroad. Mary did not want to do so and remained with the family at Mount Ellis and James returned to Great Falls. Shortly after their separation James divorced Mary and married again in Great Falls. After his retirement and the death of his second wife, James moved to Spokane, where he lived in a boarding house, until his death. While living in Spokane he was finally baptized into the SDA Church. I was pastoring churches in north-central Montana at that time and lived in Conrad when he passed away. Grandma Mary, after the divorce, lived in various places—southern California, Oregon, and finally in Montana. Grandma Mary was an excellent cook (she made the best buttermilk biscuits I have ever tasted) and would often "disappear" to go cook on a ranch. She was cooking on a ranch near Conrad when James died and when she learned he had passed away she phoned me, saying, "Curtis, I want you to arrange to send $200 dollars to assist James' funeral, because I know he died without adequate funds." I fulfilled her request.

Paternal Grandparents

Mary Abie Mathison-Miller, born near Bangor, Maine, in 1884; died October 5, 1979, Missoula County, Montana.

James Monroe Miller, born in Missouri November 1, 1881; died December 10, 1958, Spokane, Washington.

They were married December 19, 1905.

I am a fifth-generation Seventh-day Adventist, and am thankful for my heritage. My great-great maternal grandparents

Paternal Great-Grandparents

Zebulon William Monroe Miller, born February 10, 1841, Donegal, Westmorland County, Pennsylvania; died November 14, 1920, Helena, Montana.

Sarah Lydia McLeland-Miller, born May 28, 1853, Kokomo, Howard County, Indiana;died April 5, 1923, Helena, Montana.

are Benjamin Franklin Curtis (December 13, 1823, Scott County, Kentucky–March 4, 1916, Sibley, Iowa) and Amanda Howling-Curtis (March 1827–May 10, 1865, Iowa City, Iowa). She married Benjamin Curtis on May 4, 1844. They were Millerites who experienced the Great Disappointment of October 22, 1844, believing Jesus' second coming would occur on that date.

Amanda, which means "beloved," emigrated from Ireland in 1835. She became a Millerite in 1843, married Benjamin in the spring of 1844, and together they looked forward to Jesus' second coming on October 22 of that year. Alas! Jesus did not come on that date; William Miller had the prophetic date correct, but the event wrong. Out of the Millerite movement emerged the "Adventist" movement, believers of which still look forward to Christ's second coming today. After the Great Disappointment of 1844 Benjamin and Amanda continued to study the Scriptures. They resided in Iowa where they were visited by several Seventh-day Sabbath keepers, as can be learned from the accompanying letter dated October 1857 authored by Benjamin. From them they learned that the seventh day is the Sabbath. Amanda began keeping the Sabbath in 1851 and Benjamin six years later, as the following two letters to the *Review & Herald* indicate. Benjamin and Amanda are the first generation of Seventh-day Adventists in my family.

Benjamin and Amanda maintained a hospitable home and had many early SDA pioneers visit them, including Joseph Bates and James and Ellen White. Several children were born to Benjamin and Amanda, among them are Aurilla and Mary. Ellen once told Amanda, "The Lord is pleased with the way you are raising your children." Aurilla (born December 11, 1851) was my great-grandmother and she was fourteen when her mother passed away. She attended William Penn College, Oskaloosa, Iowa., where she trained as a nurse, which enabled her to treat successfully the sick in her family, and her neighbors as well. Mary, too, wanted an education, so Aurilla agreed to work to support Mary in going to Battle Creek to be educated. While there, Mary lived in the home of James and Ellen White. Aurilla became employed as a nanny to the children of widower James Allen Rentfro, who was a Civil War veteran. James was wounded in a leg at the Battle of Iuka, September 19, 1862, in Mississippi. After the war he had a 200-acre farm near Sigourney, Iowa. In time James and Aurilla married and had eight children of their own: John Rentfro, who died at age fifteen when he fell from a horse; Clarence Rentfro, who became an SDA minister and was the first SDA minister to Portugal in 1904 (Clarence and his wife Mary Haskell also spent twenty-nine years as missionaries to the Amazon); Bessie Rentfro married Winfred Hankins and they were missionaries in China in 1906; Harley Rentfro was an SDA minister who was departmental director in the Nevada-Utah Conference; Curtis Rentfro was a medical doctor (I was named after him and he had a positive influence on my life); Earl Rentfro lived in Florida and was involved with a labor union; Clark Rentfro homesteaded near Arlee, Montana (Rentfro Lane leads to where his ranch was); Bonita Rentfro was my maternal grandmother who married Albert Corrie Hiatt on December 25, 1912 (Corrie was the Bureau of Indian Affairs administrator of the Flathead Indian Reservation and was also a U.S. Marshal). I'll talk more about the family later, but now back to Amanda and Benjamin...

Amanda wrote a letter to the *Review & Herald*, October 1851:

> *Dear Brethren and Sisters: I feel it a duty to add my testimony to the truth. I became a believer in the Advent doctrine in 1843. I have passed through many trials and temptations. Sometimes the Lord has blessed me much, and at other times I have been almost in despair; but out of all these times the Lord has delivered me, praise His holy name. I embraced the Sabbath about six years ago, and have been struggling on alone ever since, having no one with me but my little children. How I wish some messenger of God would come and proclaim the last message of mercy to the*

Benjamin and Amanda Curtis

inhabitants of this city. Why do they not come? Dear children of God, pray for me and my family, that we may be accounted worthy to escape all those things that are coming upon the earth, and most of all God's saints in the kingdom. (Signed) Yours striving for eternal life, Amanda Curtis

In October of 1857 Benjamin wrote, from Iowa City, his letter to the *Review*:

Bro. Smith [then R&H Editor] I feel constrained to add my testimony to the truth. Seven and a half years ago, while residing in Aurora, Ind., a Bro. Case came along and presented God's holy law, and some facts concerning the Third Angel's Message; but I could not get any faith in him. Some months after, Br. H. Edson (God bless him) came along, and as he came up to my front door, said to me, "Is the love of God in this house?" I replied, "It is said, If ye love Me, ye will keep My commandments." The brother spends his time and money, it seemed, just to save me and my companion. He talked until eleven or twelve o'clock that night, and we parted; and I commenced to fight the Sabbath. But my dear wife became firmer in the faith. Not long after, Bro. J.N. Andrews (God bless him. I always love him) came and talked of the commandments, and the faith of Jesus, and so on, to us; and he almost persuaded me to be a Christian. I believe if he had stopped one day longer with me, I should have taken hold of the Sabbath. Now some six years ago, from Aurora we moved to Cincinnati, and from there to Glendale, Ohio, and spent nearly three years; and about this time our brother H.E. Carver moved to Iowa City. I took a notion of following, telling my wife that when we got there, if she would go, I would keep the Sabbath; but alas! I began build and get gain, and forgot my promise. But thank my heavenly Father, Brn. Waggoner [Joseph Waggoner, father of Elet Waggoner who sparked to "Righteousness by Faith" movement at the 1888 General Conference session in Minneapolis] and Hull came along with the Tent, though against my will. After the tent meeting; when we came to part, I told them I was sorry to see

> *them go away. We had a good meeting. Several came out, and there are several convinced that the Sabbath of the Lord is truth, that I think would come out if we could have some more preaching. I hope my dear brother Waggoner will come this way soon. May the Lord direct Bro Hull so that he can spend some months with us again.*
>
> *I wish to say that for fourteen years or more, I have used the filthy weed, tobacco; but through Bro. W's influence, and the grace of God I threw it to the winds. That night I had a hard struggle. I recollect one gracious prayer we had at my house, while Bro. [James] White led in prayer, especially for me. Well, praise the Lord, the Review, though once I hated it, and took it up to make sport over it, it is now a welcome messenger, and you may send it along in my name. O I can sympathize with the lonely ones of the faith of Jesus. I pray God to keep me in that hour of trial, and from the plagues of the seven last vials. Your brother in love. Benjamin F. Curtis*

Thus, Benjamin and Amanda were "Seventh-day" Adventists even before the Seventh-day Adventist Church was formally organized in 1863. Benjamin and Amanda had two daughters who also contribute to my heritage: my great-grandmother, Aurilla Curtis-Rentfro (November 11, 1851, Cincinnati, Ohio to June 12, 1925, Arlee, Montana), and Mary Eliza Curtis-Northrup (January 19, 1856, Iowa City, Iowa to January 16, 1912, College View, Nebraska).

Both Aurilla and Mary desired to go to Battle Creek College, but necessary funds for both attending simultaneously were lacking so the sisters agreed Aurilla would work to support Mary going to Battle Creek, then Mary would work to enable Aurilla to go.

While in Battle Creek Mary lived in the home of Ellen White. Her behavior was problematic to the Whites, which resulted in the following letter being penned to Mary, when she was sixteen:

Aledo, Mercer Co., Illinois
June 2, 1878
Dear Sister Mary,

I feel anxious in regard to you. I am fearful you will cause Sister Abbey anxiety and care by your careless forgetfulness and your reckless, lawless ways. This we cannot have. If you have not at your age respect enough for yourself to try to improve your habits, it is no use for others to have the burden of you, and they be constantly harassed and perplexed by your course.

It is too bad, Mary. You know how to behave if you would only do as well as you know.

I have talked with you much in regard to correcting some of your habits. First you need to improve in regard to talking too much. Your tongue is in motion so much of the time you have no room for thoughts. You should know that nearly all that are acquainted with you think you a hopeless case. They do not hesitate to say, "You cannot make anything of Mary. You may talk and talk, and she will regard your words only while you are saying them. She will do just the same in two days after you have talked with her." I have found this to be entirely correct, to my sorrow.

Second, I have learned by experience that you are lawlessly free and reckless if you dare to be. You take liberties you should not. You do not consult or ask for advice, but move forward on your own responsibility, glad of an opportunity of having your own way. This you will have to correct or be homeless.

I noticed you have a habit of being determined to have your own way, and you are in danger of coming to womanhood undisciplined, with all your bad habits confirmed upon you for life.

Now is the time, Mary, for you to act; to be earnest, sincere, and faithful. I am sorry that things have occurred that have led me to greatly distrust you. I am constantly fearful you will take things not your own and appropriate them to yourself. You take liberties that I cannot have, Mary. Your habit of loving to eat the good things, is a temptation for you to indulge your appetite and choose not to come to the table when others eat.

Now, Mary, we love you too well to let you have your own way. We will lay down some rules for you to heed strictly. If you do not, we can no longer provide a home for you or take any interest in your obtaining an education. If you are determined to go to ruin, you must go.

We now want you to go to the Health Institute and there be disciplined. You have strength, and you can employ your strength to good account if you are so disposed, but if you prefer to follow your own inclination rather than duty, we can no longer interest ourselves for you. We mean what we say when we tell you that you must change your course or be left homeless. If you feel under no obligation to do as we feel, then it is our duty to tell you, we feel under no obligation to have any further care in your case.

Ellen G. White

Mary evidently mended her ways, for she stayed on in the White home. Her obituary was recorded in the *Review and Herald*, March 21, 1912:

Mary Eliza Curtis was the daughter of Benjamin Franklin and Amanda Howling-Curtis. Her father and mother were pioneers of the 1844 Seventh- day Adventist movement. At the age of twelve Mary was baptized into the Seventh-day Adventist Church, and remained a faithful member throughout her life.

When Mary was nine years old her mother, Amanda, died. While a young woman, Mary spent some time in Battle Creek, Michigan, making her home with Mrs. E.G. White and in the home of other families. At the age of 20 she was married to George Northrup. They had two daughters, and an adopted daughter.

Mary's life was devoted to the service of humanity, as she was possessed with the one purpose of making the world better by serving others.

My Great Grandparents James Allen and Aurilla Dunning Curtis-Rentfro
They had nine children together; Rentfro is a Scottish family name.

Aurilla was never blessed by studying in Battle Creek, for at the time Mary was there, Aurilla took a position as a nanny for a widower, James Allen Rentfro (January 10, 1834, Sangamon County, Illinois—March 14, 1908, Mount. Pleasant, Iowa) and his several children. Ultimately Aurilla married James on September 1, 1874, in Oskaloosa, Iowa. In addition to her step-children, she gave birth to sons Harley, Clarence, and Curtis, and daughters Bess, and my Grandma Bonita (May 3, 1891, Sigourney, Iowa—March 26, 1964, College Place, Washington). James was a Civil War veteran who was wounded in battle. After the war he acquired a 200-acre farm near Sigourney, Iowa, where he lived and farmed until his death. (In the early 1990s I visited Sigourney and found a plat map showing the location of the farm, which showed a creek running through it, with a significant "Ox-Bow" in it, right in the center of the plat. I climbed a hill that looked out on the area and spotted that ox-bow. In the local cemetery I also found a grave marker that simply said, "Civil War Veteran."):

Birth: January 10, 1834

Sangamon, Illinois

Death: March 14, 1908

Mount Pleasant

Henry County

Iowa, USA

Civil War Veteran

Co F 5th Iowa Infantry

Co H 23rd Veteran Reserve Corps

From military records:

Rentfro, James A. Age 27.

Residence Keokuk County, IA,

Nativity Illinois.

Enlisted July 3, 1861, as Corporal.

Mustered July 15, 1861.

Promoted Sergeant Aug. 10, 1862.

Severely wounded in calf of left leg Sept. 19, 1862, Iuka, Miss. Transferred to Invalid Corps March 15, 1864. No further record.

Based on enlistment participated in the battles of New Madrid & Island # 10, Siege of Corinth, MS (Apr 2-May 30,1862) Battle of Iuka (Sep 19) where regiment won high honors by holding its ground against four times its numbers, making 3 charges with bayonet when all ammunition was exhausted. Out of 480 engaged, the 5th lost 220 killed and wounded.

From Civil War Pension Index:

James applied for invalid pension Jun 9 1873 in Iowa. His widow, Aurilla Rentfro, applied for his pension May 8 1908 in Nebraska.

Rentfro Home in Sigourney, Iowa

In Front of Farmhouse in Sigourney, Iowa

Back Row, Left to Right: Three brothers of James Allen Rentfro—John, William, Joseph, then Charles Curtis Rentfro.

Middle Row, Left to Right: Aurilla Dunning Curtis Rentfro, James Allen Rentfro (white beard), Bessie (with shawl), Harley A. Rentfro, Earl Rentfro, Clarence Emerson Rentfro (far right).

Front Row, Left to Right: J. Clarkson, Bonita N.

Clarence Emerson Rentfro—
Parents: James Allen Rentfro, Aurilla Dunning Curtis Rentfro
Uncles: John, William, and Joseph
Brothers: Charles Curtis Rentfro, Harley A. Rentfro, Earl Rentfro, J. Clarkson
Sisters: Bessie, Bonita
The Four Rentfro Brothers: James Allen, William T., Jospeh, and John are here

Granddad Corrie was the Bureau of Indian Affairs Administrator of the Flathead Indian Reservation, until he retired in 1932, when he built Hideaway Lodge.

Elizabeth's brother was Captain Stidham of the Union Army during the Civil War; he was killed in the Battle of Kennesaw Mountain, June 27, 1864. I have a framed portion of his shirt that he wore.

Grandparents Corrie and Bonita Rentfro Hiatt

Albert Corrie Hiatt born February 1, 1870, Indianapolis, Indiana; died April 30, 1938, Missoula, Montana. Married Bonita December 25, 1912. Bonita born May 3, 1891, Sigourney, Iowa; died March 26, 1964, College Place, Washington.

Hideaway Lodge, near Arlee, Montana, where the Hiatt Family lived until Corrie died in 1938. This picture was taken the day of my Granddad Corrie's funeral.

Home of Corrie and Bonita on Flathead Reservation.

Grandma Bonita, in 1906, became a student at Union College, where her Aunt Mary was living. When her father, James, passed away in 1908, she went to Arlee, Montana, to live with her older brother, Clark Rentfro, who had homesteaded there. Rentfro Lane, where he lived, is still on the map of Arlee. While living in Arlee, Bonita became engaged to a young Seventh-day Adventist minister serving in that area. One day Corrie Hiatt,

Great Grandparents Riley and Elizabeth Stidham, Corrie's parents

a United States Marshal and Bureau of Indian Affairs for the Flathead Reservation, came knocking at her door, saying, "I have a message for you to give your fiancé. You tell him that if he is not out of Montana territory within 48 hours, I will arrest him for bootlegging whisky to the Indians." Grandma relayed that message to the minister, who said, "I will go north, into Canada, and when I am settled, I will send for you." Bonita never heard from him again.

However, Marshal Hiatt continued to call on Bonita, and courted her. They were married on December 25, 1912. They then traveled by train to Spokane, for their honeymoon, where Corrie wanted to buy her an ostrich-plumed hat—such hats were very much in style at the time. Bonita declined the offer, saying, "Adventist ladies do not wear such showy hats." The following Sabbath Corrie and Bonita attended an SDA church and were seated behind a lady with an ostrich-plumed hat that was so large it blocked their view of the pulpit. That woman wearing it was the pastor's wife. Corrie looked at his new bride, then at the hat, and went "Humpt!"

Grandad Corrie, since he was a government employee, was given a very fine house to live in. While living there, my mother,

Cora Lynn, and her younger sisters, Joelle and Jean, and younger brother, Ross, were born.

> *"I will go north, into Canada, and when I am settled, I will send for you." Bonita never heard from him again*

As a marshal and reservation administrator, Corrie was challenged to deal with bootleggers of illegal alcoholic beverages to the Native Americans. He carried a Smith & Wesson .38 caliber pistol. Corrie, born of a Quaker family in Richmond, Indiana, was a pacifist, and in his duties of combating bootleggers, he was in several gun-battles. In these gun fights he never shot to kill, but he did wound. His philosophy was, "If I wound them, and they get away, sooner or later I will catch them," and he often did.

As a U.S. Marshal, Corrie had a deputy by name of Perkins. One day as Corrie and his deputy sat in their office in Arlee the marshal from Polson, Montana, came stomping into the office, shouting at Perkins, "I have learned you are keeping company

Great-great Grandmothers Hiatt and Stidham

with a woman that I want as mine, and I demand you stop seeing her."

Perkins stood up to calmly answer, "I will keep company with this lady, if she will have me."

"Oh, no you won't," declared the marshal from Polson, as he started to draw his gun to shoot Perkins. Perkins, however, was quicker with his draw and shot the Polson marshal who then fell to the floor, dead.

Perkins was tried in court for murder. Corrie, being the only witness to the shooting, said on the witness stand, "Yes, my deputy Perkins killed the Polson marshal who started to draw his gun first. But my deputy, whom I trained myself, was quicker on the draw. Yes, he killed the Polson marshal, but it was a case of 'self-defense.'" Perkins was acquitted of murder.

Both Corrie and Perkins married ladies who were Seventh-day Adventist. Both would say, "My religion is in my wife's name." Many years later, when I was a student at Walla Walla College, Perkins had a barber shop in College Place. Once, when my mother, Cora Lynn, visited me while I was in college, she took me to Perkin's home and introduced me to him and his wife. Still later, when I was a SDA minister, I visited Perkins. His wife had passed away, with him still having his religion in his wife's name. He told me that after her passing he thought, "My wife will be in heaven, but I have never given my heart to God. I need to be baptized and prepare to meet her in heaven." Perkins was baptized soon after, but he lamented to me, "Oh, how I wish I had been baptized before she passed away so that she would have the comfort of knowing I plan to meet her in heaven."

Charles Curtis

My grandfather Corrie lived twenty-six years with Grandma

Bonita, with his religion still in her name. He supported Grandma in her faith, even sending his three daughters to Mount Ellis Academy. After he retired from administrating the Flathead Reservation, Corrie purchased eighty acres along the Jocko River, nestled along the foothills of the Bitterroot Range of the Rocky Mountains. Here he and Grandma built a house they named "Hideaway Lodge."

Here is an interesting family footnote from that era:

Charles Curtis (January 25, 1860—February 8, 1936) was an American attorney and Republican politician from Kansas who served as the 31st vice president of the United States from 1929 to 1933, becoming the first Native American and the first person of color to hold the office of vice president. He also previously served as the Senate Majority Leader from 1924 to 1929. A member of the Kaw Nation …

Born on January 25, 1860, in North Topeka, Kansas Territory, a year before Kansas was admitted as a state, Charles Curtis had roughly 1/8 Native American ancestry and 1/8 European American. His mother, Ellen Papin (also spelled Pappan), was Kaw, Osage, Potawatomi, and French. His father, Orren Curtis, was of English, Scots, and Welsh ancestry. On his mother's side, Curtis was a descendant of chief White Plume of the Kaw Nation and chief Pawhuska of the Osage.

Charles Curtis is a distant cousin of my maternal family.

CHAPTER III

B-R-R-R! I'm Cold!

The Montana Years of Childhood

It was thirteen minutes after mid-night, Tuesday, January 1, 1935, that I was propelled into life. Although the family home was near the small town of Arlee, Montana, my mother, Cora Lynn Hiatt-Miller, went to Missoula and the Thornton hospital for my birthing.

Outdoors it was twenty-eight degrees below zero. Dr. Charles Thornton, who had delivered my mother twenty-two years previous, did not follow the usual method of stimulating a new-born baby to take his initial breath by smacking me on my little fanny. No! His method of stimulation was to plunge the new-born into a basin of cold water, and that is what he did to me. I was told that I gave a convulsive gasp at the cold-water shock. To be born so early, on such a cold morn, then to be plunged into cold water, must have stunted my growth; I was an eighth-month baby and small to begin with, weighing in at four pounds twelve ounces and measuring eighteen inches long.

I made headlines in the section of the Missoulian newspaper that listed birth records, for it was recorded I was the first baby born in the State of Montana, in 1935, at thirteen minutes after midnight. The news article quoted the attending nurses:

"However, that light weight or not he is a lusty infant and bids fair to be a husky world-beater."

My mother did begin a "Baby Book" about me, but scant information did she record. Here are a few notes she jotted in the book:

> *"Curtis went to see the doctor when he was three weeks old ... and has gained 1lb-4oz."*
>
> *"At nine months Curtis could no longer bathe in his little tub. He takes his swims in a small wash tub ... one time her slipped over the edge and his mother caught him by one leg before he reached the floor. "*
>
> *"His first trip far from home was to see Grandma Mary and Grandpa James Miller at Bozeman where he was proclaimed 'the very best grandchild in the world.'"*

Years later, after Mother passed away, I found that baby book learned there was a brief note, typed on his ancient portable Smith-Corona typewriter, on "Hotel Leonard Honolulu, Hawaii," stationary. It was from my great-uncle Joe, my maternal grandfather Corrie's older brother. The letter said, "Dear little Curtis: I completely forgot you until I had boarded the bus and was on the way to Missoula the day of my departure, so here will try and square myself by enclosing something more substantial than what a mere apology would count for, but do not let any other member of the family get their fingers on it or, well, you may never even have an opportunity to kiss it good-bye, Uncle Joe." And he was right, for I have never learned what happened to that $5. Of note: that five-dollar bill would be valued at least $100 in 2021.

Uncle Joe was an engineer who designed parts for early Chevrolet cars. He was a world-traveler, circuiting the globe by ship, rail, and even rickshaw, at least two times. His records tell that on one world-voyage he was a table mate with Queen Ioanna of Bulgaria. Uncle Joe had quite a "bucket-list" of things and places he wanted to visit on his world-travels. One was to visit the sites of the Mayan Ruins in Mexico, but I can find no record that he went there.

Joe had an interesting experience while in London during one of his trips. He checked into a hotel in the city center, noting an advertisement for a spiritualism séance in a parlor nearby. That evening, out of curiosity, he decided to visit the site. Before leaving his room, he placed a Bible in a pocket in his suit coat. Upon arriving, he sat down in the rear of the room; there were already several persons present and shortly the spirit medium took a seat at a small table from whence he asked if anyone in his audience had a request for a specific spirit of a deceased person to be summoned. Upon being given a name the medium began to conjure the spirit of that departed person.

Several times he repeatedly endeavored to have contact with the spirit but failed. The medium ran his eyes over the group, then said, "Someone in this room is doubting a spirit will come. I cannot succeed while that person is present, so I am requesting you leave, if you are that person." The medium waited, but no one left, so he tried again to summon the spirit, but to no avail.

The medium closed his eyes a moment, then again swept his eyes over the group, as he pointedly declared, "One of you has a Bible on him, which prevents the spirit from coming; will that person please leave?" Again, no one stirred. The medium tried still again to summon the spirit, but again it was to no avail.

Once more he implored the spirit to manifest himself, and again he failed. Again, he closed his eyes, then opened them to look carefully at each person present. He finally fixed his eyes on Uncle Joe, uttering these ominous words: "Mr. Joseph Hiatt, you have a Bible in your right coat pocket, right over your heart. I order you to leave the premises, for I cannot make contact with the spirit until you leave."

Uncle Joe left that séance!

Now, back to Uncle Joe's birthday gift to me of five dollars, which in 1935 was a generous amount. I was born about midway in the "Great Depression" that began with the infamous stock market crash in the fall of 1929. Unemployment was very high, and there was much poverty. Compared to the current economy, many things were comparatively cheap in 1935: average yearly salary was $1,500; average automobile was $580; gas cost only eighteen cents per gallon; average house was $6,300; bread eight cents a loaf; a gallon of milk forty-seven cents; while a soda pop, Hershey bar, or one scoop of ice cream were all only five cents. My birth certificate, which indicated I was born "legitimate," cited my father, Lyle Miller, to be an unemployed "carpenter's helper."

The medium closed his eyes a moment, then again swept his eyes over the group, as he pointedly declared, "One of you has a Bible on him, which prevents the spirit from coming; will that person please leave?"

My parents met at Mount Ellis Academy, near Bozeman, Montana. Although my dad never graduated, mother graduated in the class of 1932, and she was one of three of the all-female senior class of that year. Mom and Dad were married September 18, 1932. Her father, Corrie Hiatt, was not in favor of the marriage—not that he objected to my father as a person but Granddaddy simply felt it was not timely for a young couple to marry in the midst of one of the worst depressions in U.S. history.

Neither of my parents were then employed. My mother, eighteen years old at the time, was determined to marry my father "right now." The "family story" of how she prevailed upon her father to gain his permission was that Cora Lynn barricaded herself in her upstairs bedroom, clutching Granddaddy's .270 caliber hunting rifle in her hand, as she told her father, through the closed and locked door, "If I can't marry Lyle, I might as well shoot myself." Corrie Hiatt quickly gave his permission for his daughter to marry, but it was surely under extreme duress.

Knowing how much "true grit" my mother had, I doubt she would have shot herself, and the rifle was likely not loaded anyway, but how was Granddaddy to know? A quiet garden wedding shortly took place at my grandparent's rural home, which was known as "Hideaway Lodge."

Having a Seventh-day Adventist heritage and academy education, my parents desired to equip themselves "to be in the Lord's work," and, shortly after their wedding, they drove to Madison College, located in Madison, Tennessee. Madison was a SDA "self-supporting" college, where students would participate in a "work/study" program and earn their way through college.

Mom enrolled in the "Normal School," to become an elementary school teacher, while Dad entered the School of Nursing. His training included working as a male orderly in Madison Sanitarium. W. C. "Willie" White, son of Ellen G. White, was living his last days at the Madison "San." Dad often took care of Willie White; I remember him telling numerous stories about the White Family that Willie personally told him, many of them specifically about Ellen White and her visions.

Alas! My parents were only a few months at Madison, when Dad was stricken with appendicitis and had his appendix removed—the medical costs sank their hopes of continuing their schooling, at that time. Mom once described to me their drive back to Montana, saying, "We hardly had the money for gas for the trip. When we reached the Mississippi River, there was a fifty-cent toll to cross the bridge, so we dug down deep into our purse for that fifty-cents, which left us with hardly any money for food the rest of the journey."

There are several early childhood memories that I have retained into my senior years. Some are primal memories that are my own, while others were told to me, sometimes by Mom or by Grandma Bonita, her mother.

Upon their return to Montana, Dad worked off and on doing odd jobs, including being a "Carpenter's Helper," about the time I was born. My mom was a full-time, stay-at-home mother, as was the custom of that generation. A very protective mom was she, keeping me safe in a small crib near her bed. Dad was away from home searching for work wherever he could find it during to depression years. Mom, for our mutual protection—she heard a cougar scream one night when Dad was away—slept with a loaded, cocked .38 caliber Smith & Wesson revolver under her pillow. Thank goodness it never was triggered when she moved her head or arms during sleep, for a slug could have hit me in the head!

I was subject to a number of childhood maladies, including whooping cough and pneumonia. Dad, Mom, and I lived in a log cabin on the banks of the Jocko River,[1] near HideAway Lodge (the home Granddaddy Corrie Hiatt built at the base of the Mission Range of the Rocky Mountains, after he retired from being a United States Marshal and Bureau of Indian Affairs agent for the Flathead Reservation). When I was nine-months-old I was stricken with pneumonia. Mom rubbed my chest with Vicks—the popular over-the-counter medication of the time—while Grandma Bonita saddled Mom's Indian pony, named Buck, and rode three miles to Arlee to summon a doctor for me.

Around this time my father, Lyle, was working for my great-uncle Clark Rentfro, Grandmother Bonita's older brother, who had homesteaded a ranch on the west side of the Jocko Valley from the Hiatt Ranch on the east side. The distance between Corrie and Clark's ranches is about five miles. Dad worked six days a week for Uncle Clark. He was paid $25 per week, with room and board. My mother stayed with her parents, Corrie and Bonita.

The following story occurred during this time; it demonstrates to me that God's miraculously protective hand was upon me throughout my life. It concerns an incident during the time the

---

1 The Jocko River (Salish: nisisutetk) is a roughly 40-mile tributary of the Flathead River in western Montana. It rises in the foothills of the Rocky Mountains. It is named after Jacques (Jocko) Raphael Finlay (1768–1828), an early Metis fur trader, scout, and explorer.

Bureau of Land Management was constructing an irrigation canal on the Jocko River that flowed through the middle of Grandfather Corrie's eighty-acre ranch. Mother, Uncle Ross, and I had gone to Missoula one day. Missoula was about thirty miles from HideAway Lodge. [I began writing this autobiography during my years of mission service, while I was living in Beirut, Lebanon. In order to learn more of my childhood, I often wrote to my mother to obtain information about my early childhood. She wrote the following letter, dated February 29, 1969, which specifically answers a question I posed to her about what I consider to be a significant event in my life]:

> *The soil was quite rocky, which was the reason for the enlarged cemented ditch to be constructed to prevent the loss of so much water enroute. It was almost a yearly routine to "pick rocks" and pile them along the fence line. With the constant freezing each winter, the result was rocks were continually coming to the top of the ground.*
>
> *The road into our place from the regular Jocko Road was about a mile. It was a winding road around a mountain side and only part of it could be seen from the house. ... So the road curved all the way, following the hillside.*
>
> *The car [we drove to Missoula that day] was a '29 Model A Ford, with a soft top, a "California-type," known as a "Run-About," as the top could be put up or down, and it had a "rumble seat."*

The Jocko River had tall trees along it, where to canal was being built behind our house. Below the trees was the house and barn, an alfalfa field, and a hay stack. The canal was at the foot of the hill.

> *Our house was completely covered by 8x8 inch timbers to protect it from rocks falling from the dynamite blasting necessary to build the canal. Every time a blast was to go off, the crew foreman*

yelled "Fire!" It got to the place that all the livestock raced up to the north end of the pasture and all the chickens and turkeys ran into the barn, every time they heard the shout "fire."

That day the foreman informed Granddaddy [Corrie] that they would set off the biggest blast of the day around 5:00 pm., as the crew left for the day. Knowing that was about the time Mom, Ross, and I would be returning home from the shopping trip in Missoula, Granddaddy requested the foreman to place a flagman at the head of our mile-long lane that lead from the Jocko Road to our house.

When Granddaddy heard the shout of "fire" he was looking out the kitchen window at our car that was coming around the curve near the blast-site. He heard the blast, and cried to Grandma H, "My God, there goes our family." Grandma joined him at the window, as they waited for the heavy dust, dirt, and rocks to settle. They expected to see a very flat Model A Ford and lifeless bodies.

Ross had just opened the last gate and gotten back in the car when the blast occurred. Thank God, the blast blew the heavy rocks clear over the car, but some rocks came down on the soft roof, pushing it down so the doors could not be opened. Ross crawled out of the car window. I handed you to him, then crawled out a window myself. Granddaddy and Grandma were very relieved and thankful to see that we were all safe.

Your father [Lyle Miller] thinks the blast was about 300 yards from the house. After the blast there were rocks and trees all around the house, from the blast. Had we been a little way off either side of the gate, we would have been under the heaviest part of the exploding rock. God's protecting hand was surely over us to protect two future church school teachers [both my mother and uncle Ross taught many years in SDA church schools] and a future overseas missionary to the Middle East [meaning me].

Granddaddy was very angry with the foreman and the blasting crew. He had very colorful language that would make the air blue with his cursing when he was angered. He lit into the foreman and the flagman he was supposed to station at the head of our mile-long lane. The flagman forgot to stay at the place where he was to hold our car until the blast was over. Granddaddy let him have a real blast of his anger the next day when the crew returned to work!

Some of my earliest memories, dating back to when I was two to three years old, are connected to that log cabin just a short way down the Jocko River from HideAway Lodge. The cabin was right on the riverbank.

The first memory is of me being on the rather steep riverbank, struggling to climb up the bank to get back to the cabin. I don't remember going down the bank, but I have a keen memory of crying, literally, and crying for help. I still wonder why no one was watching me more closely—whoever that was supposed to be—for it surely was not safe for the small boy I was to be alone on that bank. I do not remember how I got safely up the bank.

There was a path from the cabin to HideAway Lodge. One day, when I was about two-and-a-half years old, I decided to walk, alone, to my grandparents' home. Again, I wonder who was or was not watching me. I started "by-my-lonesome" on that dirt path. It meandered through a short-wooded area, then came to a wooden gate opening to the cow and horse pasture. I was able to slide the wooden bar to open the gate; I went through the gate (did I close it?) and entered the pasture. Shortly I heard the "moo—ooh" of a cow; it was close by, but I didn't wait for the cow to come towards me. That moo—ooh was enough to scare the bejeebers out of me, and I turned tail to scamper back through that gate! Still, I can't remember if I closed that gate ... hmmmh.

One cold evening I was playing with a toy truck by the warm fireplace in HideAway Lodge. Granddaddy Corrie was seated nearby, reading a book or newspaper. He saw I was intrigued by the brass andirons; he warned me they were hot and that I should not touch them. He must have been watching me closely, for despite his warning—or was it because of it—I reached a hand to touch an andiron. Graddaddy must have decided experience is the best teacher, for he saw I was not heeding his warning; he let me touch it, then comforted me when I quickly drew back my hand, crying and smarting, because it had been mildly burned. I must have learned from that experience, for I don't remember ever touching a hot andiron again!

It must have been the spring of 1937—time for spring plowing and harrowing time. Granddad Corrie had hitched his team of draft horses—he had a matched team of giant Percheron horses, Kit and Polly, that were his pride and joy—to a harrow. A harrow was a metal frame equipped with steel "teeth" that broke up the ploughed ground, making it ready to be seeded. Oh! I wanted to ride that harrow. I climbed up on it, only to be told, "Curtis, you can't ride the harrow; it's too dangerous; you might fall off, or slip through the frame, and be cut-up by the harrow teeth." I got off the harrow, but as soon as Granddad Corrie wasn't looking, I climbed back on. He proceeded to address me firmly and sternly, "Curtis, go back to the house and stay with your mother." I remember him telling me that, but I don't remember complying, but logic tells me I probably obeyed.

Granddad Corrie loved horses. His giant Percherons, Kit and Polly, were his favorites. One day he was yarding logs to build with. The logs were across the Jocko River from his building site, so he used Kit and Polly to pull the logs through the river. When lunchtime came around, Grandma Bonita, my mom, and I took his lunch to him. We found him right by the river, with the horses hitched to a log. When we arrived, Granddad dropped the reins on the ground. Kit and Polly did not move. They were trained to stand in place when the reins were dropped.

I still remember Granddad Corrie lifting me up to place me on Kit's back. I took hold of the hames of the harness, thrilled to be on a horse—I have loved horses ever since this event—feeling I was a real horseman. Then Granddad, Grandma, and my mom sat down to eat. About that time I kicked by heels against Kit and shouted, "Giddyap!" Obediently Kit and Polly settled into the harness and started forward, pulling the log behind them. Granddad made a lunge for the reins but missed them. Kit and Polly started into the Jocko, with me happily urging them on. With bated breath the adults watched, fearing I might fall into the Jocko. Granddad was poised to dive into the river if need be to save me. However, I triumphantly rode Kit and he and Polly successfully yarded that log across the river. I guess that experience prepared me to work as a logger to earn money to attend Walla Walla College years later.

Here's a bit of history of Granddad Corrie and his team of Kit and Polly. He very much wanted to raise a pair of colts from them. One year the foals were dropped early on a very cold night, and they froze to death. The next year the new foals fell into the canal and drowned. The third year they were born during Granddaddy Hiatt's funeral in Missoula. When Grandma Bonita, her daughters Cora Lynn, Joelle, and Jean, along with Ross and I, arrived back at HideAway Lodge, after Granddaddy's funeral service, the spring of 1938, they all sighted the newborn foals. That year they survived, but Corrie never saw them.

CHAPTER IV

The California Years

1938–1946

Towards the end of the Great Depression, in 1938, my parents and I moved to Salt Lake City, Utah. Grandma Bonita's older brother, Harley Rentfro, an SDA minister, was a departmental director for the Nevada-Utah Conference of Seventh-day Adventists (NUC). At that time the NUC wanted to enlarge the SDA membership in Salt Lake. Uncle Harley invited my father to open a bakery there. I do not remember traveling to Salt Lake, but I do have some memories of the time we lived there, and I clearly remember my father telling me about his bakery.

We were very hard-up financially, and food for us was scarce. I learned how to make a mayonnaise sandwich with one slice of bread. I would take a slice of bread, spread a very thin layer of mayonnaise on it, then fold the slice in half—presto, the sandwich! I remember making them several times.

Dad and his bakery partner rented a small building for their bakery. Somehow my dad had found the recipe for X-Cell Donuts, which were famous at that time, and name X-Cell was the featured name for their bakery. Dad and partner also baked bread, dinner rolls, and other baked goods. In order for their baked goods to be fresh, they had to get up in the middle of the night to begin their baking process, but the dough had to have time to rise before the loaves were put in a large oven.

Early one morning uncle Harley came to visit the small apartment where we were living. I know not the reason for his visit, but a playmate and I found his automobile unlocked, so we proceeded to climb inside, where we found a whole box of a dozen X-Cell donuts, and I remember the two of us quickly made a meal of them. That was probably the only time in my life I ate six large donuts in one meal! They tasted good, too. My mouth is watering as I write this.

The bakery opened at 7 o'clock in the morning, so walk-in customers could have fresh bakery goods. The partner would stay at the bakery all day, while dad drove a delivery truck to take baked goods to homes and shops. The bakery was a great success from the beginning, with sales producing what dad hoped would enable him to make sufficient funds to support the Miller family. Then, suddenly, sales drastically dropped off, overnight. The baker partners were puzzled, but dad was soon to learn the reason. He started on his bakery route one day, stopping first at a gas station where he usually fueled the bakery truck. The proprietor came out to gas up the truck, and while doing so casually asked dad, "Well, how is the bakery business going?"

"It was going great until yesterday," replied dad, "but then business plummeted to almost nothing, and I don't understand why."

"Because that's the way we planned it," rejoined the gas station owner. "You understand, I am also a Bishop of the Mormon Church, and most of your customers are Mormon. I let you start the bakery, then suddenly stopped buying from you, so that we can offer you a business deal: You join the Mormon Church and we guarantee you will make a good living; but if you don't join you will go bankrupt, simple as that."

Dad and partner did not become Mormons, and the X-Cell Bakery was forced out of business. However, during our short sojourn in Salt Lake the NUC held evangelistic meetings in a large tent. From a lumber yard 2x12 inch boards were borrowed with the understanding they would be returned after the meetings were over; these boards were used for benches for the attendees to sit on during the meetings. I remember dad taking me to one of the meetings. It was a very rainy night, so the speaker was challenged to be heard above the rain pounding on the tent. The ground inside the tent was covered with several inches of sawdust; this was during the time when many public evangelists of various denominations encouraged folks "Follow the Sawdust Trail to find Jesus."[2]

Since my father wouldn't compromise, we had to leave Salt Lake, but where would we go?

At that time Dad's younger sister, whom I have always called "Aunt Floy," was a registered nurse working at the White Memorial Hospital, in an area called Boyle Heights in the large metropolis of Los Angeles. She encouraged us to come stay with her while Dad looked for work.

There was a small sandbox in the backyard for me to play in. That sand got me in trouble! I remember parts of the event, and Mom informed me of the rest of the story. It seems I had a small sand shovel and bucket, which I filled with sand. According to Mom's account, I emptied the bucket of sand into the toilet, causing it to overflow when I flushed it. For punishment Mom locked me in a small shed in the backyard, leaving me there quite alone.

I began to scream and cry, as only a three-year-old boy can. I screamed so loud Mom and Aunt Floy could hear me inside the apartment. Floy was alarmed by my loud screams, telling Mom, "You let Curtis out of that shed. What will the neighbors think when they hear his screams?" God bless Aunt Floy, for Mom acquiesced and let me free.

---

2 "Sawdust Trail," Wikipedia, https://1ref.us/1ue (accessed August 28, 2021).

We did not stay long with Aunt Floy, for Dad found work caring for a very rich man who was an invalid, in the then small town of Orange, California, near the present site of Disneyland. The man had made a fortune as an orange-grower but suffered a crippling stroke. Dad had qualified as a "male orderly," likely the same as a Certified Nursing Assistant today, while at Madison College where he was hired to work the 12-hour night shift caring for the rich man, Mr. Hayward.

Initially we lived in a "Tourist Camp," wherein were a hodge-podge of trailers and small cabins. We lived in a very small cabin. I had to be quiet during the day, inside our living quarters, for Dad worked nights and slept during the day. Right next door to us lived an old codger who kept a raccoon in a small nail keg, tethered there by a chain. I was intrigued by that coon. When given food he would industriously proceed to wash it in his water bowl.

Eventually we moved into a very small rental house on Glassell Street which we rented from a kindly old man, Mr. Shaffer. The local grade school was on Center Street where in 1939 a kindergarten was started. Kindergarten enrollees were evidently sparse, so four-year-olds were encouraged to come, and my parents enrolled me in 1939–40 schoolyear. The teacher was Mrs. Baker who had had beautiful white hair and who ran herd on about a dozen kids. In kindergarten we mostly played games, learned our colors, and colored lots and lots of pictures. We were challenged to "make sure you color within the lines."

My favorite kindergarten class was "Skipping." The girls would form a circle, facing out, then the boys would choose a "Skipping Partner." Joining hands, like for couples' skating, we would skip around the room to the music Mrs. Baker played on the piano.

I always did my best to choose a girl named Kay Watson. I thought Kay was really cute, with her curly black hair and blue eyes. There was keen competition among the boys to skip with Kay.

I liked Kay for another reason—her father was a pharmacist who owned a drug store with an old-fashioned soda fountain at the back. Burgers and shakes were the main menu items, along with Pepsi-Cola® and Coca-Cola®. The counter was high, and little boys such as I would perch on a revolving stool to place our orders. A single scoop ice cream cone was five cents, as was soda pop. Burgers were fifteen cents, as were chocolate malts, which were my favorite. Mr. Watson would scoop up big balls of chocolate ice cream into a thick-ribbed glass malt container then whiz it in a blender. He would then pour the malt from the ribbed glass into a smaller glass, set it down in front of me, with the ribbed glass having a nice amount still in it. That way I could slowly drink from the glass, while keeping my eye on the larger container, knowing when I finished the glass the larger container would still have a second helping for me. Watson's chocolate malts and his cute daughter Kay are among my fondest memories from Orange, California.

Achieving success in kindergarten, I entered first grade in 1940, when I was five-and-a-half years old. Miss Donaman was first-grade teacher and school principal. She divided first-grade students into three groups, based on their reading ability. The lowest level was named "Robins," the mid-level "Bluebirds," and the highest level "Brownies."

I began in the Robin group, but being upwardly mobile, even back then, I was promoted to be a Bluebird after a few weeks. I persisted in developing my reading skills. I have always been a voracious reader and even today I have books in about every room in the house, books in my car, and during the years I worked at Linn County Mental Health I had books in my office, to read between seeing patients, and during breaks and lunch time. As a kid I began laboriously reading the comic section

I began in the Robin group, but being upwardly mobile, even back then, I was promoted to be a Bluebird after a few weeks.

of the Sunday newspaper and other kid books, so by mid-year I became a Brownie!

Based on my later clinical skills in assessing youngsters for Attention-deficit Hyperactivity Disorder, in retrospect I believe I was ADHD, often restless, needing to have something fulfilling to occupy my time. If I was not adequately motivated, I was mischievous and probably disorderly in class.

One spring day during my tenure in first grade, my mother informed me, "Curtis you come right home after school today, because we are going to visit Grandma Bonita," who lived in L.A., near the White Memorial Hospital, where she worked in the laundry. Mom probably tried to impress that on my mind, but remember, I was attention-deficit back then (my good wife, Joy, believes I still am!), and by early afternoon going to visit Grandma was probably gone from my mind.

I must have done something which warranted Miss Donaman to place me in "Kid Jail." Don't ask me what I did, for I don't remember now more that eighty years later. Miss Donaman placed me in the school supply room, and sternly ordered me, "Now, Curtis, you stay in this closet until I tell you to come out. And you better be quiet while you are in here."

School let out at 2:30 p.m. and Mom expected me home by 2:45. When I did not present myself at home by that time, Mom and Dad drove slowly from Glassell Street to the school on Center Street, but found no sign of me. While Dad waited in the car, Mom went to the first-grade classroom to ask Miss Donaman if she knew where I was. "No, Curtis is not here. He must have gone home when the rest of the students were dismissed."

Mom and Dad searched the route from school to home again. They even explored alternate routes. They went to homes of my playmates. They particularly questioned Billy, a fellow classmate and the boy who lived next door to our house. Billy was home, as was his older brother, Jerry. Neither had seen me after school.

By supper time there was still no sign of me. It was my habit to never miss supper! The local police were notified that "Curtis Miller, age five and small for his age, is missing." Shortly many police were ordered, "Be on the lookout for Curtis Miller."

"Curtis Miller, age five and small for his age, is missing." Shortly many police were ordered, "Be on the lookout for Curtis Miller."

By 8:00 p.m. I still had not been located. My parents were very fearful I had been kidnapped. Many persons continued to search for me in nearby parks, at grocery stores, and wherever it was thought a small boy might have wandered.

Now, back in that supply closet. I was still there. Miss Donaman had sternly told me, "Curtis, you stay here until I tell you to come out." For once I was obedient and stayed put. Time went by and went by. I was unaware school had dismissed. I was unaware that around 4:00 p.m. Miss Donaman had turned out the lights, and with the other teachers left the school building. The closet had been dark when I was incarcerated there and I fell asleep so I was unaware the town of Orange was cloaked in darkness.

Finally, the police decided to search the school, for by this time Miss Donaman remembered she had placed me in the closet. She remembered she had ordered me to stay in that closet "until I tell you to come out."

Two police officers, Mom, Dad, and even Miss Donaman, entered Center Street School, to begin a room-to-room search. They searched the first-grade room first, and I was found fast asleep, on the closet floor. I was sprung from "Kid Jail."

It was too late to visit Grandma Bonita. At home I was given supper and put to bed. I do not know how, or if, Chief Jailer Miss Donaman was prosecuted for her violation of sentencing a little kid to "inhumane and unjust punishment." I think she should have been sentenced to one year for each hour I spent in her jail, or about eight years, doing hard labor, and living on bread and water, with no visitors allowed. She would sleep on the cold, hard, concrete floor of her 6x6 foot cell, with no blanket, and no early release for good behavior.

That's justice, per a 5-year-old, innocent, attention-deficit disordered kid. And in my current work as a psychologist for Linn County Mental Health, I strive to protect innocent, little, even attention-deficit disordered, kids from cruel, inhumane, teachers!

I remember one last thing Miss Donaman did for me during my first-grade experience. I arrived at school one day and as I walked into my classroom she glimpsed my neck, then took me into the hallway to carefully inspect my neck and arms. She suspected I had scarlet fever and sent me home. However, I now learned that Miss Donaman did have a heart, for as she led me to the main entrance door where we passed the school's ice cream chest, which she opened, took out an ice cream cone, and handed to me. She evidently knew that I would not be returning to Center Street School again, for it was late April, and school would be over in a few weeks. I never saw Miss Donaman again, but as I strolled home, I slowly licked that cone, making it last as long as possible. I wonder if kids still lick ice cream cones like that? That cone is my last memory of Miss Donaman, and I changed the prison sentence which I had rendered. I reduced her eight-year sentence to time spent as I licked that cone. She only served a couple weeks of incarceration!

Shortly after I reached home, a public health nurse knocked at our door, examined me, and declared "This boy has scarlet fever!" She immediately nailed to the front door of our house a large sign, with bright red letters, that proclaimed:

BY ORDER OF ORANGE COUNTY PUBLIC HEALTH
THIS HOUSE IS
QUARANTINED
DO NOT ENTER

Mom immediately put me to bed, then posted herself at the front door to inform Dad and Uncle Ross, "Curtis has scarlet fever. No one can enter the house, even to take some clothes or toilet articles. I don't know where you can stay while he is quarantined, but you can't stay here."

They found lodging with some members of our local SDA church. Every few days Dad would bring necessary groceries for Mom and me, leaving them at the front door. I don't now remember how long I was quarantined, but it was long enough that I did not return to school. Keep in mind, I never actually finished first grade!

Slave Labor

While in Orange Mom's younger brother, my uncle Ross, lived with us. Being only seven years older than I, he was more like a big brother to me. Ross was one of the finest persons I have ever known, and I am ever thankful for him taking me into his life.

We had a business enterprise together selling the *Los Angeles Examiner* newspaper. Ross had a delivery route for the daily papers, which he operated on his own, but on Sundays he included me. He would station me at a prime corner in the downtown area, right by a Safeway Store, about 8:30 a.m. He would leave me there with a good supply of papers and a money bag from which I could make change. We paid three cents for each copy of the Sunday paper, sold it for five cents, making a two-cent profit, and therein is a most interesting development. I was five years old at the time, and not well versed in business management, profit/loss, or profit sharing. I would man that corner, selling papers all morning, with Ross pocketing two cents on every paper I sold. When my morning work was over, Ross would pay me my wages, but he, being the "owner" of the business, giving me the grand sum of one, get that, one solitary nickel, or five measly cents. Calculate it! If I sold twenty-five papers, at two cents profit per paper for Ross, that would make the grand sum of fifty cents. Uncle Ross was very enterprising as a "Paper Boy." There were no "minimum wage" regulations, so Ross was free to exploit his nephew! But I will declare that through the years my uncle Ross was the best uncle anyone could ever have. I miss him, for he has gone to his rest until our Lord comes to take us to our heavenly home. What a great family reunion we will have then!

Aunt Joelle's Wedding

Mom's younger sister, Joelle, had completed her nurses training at the Portland Sanitarium and Hospital, better known "The San," and was the forerunner of the current Portland Adventist Hospital, and was engaged to marry an auto mechanic, Carl Heid. Uncle Carl, in the early 1950s, opened his own auto repair shop on College Avenue, in College Place, Washington, where I attended Walla Walla College. I was to be the "Bible Boy" in Aunt Joelle's wedding when I was five years old. Dad had to work, caring for Mr. Hayward, and could not attend the wedding, so Mom drove our 1940 Plymouth to Portland and back. I was dressed in a white suit for the wedding. At the wedding reception strawberry shortcake was served—which was a real treat for me! To this day I still love strawberry shortcake!

About that time Mr. Hayward passed away, and Dad was again unemployed. We moved back to L.A. and rented a two-story house at 304½ North Boyle Avenue, only a half-block away from White Memorial Medical Center. Grandma Bonita worked there and was instrumental in Mom and Ross getting work there, both in the hospital kitchen.

My father, my very powerful role-model, took on a very heavy workload, working from 11:00 p.m. to 7:00 a.m. at the large Los Angeles County Hospital, as a nursing orderly that prepares patients for surgery. At that time the hospital was a gigantic,

White Memorial Hospital

concrete monolith dominating the western sky of the city.

Los Angeles County Hospital

Dad did not come home after his hospital nightshift, but instead he took a cross-town bus to the large Sears & Roebuck store, where he worked from 8:00 a.m. to 5:00 p.m. After working at Sears he then took the bus home, arriving about 5:45. After eating a quick supper he went to bed to sleep until 10:00 p.m., when he would start it all again at the hospital. He was like a man of iron, modeling for me the attributes of a reliable, responsible, hard worker as I functioned for nineteen years as the senior crisis psychologist for Linn County Mental Health, where I had office hours from 8:30 a.m. to 5:00 p.m. daily, and then was on-call at the emergency rooms of the three mid-Willamette Valley hospitals nights and weekends.

Lincoln Park School

Remember, the previous spring of 1941 I had scarlet fever and I missed the last few weeks of school thus not actually completing first grade. It was about four months until I was to start school in the second grade. Keep in mind, I was a year younger than the rest of the second graders. In the fall of 1941, mother accompanied me to Lincoln Park Union School, the SDA elementary school for that area of Los Angeles, to enroll me in second grade. The teacher, a Mrs. Serns, was of the opinion I was not ready for second grade, and suggested I repeat first grade. Mrs. Serns and Mother locked horns about that, so the teacher took out a *Fun with Dick and Jane* book. (Dick and Jane reading books were the standard texts of that day. You of my younger generation—grand- and great-grandchildren—have probably never heard of those ancient—often boring—reading books

The problem was, when Mrs. Serns challenged me to read that Dick and Jane book, I stumbled over the words—after all, it had been four months since I was prematurely ejected from first grade. Hearing me stumble, Mrs. Serns declared I must repeat first grade.

Mom found that quite unacceptable. She had learned that a Mrs. McFarland taught grades five and six. Mother had known her from years before, when the McFarlands taught at Mount Ellis Academy, back home in Montana. Mom sought out Mrs. McFarland, asking for her support for me to enter second grade. That kindly lady took us to the principal, Mrs. Wyant, where Mom continued her appeal for me to enter second grade.

Shortly thereafter, Mrs. Wyant and Mrs. McFarland accompanied Mom and me to Mrs. Serns. Mother made her ultimatum: "Try Curtis in second grade for one month. If he still can't keep up with the rest of the second graders, he can be put back in first." Mrs. Serns finally acquiesced. Then she began to ride me hard to see if I would fail.

I mastered the boring adventures of Dick, Jane, and Spot. I dutifully recited the Lord's Prayer and saluted the flag of the United States of America with my fellow classmates every morning. I enjoyed recess—probably my best and most favorite subject, and I never failed that class!

But there was a coiled monster that rose up before me: arithmetic or math as it is called these days. I have always been weak in math. I did learn to add, subtract, and in the upper grades, I even struggled with multiplication, long division, and eventually fractions. I am still weak in math. I try to keep score when I play a board game with G-ma Joy, but when I tally my score, I sometimes still have to use the calculator on my cell phone.

Second-grade arithmetic vexed me with another anatomical problem. I have always had a small urinary bladder capacity, and when I am in a time of stress, my bladder signals ... well, you can guess what it signals. During my second- through fifth-grade years, the teacher would not let anyone pause in an "Arithmetic

Time Test"—you know, those tests when you have 15 minutes to work as many problems as you could; and the tests were scored by the number of "rights minus wrongs." While I knew Ol' Lady Serns could not flunk me in reading about Dick, Jane, and Spot, but she could flunk me in arithmetic!

Early in my second-grade year I was in the middle of a time test with fifteen minutes to work as many problems as possible. The pressure was on. My bladder felt full. In a couple minutes it felt critically over-full. Ooooppppsss! And beneath my desk was a puddle, and not a real small one! Wouldn't you know it, Mrs. Serns spotted it right away. As soon as the fifteen minutes were up, that mean ol teacher announced to the whole class, "Curtis made a puddle on the floor. He is too young, too immature, to be in school." All the kids laughed. They teased me for days. Oh, I wanted the floor to open up and swallow me.

One thing Mrs. Serns learned, though, was that from then on, when a Time-Test in arithmetic was to be held, she made certain I went to the toilet first.

Uncle Harold

I remember December 7, 1941. It was Sunday morning. Our radio was tuned to the *Voice of Prophecy*, featuring Pastor H. M. S Richards, one of the most renowned SDA preachers. His program began with the King's Heralds Quartet singing "Lift up the trumpet, loud let it ring, Jesus is coming again." Those words are eternally engraved in my memory. Suddenly the VOP was interrupted by a news flash, "The Japanese have bombed Pearl Harbor." The Miller family was shocked. The next day the President of the United States, Franklin Delano Roosevelt (FDR), made a broadcast to America; his words are also imprinted in my memory. Here is what FDR forcefully and deliberately intoned:

Yesterday, December 7th, 1941—a date which will live in infamy—the United States of America was suddenly and deliberately attacked by naval and air forces of the Empire of Japan.

My father was one of four brothers, who all served in U. S. Armed Forces during World War II (WWII). Uncle Harold, next in birth order to my dad, had joined the United States Marine Corps several years previously. He had been a student at Mount Ellis Academy with my parents. In fact, Mom became acquainted with Harold even before she met Dad. In those days there was a fall and a spring "Week of Prayer" conducted in SDA schools. Harold responded to an "altar call," going forward when the speaker asked for academy students to be baptized. He was scheduled to be baptized the next day but was not. Harold did not have the best behavioral record at MEA. After the Friday evening meeting a faculty member made a sarcastic declaration to my uncle, "Harold, I sure hope you can behave yourself and be worthy of baptism."

Harold was deeply hurt. At the very hour he was supposed to be baptized, he went to the Armed Forces Recruiting Office in downtown Bozeman, Montana, and joined the Marine Corps, wherein he eventually became a Master Sergeant. He looked very sharp and handsome in his uniform.

Prior to the onset of WWII, Harold was aboard a Navy destroyer, one of the smallest of fighting ships. It was said battleships sail atop the water; submarines cruise below the water, while destroyers go through the water. One night Harold was standing guard duty on the destroyer's deck. I remember him saying, "Sometimes we were so tired and worn-out that we could sleep standing up!" He may have been so asleep that night that when the ship went through a wave it washed him toward the side of the ship. He came to his senses, felt the wave, and instinctively grabbed for whatever his hands might find. There was a lanyard—a short

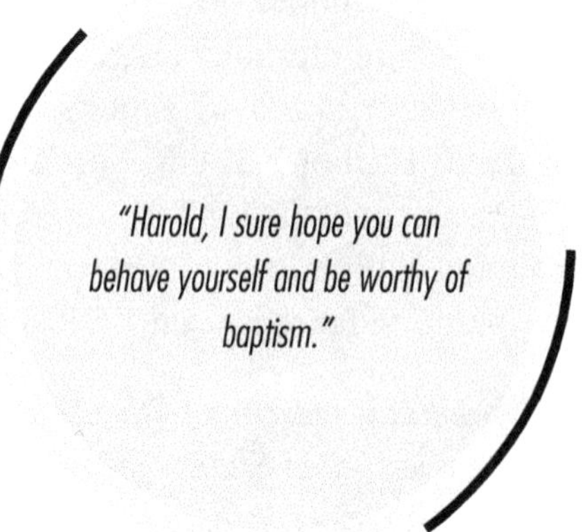

rope used for fastening rigging—that God placed within his frantic grasp as he felt himself being washed overboard.

Harold was deeply hurt. At the very hour he was supposed to be baptized, he went to the Armed Forces Recruiting Office in downtown Bozeman, Montana, and joined the Marine Corps

He told me, "I held on tight to that rope. I wrapped my legs around it. Still, I felt myself slipping downward. In desperations I even bit the rope as hard as I could, telling myself, 'If I can hold on just one more minute I can be saved.'" He held on; fortunately for him a sailor on deck heard his cries for help. Soon he was pulled safely back on deck.

Shortly after WWII started Uncle Harold was shipped to the battle areas of the Pacific Ocean. Early in 1942 his troop train came to Los Angeles. We were living at 304½ North Boyle Avenue, so he was able to visit us over night. He arrived on our doorstep one evening, carrying a full battle-pack and a Browning Automatic Rifle (aka BAR) with a bayonet. It could rapid fire 30 count, 30.06 bullets in a few seconds of time. It was a heavy weapon, weighing close to twelve pounds. I was thrilled to be able to touch it before I was sent to bed while the adults stayed downstairs to talk.

I couldn't go to sleep, for I knew my uncle Harold was no longer a member of our church. I also knew he was a smoker and drinker. I worried that he might not go to heaven. Finally, I left my bed, went to the head of the stairs to plaintively call my mother, who came to see what I wanted. I asked her, "Will Uncle Harold go to heaven?" I do not remember her answer, but I did hear her repeat my question to the adults downstairs, including Harold.

He fought in the battle to take the island of Saipan from the Japanese. After that battle he was sent to New Zealand for "R&R"—rest and relaxation. There he met a New Zealand lady, Joyce by name, who was a registered nurse. He proposed marriage, which she accepted, and a wedding was planned. Joyce indicated a Saturday afternoon was the most popular time for a wedding. Harold countered by stating "I will be married on a Sunday, or a Saturday night, but not Saturday afternoon." Joyce wondered why he would not be wed on a Saturday, but Harold refused to give a reason; he simply refused. They were married on a Sunday afternoon.

Not long after the wedding, Harold was once more sent back to battle, while Joyce remained in New Zealand. After the war ended, Joyce came by ship to the U. S. Her ship docked in a port right near Los Angeles, where we lived at that time. It was a challenge for her to find her way to our home, by a combination of trolley and taxi. She arrived at our home at 155 West Avenue 28 on a Saturday night. When she rang the doorbell, I answered the door, and was the first of Harold's family to meet her. I remember her English accent, quite normal in her native land, but strange for an American to hear.

We invited her to attend our Seventh-day Adventist Church with us, but she emphatically made it known she wanted nothing to do with Adventists, for she was very Anglican, known as Episcopalian in the States.

Harold was still in the Marine Corps, headquartered at Camp Pendleton, north of San Diego. Through the years after WWII they lived in La Jolla. Harold was often at sea, leaving Joyce alone and lonely. My Grandma, Mary Miller, a Seventh-day Adventist, sent them the Adventist periodical *Signs of the Times*; because it came in Harold's name she placed each copy in Harold's desk, where he would find it when he came home. He usually threw it in the trash, which surprised Joyce; she often took the magazine from the trash and put it back in the desk. She knew it was an Adventist magazine, and would not read it herself, but she kept putting each issue in his desk.

One day, as she was putting the latest issue into the desk her eye was caught by the magazine headline: "5 Minutes After Death,

Where Are You?" "That's an odd thing to say," thought Joyce, "Everyone knows when you die, you go to heaven." Her curiosity pricked, she began reading the article, and was amazed to learn the Bible taught when death occurs, the breath goes forth, and the deceased, if a righteous person, rested in the grave until Christ's second coming. She looked up each text and was convinced the Adventist teaching was quite Biblical. She commenced to read the rest of that issue, then every issue she had put in the drawer. Soon came the day we received a letter from Joyce which warmed out hearts: she said she was going to be baptized the next Sabbath.

Harold was at sea when she baptized, but when he learned of it when he returned home, he declared to Joyce, "I will see to it that when we have children, they can go to school functions, particularly ball games, even on Sabbath."

On June 25, 1950, North Korea invaded South Korea, starting what is known as the Korean War. Harold was shipped to Korea with the 1st Marine Division. The 1st Marine Division is a Marine infantry division of the United States Marine Corps headquartered at Marine Corps Base Camp Pendleton, California. It is the ground combat element of the 1st Marine Expeditionary Force. It is the oldest and largest active-duty division in the United States Marine Corps, representing a combat-ready force of more than 19,000 men and women. It is one of three active-duty divisions in the Marine Corps today and is a multi-role, expeditionary ground combat force. Later generations have nicknamed it "The Old Breed."

From Harold I directly learned about two life-changing events during his Korean War experience. The first was when he and his cohorts set up an ambush on a hillside overlooking the road where a North Korean truck convoy was to pass. He was in a foxhole with two other Marines. What they did not know was that while they were setting up their ambush, further up the hill from them a group of North Koreans had set up an ambush against them. As the convoy came into sight, Harold and his fellows were set to open fire, when suddenly the North Koreans above them began to fire at them. Suddenly Harold saw a grenade land right in front of him; before they had time to duck, the grenade exploded, killing the marines on either side of him, while he was unscathed. "Why," he wondered, "Did God spare me and not my fellows also?"

On November 27, 1950, the Chinese 9th Army surprised the US troops at the Chosan Reservoir area. A brutal seventeen-day battle in freezing weather soon followed. In the period between November 27 and December 13, 30,000 troops (later nicknamed "The Chosan Few") were encircled and attacked by approximately 120,000 Chinese troops under the command of Song Shi-Lun, who had been ordered by the Chinese Premier Mao Zedong to destroy the U. N. forces. In those surrounded by the Chinese, who were fighting allies with North Korea, were 1,000 Marines of Harold's corps. The Marines radioed to be rescue, but word came back from the U. N. High Command that they were unable to rescue them; if they were to get out from the encirclement, they would have to get out on their own.

Harold related to his family, "I began praying, God, if You get me out of here alive, I will be baptized at the first opportunity I have when I get back home. I am thankful we have a prayer-answering God, for a dense fog descended over the Chosan area. There was snow on the ground when I began to crawl out of the area. As I crawled I could see the feet of the Chinese troops on either side of me, but I kept crawling to safety, and I made it!"

I was in my second year of college at Walla Walla College when one Friday I received a phone call. It was from Uncle Harold, who said, "Curtis, I have arrived in College Place, and tomorrow I am going to be baptized in the Walla Walla Church by my Mount Ellis Academy classmate, Pastor Clifford Rouse (Rouse is author of the now out-of-print book *Montana Bullwhacker*, the story of how his ancestors came to Montana and helped found Mount Ellis Academy; he also performed my first wedding).

It was a joyful thrill to witness Uncle Harold's baptism.

My dad's next younger brother, Uncle Jim, was also at MEA prior to WWII. He wanted to marry one of his classmates, but her father opposed that. Shortly after the close of that school year, Jim joined the U. S. Navy. I do not remember where he served during the war, but after the war he returned to Montana where he worked for the Great Northern Railway as a "Fireman" (the crewman who shoveled coal into the firebox of boiler-driven locomotives) for the GNR; he likely obtained that position because his father, James Monroe Miller (my paternal grandfather) was a Chief Engineer for GNR. Granddad James retired after many years as an engineer. I will relate stories about him elsewhere in this autobiography.

Uncle Bill

Dad's youngest brother was my uncle Bill Miller, who saw his older brothers were in U. S. Armed Forces. He, too, joined the military, choosing to join the Marine Corps. I believe that he likely lied about his age in order to join, for he was only eighteen-years-old the day he landed on a beach on the Island of Guam. Bill, too, was issued a BAR. During the battle for U. S. Forces to capture Guam, he was in a fox hole, in which he survived three successive "Banzai Attacks"—a Japanese battle cry, especially used by Japanese troops attacking fiercely and recklessly—after which an artillery shell hit so close to him he was buried chest-deep and had to be dug out by his fellows after the last attack. Bill was rotated back to the U. S. after the battle of Guam and was diagnosed with "Battle Fatigue," which is now known as Post-Traumatic Stress Disorder, or PTSD.

For most of WWII the top draft age was thirty-five years-old, but towards the end of the war, the U. S. was short of draft-age males—it is estimated that 16 million Americans were in the military during that time—so my father was drafted into the U. S. Army at age thirty-eight. As a "Conscientious Objector" to bearing arms, he was placed in the Medical Corps, receiving his training at Fort Sam Houston in San Antonio, Texas. While in basic training he learned how to march, and military etiquette, which included how to salute a superior officer. Dad had difficulty knowing his right hand from his left (salutes were to be given by the right hand), so his drill sergeant ordered him to carry a rock in his right hand for three days!

I missed my dad while he was in the Army. I was nine-years-old at the time, enrolled in Lincoln Park Union School in Los Angeles, where I was learning about the privilege and power of prayer. The thought came to me that if I prayed hard enough about it, maybe Dad would come home. I prayed hard for three whole days. Bedtime in those days was 8:00 p.m., but one night, around 10:00 p.m., I was awakened by people talking in the front room. I immediately jumped out of bed to learn just who was talking. There was Dad, sitting by mom on the couch!

I was overjoyed to have that prayer answered so quickly! I learned that Dad was on a troop train that stopped by the L. A. Union Station, where it laid over for about twelve hours, giving Dad just a few hours at home. His troop train shipped out the next morning, to my sorrow. I concluded that God had answered my prayer, but my prayer was incomplete: I should have prayed that he could stay a longer time—maybe for always.

The physical stress of U. S. Army basic training took a toll on Dad, and he was physically incapacitated to the degree he was relocated to an army base near L. A., where we could visit him. Shortly after that the war was over, and Dad was given an honorable discharge.

An interesting footnote to his military service was ultimately connected to the strenuous, physical demands of his basic training. Although for years after he did hard, strenuous, physical labor at various jobs, in his older years he was declared by the Veterans Administration to have grounds for a military disability pension. I am not privy as to exactly how this happened, but a U. S. Senator from Oregon, Bob Packwood, went to bat for Dad, obtaining for him a full disability pension that gave him a good monthly income and full medical benefits for both him and Mom. These benefits lasted for the rest of their lives.

More School at Lincoln Park

Los Angeles was a large, sprawling megapolis with a vast public transit system of trolleys, buses, and inter-urban trains, which I soon learned how to navigate, often traveling by myself. Christmas season 1943, when I was eight years old, my parents thought I was lost, but I really wasn't for I knew where I was all the time.

The three of us went downtown Christmas shopping. We primarily shopped in the "Broadway," a gigantic, multi-storied department store. My parents dropped me off at a Magician Show on the second floor. As they did so, they told me, "When the show is over, you wait right here for us, and don't go wandering off."

The problem was, attention-deficit as I was, I did not hear them give me those instructions; consequently, when the magic show was over, I went to the entry way, but did not see Mom or Dad. I didn't wait there but proceeded to use the escalator system to navigate from floor to floor, searching for them. Each floor was vast and divided into sections for men's clothing, women's clothing, kids' clothing, shoes, appliances, furniture, etc. I wandered from section to section and floor to floor, searching for them, but alas, I did not find them, even when I reached the fourteenth floor. I proceeded down to the ground floor, where I waited and watched the main entrance to the building. It began to get dark, and I did not see my parents. I began to feel hungry but did not have even one cent for food. Time passed.

Now, I knew the transit system quite well. I knew what trolley would take me to within three blocks of the apartment where Grandma Bonita lived, close by the White Memorial Hospital; it was the "P" trolley—but I did not have the seven-cent fare. A gentleman had been watching me, and must have sensed I was lost, so he began to talk with me. I was not lost, I told him, for I knew right where I was—at the Broadway Store. I declared, "It's my parents who are lost, for I do not know where they are."

He suggested contacting the Los Angeles Police Department, but I saw no need of that, saying, "If I had seven cents, I would take the P trolley to my grandma's." The kind gentleman reached into his pocket, counted out a nickel and two pennies into my hand, as he said, "There, now you have trolley fare, and here comes the P trolley, so you can go to your grandma."

Unbeknownst to me, my parents had been frantically looking for me. They had gone to the auditorium where the magic show was, but they did not find me waiting where they had told me to wait. They alerted the police department when it began to get dark, and police over a wide area of L. A. were on the lookout for me.

It took half an hour for the P trolley to reach the stop near Grandma Bonita's apartment. When it arrived, I quickly got off the trolley and ran all the way to my grandma's home. I walked into her apartment to hear her speaking on the phone. My parents were phoning her from the center of that large city. She heard the door open, and the sound of my steps coming into her front room where she was on the phone. I heard her say, "Curtis just walked in; he's right here and is safe and sound."

My parents were greatly relieved and proceeded on to Grandma Bonita's place. Upon their arrival they showed their mixed feelings of being thankful I was safe, which was an answer to their frantic prayers, and upset about me not listening to them. Then they gave me a strong reprimand, admonishing me to "listen to what we say, from now on, and obey."

I was never lost again while we lived in California, but there was a time a few years later, when we lived in Oregon, but I will tell that saga about a lost son in a later chapter.

When I was nine years old, living in Los Angeles during the years of WWII, I attended the Seventh-day Adventist Lincoln Park parochial school. During that third-grade year, every Wednesday morning worship was conducted by the "JMV"—Junior Missionary Volunteers. I was one of the student leaders, and I took my role very seriously. At the beginning of each JMV meeting we recited aloud the JMV Pledge which included "I will go on God's errands" and "I will do my honest part."

One of my favorite youth hymns that school year was "The Captain Calls for You." When we sang that hymn, we would stand and sing with all our might these words:

There's another task to do, there's a battle to renew,
And the Captain calls for you, volunteers, volunteers,
Rally to the throbbing drum,
Shout the word, we come, we come,
Volunteers, volunteers, volunteers!

From that third-grade year on I determined that someday I would be a missionary.

My year in the fourth grade was different from any other school year I ever experienced. Before the school year even began, the lady who was to be my teacher came to my home to visit us. She was my mother's cousin, and during that visit she firmly stated, "I do not want anyone at Lincoln Park School to know that Curtis and I are related." Because of this, I will simply refer to her as "Teach." For some reason that I have never understood, Teach arranged the seating in her classroom by having the smarter students sit towards the front of the room, while the so-called "dumber" ones sat at the back. In those days desks were the now-antiquated style mounted on two runner-boards, one behind the other. Teach considered me the dumbest of the dumb, so I was seated at the very rear of the class. Three girls I clearly remember from my class, who were assigned the very front seats, were Dorothy Lansing, Janesta Jantzen, and Karen Olson. Janesta became a medical doctor, graduating from Loma Linda University Medical School; Karen graduated college and married a doctor who taught at Andrews University; I do not remember what happened to Dorothy, but I again was in school with her the year I went to Loma Linda Union Academy and lived with Grandma Bonita in 1950–51.

Teach, during arithmetic class, often had us go the blackboard (now antiquated by whiteboards using dry-erase marker pens; the blackboards used actual chalk). She would call out a problem to be solved, which we would quickly write on the board, do the math, then stand at attention while holding our chalk in our right hands. The three "Math Whizzes"—Dorothy, Janesta, and Karen—usually solved the problem first, and correctly. Math being my hardest subject, I was always last to finish the problem, and I was sometimes wrong. When that happened Teach would point out my slowness and my error before the whole class, thus humiliating me!

Teach was a very talented lady, musically. She played the piano majestically. She also organized the class into a choir, teaching us to sing some very high-falutin' songs. The spring of that year the entire school was practicing for a Thursday night musical concert, in which the 4th grade was to sing the lyrics below:

> *Ah, my heart is back in Napoli, Dear Napoli, Dear Napoli, and I seem to hear again in dreams, Her revelry, her sweet revelry. The mandolinas playing sweet of the pleasant sound of dancing feet. Oh, could I return, oh joy complete. Napoli, Napoli, Napoli, Zing, Zing, Zizzy, Zizzy, Zing, Zing, Boom, Boom, Ay, Zing, Zing, Zizzy, Zizzy, Zing ... and on, and on, and on.*

The morning of the concert Teach had us lined up on the school stage, practicing our Zizzy, Zizzy, Zing, Zing song. She waved her baton at us as we sang. Suddenly she rapped vigorously on her music stand as she called at us to stop singing. Then she declared "Someone is singing off-key. Who is it?" No one confessed, least of all me, for I had no idea whether I was on or off key. She started us singing again, only to bang again on the music stand for us to stop singing, the again demanding to know who was off-key. Again no one confessed to being off-key.

She started us singing again, then began to walk behind us as we sang. She stopped behind me, as I was singing as loudly as I could, and she said, "You, Curtis, are the one that is singing off-key. Tonight, during the program, I want you to just mouth the words, like you are singing, but don't let any sound come out."

Once, again, she embarrassed me in front of not only our class, but the whole school. I was already a musical dunce, for when I was in the "Rhythm Band" —a little kid's band where we played "music" by clacking sticks together, rang tambourines, or rubbed sandpaper blocks together to make musical noise—I was also a dismal failure. I was started out on the sand blocks, but they were quickly taken away from me because I rubbed a sand block on the nose of a girl who was standing next to me during practice. I was then given two sticks to bang together in time to the music. The band teacher stopped us during practice, declaring, "Curtis, you are tapping your foot to one rhythm and clacking your sticks to another." I was subsequently kicked out of the band, having been declared a "musical dunce." After Teach commanded me to be silent while singing, I knew I was once again labeled as a dunce, and since that time I have not stood on a stage or rostrum to lead singing. Oh! There was one exception to that: when I started the youth camp at Lake Abant, during my years as President of the Turkish Mission of SDA, I did lead the youth in singing songs around the evening campfire—I will tell about that wonderful experience in a later chapter of this book.

Teach not only challenged and embarrassed me in music but caused a challenge to my "Job" that I had when I was about eight years old. The Job came to me this way:

I had a Road Master bike with balloon tires that had no inner tubes. I was seven years old along about 1942, when we lived on Avenue 28. A long block away was a gas station owned by Einer Johnson, a jovial Swede. Now and again my balloon tires would need a shot of air to bring them up to the recommended pressure, and I would put air in at Einer's station. Usually his air hose had a pressure gauge on it when I filled a tire, but one day it did not. I screwed the air hose to my bike's tire stem and began inflating it. I was a bit lax at keeping a sharp eye on how much air was going in, and a moment later I saw a great bulge in the tire. I quit blowing air in and in a frenzy tried to unscrew the hose from the tire stem, when POW! The tire exploded.

This was bad news, because it was WWII and many things were rationed—including rubber! Thus, rubber tires were rationed or just hard to come by, even bike tires. I burst into tears at the sight of that exploded tire. Einer heard me and came running to where I was. "What's wrong, Curtis?" Einer knew me by name, for we were friends. He didn't need my explanation, for he saw the shredded tire.

I quit blowing air in and in a frenzy tried to unscrew the hose from the tire stem, when POW! The tire exploded.

Right across the street from the gas station was a bike shop. Einer quickly took me to that shop, asked the proprietor if he had a tire the size I needed, and found there was only one in stock. Einer used his own ration stamp, paid for the tire, mounted it on the rim, filled it with air, and handed me my bike. To say I was thankful would be an understatement.

I was so thankful that the next day I went to Einer's gas station to ask, "Einer, do you have anything I could do to pay you back for the tire?" I asked that for my sole income was twenty-five cents a week, an allowance my parents gave me, so I had no money I wanted to part with to pay Einer back.

He pondered my question a bit, then took a roll of Kodak film—yes, cameras back then were not digital and actual film was used—and directed me to take it the Thrifty Drug store to be developed. A few days later I again asked Einer, "Do you have any errands I can do?" He sent me to Thrifty to pick up his developed film and pictures.

After that, every few days I would be back at the station, "Any more errands, Einer?"

One day he had a brilliant idea and offered me a job! Every Tuesday and Friday Einer would deposit the monies earned by his station, along with withdrawing the money he would need to make change for purchases made at the gas pumps. He had a formula of so many pennies, nickels, dimes, quarters, half-dollars, along with paper bills of one, five, ten, and twenties. Einer's idea was ingenious, for he reasoned, "Who would ever suspect a little eight-year-old kid would be carrying a bag full of money?"

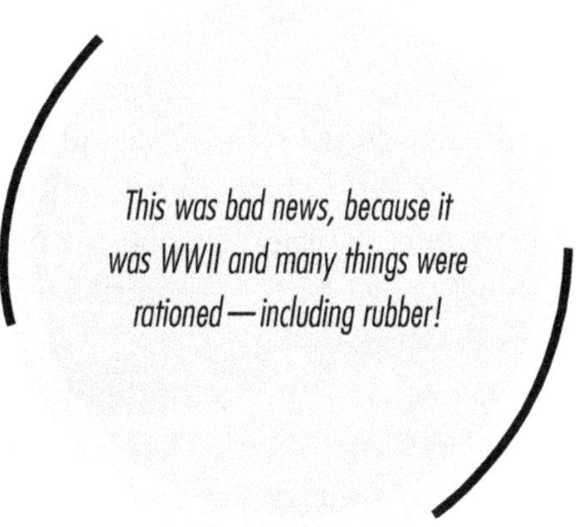

"No one," he surmised. Thereafter every Tuesday and Friday I would ride my bike as fast as I could from Lincoln Park School to Einer's gas station. School was out at 2:30; I would race to the station, arriving by 2:40, grab the money bag to be secreted in my pocket, and pedal as fast as I could to the Bank of America, about a half-mile away. I had to reach the bank by 2:59.59, for banks, in those days, were open from 10:00 a.m. to 3:00 p.m. Never did I fail to reach the bank on time, but often I was the last customer through the door, before it was locked.

Once inside, I would proceed to the window where Nicole, the daughter-in-law to our Italian landlord, was teller. Nicole was one of the most beautiful ladies I have ever seen, so I wanted to have her manage the bank deposit and cash withdrawal for me.

I would be back at Einer's by 3:25, and he would pay me twenty-five cents for my services rendered. That salary equaled fifty cents per week, added to my twenty-five cents allowance, gave me the grand income of seventy-five cents per week. My mom, being a good SDA who gave tithes and offerings to the church, had me put ten cents a week into tithe, five cents into mission offering, fifteen cents for me to spend on whatever I wanted, which was often a Hershey bar or a one-scoop ice cream cone which cost only five cents each. And the last fifty cents went into a savings account.

Now, let's not forget Teach. One Tuesday, in the early afternoon, I broke some rule or other that Teach had laid down for me. For whatever infraction I committed that day, she placed me in the corner, behind the classroom door, with the command, "Now, you stay there until I tell you to leave." She likely forgot I was there.

I was very aware of the time, for Teach dismissed class at 2:30, but failed to dismiss me. And I needed to reach Einer's station by 2:40, grab the money bag, and pedal as fast as I could to the bank. About 2:35 I heard Teach leave the classroom. I sneaked out the door, jumped on my bike, made it to the station by 2:42, grabbed the bag, and raced the clock to the bank. I arrived at the bank door just as it was being locked, but the bank person let me in. I made it in the nick of time, for which I thanked my Guardian Angel.

I wondered if Teach would remember that I was not standing in the corner when she returned to the classroom? I wagered I had a 50/50 chance she would, but I was 100/100 wrong. When I got to her school room on Wednesday, she grabbed me by the ear, twisted it, and propelled me into that corner, saying so all the class could hear, "Now, this time you stay in this corner until I say you can leave it!" I was in the corner until first recess was over—that's how cruel Teach was. I thanked my lucky stars when that school year was over and I once and for all was free from her claws.

Years later Teach bragged, when I became a minister, that she was the one who made me into what I became! Hah. Right. I became what I became not because of her, but *in spite of* her.

There were some pleasant times at Lincoln Park School—it wasn't all misery caused by Teach. In grades five/six a Mrs. Campbell was my teacher, and she had a different seating arrangement, one that had me at a special solitary desk which she placed right in front of her desk. Attention-deficit Hyperactivity (ADHD) had not been fully understood, but Mrs. Campbell must have sensed I needed to be placed where I would be least distracted by activities other students were doing. I began doing better scholastically.

Mrs. Campbell also had a motivating program to encourage all her students to do their best scholastically and behaviorally. She had a chart on the upper-left corner of the chalk board that listed all the names of her pupils. At the end of each day she would draw a star by the names of students who had stayed on task for doing their studies and who had behaved properly. In those days report cards delineating scholastics and behaviors were sent home to parents every six weeks. During that same six weeks our teacher would tally the stars by our names, with the ten highest scored students being eligible for very special events during non-school times. Examples of some of these special treats were a trip to the beach on a Sunday with Mrs. Campbell, her sister, and the "Honor" students; going to a swimming pool to learn swimming strokes and water games; or a trip to the Griffith Park Zoo. Mrs. Campbell's Honor Student program both inspired and challenged me, for I studied harder and behaved better. During that school year I was an honor student every six-week period.

It was a great school year—one of the happiest of my elementary school days.

I must admit that even though I despised Teach, every once in a while, we almost got along. Here is that *rare* story...

It was noon recess, after we had eaten our lunches. Oops! I just remembered something about school lunches—again, connected with Teach. She was from my maternal side of the family which included several missionaries to China, Portugal, and Brazil, most of whom were complete vegetarian in their diet. On my mom's paternal side of the family there were no vegetarians. When Granddaddy Corrie was in his prime, in Montana, a hunter/fisher was allowed five deer, two elk, many game birds, and there was no limit to the number of fish, mainly trout, that a person could harvest. All that game was augmented by the beef and mutton the family raised. We were definitely not "Veggies."

Lincoln Park School had no hot lunch program, so all the students had lunch buckets, as we called them. For several years mine was a shortening can, brand name was Crisco. Mom would put in an orange, banana, or other fruit, maybe a cookie or two, and a sandwich made of two whole slices of bread, filled with bologna and mayonnaise. That sandwich was the focus of Teach at lunch time.

Teach was a crusading vegetarian who was adamantly opposed to any meat in our lunches. When she determined several of us brought meat sandwiches to school, she unilaterally issued her pharisaical decree: NO ONE IS TO BRING ANY MEAT IN YOUR SCHOOL LUNCH! I told Mom of the new school commandment, but she continued to make me bologna sandwiches.

Then came the day when Teach was on her anti-meat prowl, stopping by each student's desk to check whether anyone had a meat sandwich. She found the bologna sandwich in my lunch, grabbed it, held it aloft to declare, "Look at Curtis. See his meat sandwich. Curtis, will you ever learn to follow the school rules?" She threw my sandwich in the trash bin.

After that episode, I would discretely take my bologna sandwich from my lunch pail, cup my hands around it so no one could see what was in it, and eat it fast, keeping my eye on Teach while I did so. If I spotted her looking my way, I would hurriedly put in back in my pail. You, my reader, can again easily see what kind of a teacher Teach was.

Now, where was I in this narrative? Oh, yeah, noon recess, after lunches were eaten. Usually we played dodgeball or softball. On this day it was softball. Teach was the teacher on playground duty and standing with her back to our softball game. I came up to bat, little fourth grader that I was. For once the pitcher lobbed on over the plate within the strike zone. For once I swung my bat, made a solid connection with the ball, hitting it into a high pop-fly. I started to throw the bat down and sprint to first base, but my eye was watching the trajectory of the ball. I saw that it was falling right towards the back of Teach's head!

Numb struck, I stood rooted to my spot by home plate, bat still in hand. I watched that ball reach its zenith, then descend, whacking Teach on the top of her head. She whirled around, screeching, "Who hit me on the head with that ball?"

Seeing me still standing by home plate, bat still in my hand, she came at me, grabbing me by an ear, twisting my ear, propelling me off the playground and towards the classroom, as she decreed, "For that you are going to sit with your head on your desk the rest of recess." Common sense should tell Teach that her positioning at recess had something to do with the result, but NO. Reaching the edge of the playground, Teach realized I had accomplices in my criminal behavior: the pitcher, the catcher, the three basemen, and the shortstop. She called them into the classroom also, declaring that they too had to come to the classroom and place their heads down on their desks also. We bemoaned our sentence, for noon recess had scarcely begun before we were sentenced for our collective crime of hitting Teach in the head with our softball.

I, however, was not feeling guilty. Secretly I was very happy, wishing I truly was a sufficiently skillful batter who could deliberately hit a ball to hit Teach in the head. I am still chuckling seventy years later at that story.

Now, in my old age—my mid-eighties—I do remember one very positive action Teach had on me: every morning, in our SDA church school, we had worship, the very first item of our school agenda. Teach played the piano as we sang a beautiful and blessed hymn "There Is a Place of Quiet Rest." Here I quote that hymn, for it was indelibly scripted in my memory, and singing it throughout that school year was truly a blessing to me, and when I get to heaven, I will surely thank Teach for leading my class in singing,

There is a place of quiet rest,
Near to the heart of God,
A place where sin cannot molest,
Near to the heart of God.

O Jesus, blest Redeemer,
Sent from the heart of God,
Hold us, who wait before Thee,
Near to the heart of God.

There is a place of comfort sweet,
Near to the heart of God,
A place where we our Savior meet,
Near to the heart of God.

There is a place of full release,
Near to the heart of God,
A place where all is joy and peace,
Near to the heart of God.

Oh, yeah, I had another "job" in addition to being the bank runner for Einer Johnson—I sold the Los Angeles Herald newspaper at a busy intersection called "Five-Points" where five busy streets came together. I stood on my corner, shouting, "Herald Paper, Heerraalldd!" as loud as I could shout above the very busy traffic noise.

When the traffic light would turn red, I would dash between the double lanes of cars, still yelling, "Herald Paper," selling as many as I could before the light turned green. I would be on my corner for a couple hours, making about one or two dollars. I tell you, I was one big newspaper entrepreneur!

While living on Avenue 28 I met the large Davis family, who lived on the corner of our street. They had eight children, but the ones I played with were John, a year older than I; James, a year younger than I; and Mary, just my age. We played a variety of games, including kick-the-can, hide and seek, dare base, and baseball. In warm weather we would go to a swimming pool in South Pasadena. We took a trolley to get there, at seven cents fare each way; paid twenty-five cents entry fee, making a total of thirty-nine cents. To this add five to ten cents for ice cream, candy, or pop. We would stay at the pool about four to five hours, so we were hungry when we came out. The pool days are among my happiest memories of that period of my life. Being an only child, I sorta envied the Davis family with all those kids. I missed them when the Miller family moved to Oregon, the summer of 1946.

In going through my files, I have come across my Certificate of Baptism, dated May 26, 1945, over seventy years ago. I was baptized in the Lincoln Park, California, Seventh-day Adventist Church by Pastor B. W. Brown, who was the first SDA minister to take the Adventist message through the Cumberland Gap, which is a narrow pass through the long ridge of the Cumberland Mountains, within the Appalachian Mountains, near the junction of the U.S. states of Kentucky, Virginia, and Tennessee. Famous in American colonial history for its role as a key passageway through the lower central Appalachians, it was an important part of the American wilderness.

Pastor Brown was aged and a retired pastor when he pastored the Lincoln Park church. He lived well into his nineties. I will always fondly remember him for baptizing me. The baptistry was beneath the floorboards of the rostrum. When a baptism took place, the boards were taken up to gain access to it. When Pastor Brown raised me up from the water, I opened my eyes to a beautiful sight, for high above his head was a circular window, and at that time the sunshine was streaming through, causing his head to be illuminated in a halo. I saw his snowy white head of hair, and I desired to someday have a head of white hair just like Pastor Brown. Perhaps I will eventually achieve that, for my hair is now turning white, too!

CHAPTER V

The Oregon Years

1946-1950

My parents, born in rural communities in Montana, found living in the megalopolis of Los Angeles quite foreign to their historical roots. Dad, for reasons unknown to me, began looking to relocate to Oregon after WWII ended. Somehow, he learned of Oregon Realty selling property in Lane County. I remember a man, a realtor, visiting our house several times while we lived on West Avenue 28. He showed my parents pictures of properties in the foothills of the Coast Range northwest of Eugene. One picture showed a farm scene with a large pen of turkeys, while others featured sheep or cattle.

One evening I heard the realtor say, "Mr. Miller, you have just bought a ranch in Oregon." Already I had been fantasizing about living on a ranch with a large house, barns, fields, woods, with a stream in the background. I also picture a beautiful horse, a dog, and an imaginary twin brother, Scott by name—I was still wrestling with being an only child!

Dad bought ten acres of wooded land near Lawrence Road, two miles west of Fern Ridge Lake. The problem was, he bought it "sight unseen," meaning he had never actually seen the property. After he was discharged, we traveled to Oregon to see the property. In 1946 most of the rural roads on the western slope of the Coast Range were unpaved gravel roads, and such was the four-mile-long, east-west Lawrence Road, which linked Territorial Road with Oregon State Highway 36. Butler Road, running north-south, bisected Lawrence Road at its midpoint and its highest elevation. Dad's ten-acre "ranch" was about a half mile southwest of the intersection of Lawrence and Butler Roads. A very short dirt track branched off Butler, but petered out a quarter mile from dad's acreage—hence no vehicle could be driven all the way to the tract. The ten acres were all on a slope, with no level land. Dad was very disappointed in the land he bought "sight-unseen," and reluctantly concluded it was not suitable for the farm he had envisioned. He began looking for another tract of land.

His search for land brought him in contact with Glenn Norris, who lived on the southeast corner of where Lawrence Road tied into Highway 36. The Norris family became our close family friends. Glenn was involved with several sales of property in the area of Lawrence Road. Dad looked at an approximate sixteen-acre tract that was very close to the mid-point of that road. I remember walking over that tract of land with a realtor friend of Glenn's, a man named Emil Vejanski. The rear of the tract reached to a steep hill. There was a spring at the bottom of that hill that became important to Dad, for it would be a good source of water for both irrigation and household water. Dad was not certain that spring was on the sixteen-acre tract, and challenged the realtor regarding whether the spring was, indeed, a part of the tract. I remember Vejanski saying, "If the spring is not a part of the sixteen acres, I will give it to you."

Glenn Norris had been born into an SDA family, but was in 1946 a "backslider." His wife, Veda, and his children Billy, Anna, and a still younger sister all attended church at Junction City. Glenn's father, whom everyone called "Old Man Norris," was SDA. The Millers became close friends to him, too.

Old Man Norris knew the environs of Lawrence Road like the back of his hand. Dad asked him to walk over the sixteen acres with him. By that time dad had actually purchased the acreage, but he still had a question as to whether the spring was on his property. There had been two different surveys of the land, one showing the spring on the tract, while the other did not. Dad, Old Man Norris, and I walked around the tract, both surveys in hand. Norris looked very carefully at the location of the spring, and at the surveys, then concluded, "Lyle, this spring is not on your land." Dad was sorrowful. He appealed both to Glenn and Vejansky, to no avail, and the spring was not ours.

Dad had to purchase a small tract of land with the spring. A new survey was done, the spring became ours, but with a new development—a house on the eastern side of our tract was now on land owned by dad. This was a shock and concern to the family who lived in that house, for legally it belonged to Dad. My father was one of the kindest, most generous men I have ever known, and he drew up a deed, giving a small portion of his land, with that house, to the neighbor.

Moving to Oregon

After purchasing the sixteen acres, the Millers made ready to move from West Avenue 28 to Lawrence Road. However, there was no house on the land for us to live. I now became involved in actually building a house, which we later called "The Shack." What an almost comical structure it became. We purchased rough, green lumber from Glenn, who had a "Gypo" sawmill up the south end of Butler Road. A "Gypo" mill was very small, with one large circular blade. In those days it was often easier and less expensive to have a small mill that could easily be moved to where timber was readily at hand, than to truck the logs to a larger mill that was often miles away.

The slogan was "Wagons West" when rugged pioneer trails led across snowy mountain peaks to the grassy plains of big-sky country, where I was born in Montana. Rich mines of fabulous gold lured dreamers and desperados to stake their claims in this lawless territory. There, brave ranchers fought for their homesteads against outlaws and natives who tried to plunder their wealth. Like some of you, I had ancestors who came west in covered wagons. Many more wagons west had headed to Oregon and the bountiful Willamette Valley by the 1840–50s.

I, however, did not have the pioneering experience of coming west in a train of covered wagons, but I did have the exciting experience of "Wagon North" in 1946. Dad was discharged from the U.S. Army in 1945. During WWII we lived in the greater Los Angeles area of southern California, a place of exile for a family born in the wide-open and beautiful spaces of western Montana. Now our family dream of living on a farm in Oregon became a reality on that sixteen acres of land in the foothills of the coast range.

My father was one of the kindest, most generous men I have ever known, and he drew up a deed, giving a small portion of his land, with that house, to the neighbor.

Classmates of Dad and Mom, Alvin and Flora Kincaid, from their years at Mount Ellis Academy in Bozeman, Montana, had recently moved to Loma Linda, where Alvin was attending the College of Medical Evangelists, now known as Loma Linda University Medical School, to become a medical doctor. Flora Cooley Kincaid had been Mom's roommate at Mount Ellis Academy. In order to move to Loma Linda, Alvin had built a monstrosity of a trailer. It was made of wood, was six feet wide by twenty feet long, mounted on two old truck axels, equipped with nineteen-inch size wheels of which were an odd, uncommon size, and hard to find, if you had a flat tire. The summer of '46 we loaded our few possessions into that trailer, hitched it to our '46 DeSoto, and began the move to Lawrence Road, a distance of about 900 miles. The interstate highway system started by President Eisenhower was not built at that time, so the route we followed was Highway 99, where Interstate 5 is now.

Mom's youngest sister, Aunt Jean, traveled with us, as well as my newly acquired mongrel dog Kazan. About 110 miles north, near Bakersfield, the first of several of those obsolete tires blew out, causing the wagon to wildly fishtail on the road behind the De Soto. Dad guided the car and trailer to the edge of the road where we surveyed the tire. Somehow Dad jacked up the trailer, removed the tire and rim, and put on the spare tire. We had not driven far until another tire blew. We unhooked the trailer, leaving Mom and Aunt Jean to watch the trailer to prevent theft of our household items while Dad and I drove to tire shops around Bakersfield, looking for a replacement for that outdated size. We had to go to several places before we finally found a used one which had very little tread left on it.

We returned to the trailer, put the tire on, and hit the road again. A few more miles down the road another tire blew. That was how the trip went: a tire would blow out, we would disconnect the trailer, then go to a nearby town to search for another tire. During that 900-mile trip we had a tire blow about every 100 miles. I will never forget the rest of that journey! Memory has it that eventually each of the tires that were on the trailer blew out. Each time we had to search and search for a replacement tire, which often took hours and delayed our journey. We slept in that crowded car two nights along the way. Aunt Jean and I took turns sticking our heads out the window to look at the tires as we drove, hoping to avoid another blow-out.

The trip thus took twice as long as we had planned, sleeping two nights in that crowed car, but the Millers finally arrived at Lawrence Road to unload our meager possessions into the Shack.

When wagons bound for Oregon, way back in the mid-1840s, were found to be overloaded, the pioneers discarded by the Oregon Trail items they deemed non-vital to their needs, but not so the Millers on their trek north, for Mom tenaciously declared every single item in our wagon was vital to our survival in Oregon.

Building the Shack

In Oregon Dad, Mom, and I built a rough cabin—rough because Dad was certainly no carpenter! —out of 1-inch rough fir boards. The boards were still "green" and as they dried one-inch gaps were left between the boards. After we moved in, the cold wind blew through those cracks, so we lined the inside of the cabin with black tar paper to keep out the cold drafts. The cabin, which Mom quickly dubbed "The Shack," was roughly twenty feet square, partially divided into two rooms, a living room/bedroom for my folks, and a kitchen/bed area for me.

When we finally were settled in the shack fall rains began and the weather turned cold. We initially heated the shack with a wood cookstove. Mom struggled to keep the shack warm during the day while Dad worked and I was in school. Wow! Did Mom ever burn the wood! Every Sunday, that first year, Dad and I cut firewood, hoping we cut a sufficient amount to last Mom throughout the rest of the week.

Before we were even settled in the shack, Mom wanted a permanent home built, for she had a pressing reason to move out of the shack. We planned to turn it into a barn when we moved out, but before that happened, "Elsie" tried to move in! Shortly after moving to Lawrence Road we bought a cow, a fine Jersey cow which we named Elsie. She was quite a cow, giving about five gallons of good, rich milk a day. Our sixteen acres were fenced to keep animals away from the shack. One day Elsie sought to prematurely take possession of the shack by breaking through the fence and entering the kitchen through the back door. Mom indignantly drove her out by waving a broom in her face.

One last comment about the shack. My small sleeping quarters was partially portioned off the kitchen. Kazan was a relatively small pup when I acquired him. I had longed for a dog to sleep at the foot of my bed, and he quickly learned to sleep there. But over time Kazan grew and grew, eventually coming close to crowding me out of my own bed. I would order him out of the bed at night, but while I slept, he would creep back onto it, sleeping like a log across my legs. I finally had to put a barrier up to bar him from my bed. Kazan was quite a dog, one of the most intelligent I have ever had.

Mom later named those sixteen acres “Linda Vista”—Linda meaning “beautiful” in Spanish and vista meaning “view.” And those acres were very beautiful to the Miller family.

Eugene Junior Academy

Dad had worked several years for Sears and Roebuck in Los Angeles. When we moved to Oregon, he was able to transfer to the Sears store in Eugene, which was under construction at that time. Dad became the first employee of that store, and he truly needed the job, for contrary to Dad’s dream, that acreage never came near to supporting the Miller family. He also wanted that job at Sears so that I could continue my education in an SDA parochial school, Eugene Junior Academy (EJA), were I attended grades seven through ten. Dad worked for Sears a couple years, as shipping clerk, keeping the job so he could drive me the fifteen miles each way from Linda Vista to EJA.

I entered seventh grade at EJA the fall of 1946. My teachers were Wallace and Floy Haraden. Mrs. Haraden was a teacher quite unlike Teach of Lincoln Park School, and school became an enjoyable experience for me. My grades began to improve.

Mrs. Haraden allowed a student to read a book of choice if your school assignments were complete. I read a lot! One day I was intently reading a book and was oblivious to anything going on around me. I so was immersed in the book I was reading that I did not notice Mrs. Haraden calling the class to order for a spelling test. She would call aloud the word to be spelled, give a short time for students to write the word before calling the next word. I had not heard the spelling test was announced and just kept on reading. Mrs. Haraden, as was her wont, walked the aisles as she called out the words. She came upon me as I read, where upon she quietly whispered to me, “Curtis, you are not to read during a spelling test.” I looked up, surprised that a test was in progress. Mrs. Haraden sized up my situation, then told me, "As I call out each word for the class, you write that word, and I will stay right here by you to whisper the words you missed, one by one, until you are caught up."

Now, if that had been Teach, she would have embarrassed me before the whole class, saying loudly, "Here is Curtis, again, still not able to follow instructions. Curtis, go stand in the corner until I tell you that you can leave." Mrs. Haraden simply and quietly took care of me without any embarrassment. I say, "God, give us more teachers like Mrs. Haraden!"

In order for Dad to get to work on time at Sears at 8:00 a.m., he had to drop me off at EJA at 7:50 a.m., but the school was still locked so I waited on the front steps of the building. The Haradens lived a long block and around a corner from the school, so I would wait until 8:15 when they arrived to open the school. When school was out at 3:20 p.m., I had plenty of time to walk to the Sears store to wait for Dad until he got off work at 5:00 p.m. Then it was off to home, arriving by 5:30, to do chores of feeding the rabbits, feeding the chickens, gathering their eggs, and milking cows.

A school buddy of mine was Norman Parmenter. (He married a lady who was half Filipino/half Caucasian. They had a son named Curtis, named after me, who died of an automobile accident in his early adult life, thus ending anyone ever being my namesake.) Norman lived midway between EJA and Sears. One day I walked with him to his home, where we played with his electric model train. I was oblivious to the time as we continued playing. Belatedly I looked at a clock, realizing it was past 5:00. I hurriedly left Norman's and ran to Sears. By this time, it was dark, but I still found the usual place Dad parked our car for the day, but the car, and Dad, were gone. He had no idea where I was, but drove the route I walked from EJA to Sears, carefully looking for me. He went to the school, which was locked. He went to the Haraden's house, but they had no idea where I was.

Dad drove home, picked up Mom, and drove back to Eugene to look for me. I stood by Dad's parking spot for a long, long time.

I didn't know what to do, or how to get home. I finally walked a number of blocks to the Lane County Sheriff's Office and Jail. I knocked on a door, which happened to be the jail. No one came to the door, so I knocked louder and finally the jailer opened the door. "I'm lost," I told him. He didn't know what to do with me, but he invited me into the jail office. "Are you hungry?" he queried. I was so worried about being lost that I had not even thought of food. The kindly jailer continued, "I have already fed the prisoners their supper, but I can wrestle up a peanut butter and jam sandwich for you." Quickly he made that sandwich, put it in front of me, and I ate it while he contacted the sheriff by phone.

I stood by Dad's parking spot for a long, long time. I didn't know what to do, or how to get home.

The sheriff was off-duty at that time, but when the jailer explained my plight, he called to his wife, "There's a lost boy at the jail. Come with me while I check out what I can do for him." They shortly arrived at the jail, listened as I told them my story, then he asked, "If I take you home, can you show me the way to your house?" I assured him I could.

About 8:00 p.m. we arrived at Linda Vista, but no lights were on at home. Dad and Mom were still in Eugene looking for me. The sheriff dropped me off, and my parents arrived home an hour later, and we concluded "All's well that ends well."

Elsie the Cow and Her Family

Dad's "Ranch Dream" included cows, chickens, and rabbits. About as soon as the shack was built Dad went to an auction where a farmer was selling off farm equipment and milk cows. Dad examined the herd of cows and selected a fine-looking Jersey cow, which he bid on and succeeded in buying. This was in the days when the Borden Company had a Jersey-looking cow as trademark. The Borden cow was named Elsie and our cow was a look-a-like for the Borden cow, so we named our Jersey Elsie.

When we purchased Elsie, she was in-calf from a Hereford bull. We watched her carefully as her calving date came closer. One evening she did not come when called, so we set out to find her. After a long search we found Elsie but no calf. We searched more until we found where she had hidden her heifer-calf in a thicket. The heifer looked just like a Hereford, with no Jersey look in her. We raised the calf up to market size and sold her at a livestock auction.

When Elsie came in "season" again, we took her a couple miles down Lawrence Road to a dairy farm that had a pedigreed Jersey bull. Nine months later she delivered a heifer that definitely looked like a Jersey, so we again looked to the Borden Company for a name. Their Elsie's calf was named Beulah, so we named our new heifer Beulah, also. My readers are probably aware of "Elmer's Glue," a white glue used primarily for wood. Borden's bull was named Elmer, for which they named their famous glue.[3]

Angora Rabbitry

Prior to moving to Oregon Dad and Mom subscribed to an agricultural magazine called *Farm Journal*, from which they learned about Angora rabbits, which were raised primarily for their wool. An Angora would produce a pound of wool a year—wool that was very soft, fluffy, and warm, and was often used for sweaters. Dad and Mom went into raising Angora rabbits in a big way, purchasing a buck and two does for breeding stock, and over a period of just a few years we had over three hundred Angoras,

3 To learn more about the story of Elsie, Elmer, and Beulah, see the following story from their "hometown": William Hart, "iconic Advertising Symbol Elsie the Cow Lived and Died in Plainsboro," *Community News, May 1, 2021, https://1ref.us/1uf (accessed September 12, 2021).*

which probably made Linda Vista the largest Angora rabbitry in all the Northwest.

At the time we went into raising Angora's the price of their wool was twenty dollars a pound. Rabbit food cost about three dollars to feed a rabbit a year, so selling the wool for twenty dollars would mean seventeen dollars profit per rabbit, per year. About the time we reached three hundred rabbits the U. S. Department of Agriculture dropped the protective tariff on Angora wool, allowing Australia to export much wool to the States, thus flooding the U. S. Angora wool market, causing the price to drop to three dollars per pound, the amount it cost to feed a rabbit a year; consequently, we made no profit, which was disastrous. We could not afford to feed those rabbits, and I well remember the sad day when we had to mercy-kill three hundred rabbits because we could not afford to feed them, and there was no local market for them.

The Hen House

Then Dad decided to try raising chickens with the aim of selling the eggs. To make the chicken coop we used log slab wood, which is the first cut made on a log during the milling process. The first cut was designed to cut away the outer bark area of a log. We built two slab-walled chicken houses that were about twenty-five feet square in size. Dad purchased an older chicken brooder, a device that produced heat that hovered over new-born chicks, thus producing heat to serve in place of a mother hen that covered her brood of chicks to keep them warm. When the chicks were large enough to leave the brooder, we placed them in the large chicken houses. Ultimately, we had about two hundred egg-laying hens of the White Leghorn breed. Leghorns were, in the late 1940s, the best laying breed of hens. We sold eggs to private customers Dad cultivated from his work-colleagues at Sears, from friends and neighbors in the environs of Lawrence Road, and a few church members. I doubt there was much genuine monetary profit made on the eggs, but Dad thoroughly enjoyed raising those chickens!

Napoleon

There was one inhabitant of the chicken house that was not a chicken. One day I found a pigeon that had sustained a non-lethal gun shot in a wing which so damaged the wing that the pigeon would never fly again. I realized the humane thing to do would be to euthanize the pigeon, but I didn't have the heart to do that, so I brought the bird home to have Dad examine it. He agreed with my diagnosis and prognosis, that the pigeon would never be able to fly. Dad did allow me to turn the pigeon, which I dubbed with the name Napoleon, loose in one of the hen houses. Napoleon quickly adjusted to life with the hens which tolerated him to live among them. Although this strange, little bird could not flutter up to the hen roosts to sleep with them at night, he did sleep on the floor very near them, proving his loyalty to his flock. There were troughs for food and water on the floor of the hen house, and Napoleon would walk amidst the hens, pecking at the chicken feed, and drinking water with them. I don't remember what ultimately happened to Napoleon, but I know he was still living amidst the hens when I went to Loma Linda, California, to live with Grandma Bonita.

Our Junction City Church

The Miller family joined the Junction City Seventh-day Adventist Church, where Dad was First Elder for twenty-five years. It was a kind, loving congregation. I began telling stories in the children's classes when I was twelve years old. I was elected youth leader of the church when I was fourteen, thus I served on the church board. Through my life I have served on local church boards as well as conference committees ranging from local conference through union, division, and the General Conference. I also taught a Sabbath School class at that same age. We had fellowship meals, outings to the coast, ski trips to Hoodoo Bowl on Santiam Pass, and swimming in the Willamette River, which ran by the dairy farm of one of our members. I also remember corn roasts in the fall.

EJA had numerous activities on Saturday nights, the most popular of which was roller skating. I even got up enough courage to ask a girl to skate with me, for I was beginning to recognize that girls were not pests, after all. I graduated eighth grade at EJA in '48, and tenth grade in '50, as class president. The years at EJA are some of the happiest of my life.

There were two families in the Junction City church that had a profound, positive impact on my life—Vern and Delia Hassell, their son Bob, and younger daughter Vivian, who were about eight years older than I. The other family was Earl and Iva Hutchinson.

Earl was discharged from the U. S. Army about the time we joined the Junction City church. He taught the junior class with me and Richard Withers. Richard's father owned the dairy farm on the Willamette River where we had church picnics, swimming, and baptisms. About the time Earl was junior teacher he married Iva, a girl he met in Michigan while he was in the Army. Initially I was not happy he married Iva, for I feared he would not have time for us juniors anymore. But the opposite happened, for Iva now joined with him in planning activities for the youth of the Junction City church. They were a great couple who had a wonderful influence on me as I was growing up.

The Hassells and the Hutchinsons formed a business named "H&H Logging Company." My summers employed by H&H Logging will be chronicled in another chapter of this book.

Farm Labor

During those years I lived at Linda Vista I worked summers in agricultural settings, mainly with string beans and cherries, with some bucking bales of hay.

First, I worked with beans, the Blue Lake variety that grew on poles or strings. The only mechanized part of growing beans was the plowing, harrowing, and seeding the fields. The rest was hand labor, first hoeing the beans to rid of weeds, then the "stoop and stretch" portion—stooping to tie a string around the base of the plant and then stretching up to tie the string on a wire about six feet in the air—and finally the picking of the beans. The hoeing and stringing paid seventy-five cents an hour, for which I worked an eight-hour shift, earning six dollars a day. That does not seem like much in 2021, but in 1947 it was good money for kid-labor. I made more money picking beans, for I was paid two and a half cents a pound. Initially I aimed to pick two hundred pounds a day, which netted me five dollars. The next year I set my goal for four hundred pounds per day, to earn ten dollars, which was good pay for a kid way back then. At the end of the picking season, I received a quarter of a cent bonus for each pound picked on condition that I picked for the bean farmer for the full season.

Between the hoeing and stringing beans came cherry season. There was a cherry orchard right near Cheshire, Oregon, only six miles from Linda Vista. The cherry season was rather short, only about two weeks, and pay was two cents a pound plus all the cherries I could eat while I was picking. Wow! Did I ever eat cherries as picked, choosing the sweetest and juiciest on the tree. To make my goal of ten dollars a day, I had to average picking five hundred pounds. The biggest and best cherries grew on the very top of a cherry tree, so we used ladders to pick the cherries. Ladies, often our moms, didn't like to precariously balance on the top of a tipsy ladder, to reach out with a three to four foot wire bent with a hook on each end, one hook to snag a top tree branch, pull it down to within arm reach, and the other hook went to the rung of the ladder to hold it while the picker stripped the cherries off the limb; consequently ladies were very happy to have us kids "top the trees," which we were in turn happy to do for we accumulated more cherries by being "top pickers."

I usually earned five hundred dollars a season from all the farm work which I used to purchase my school clothes, books, and my church school tuition. Tuition was fourteen dollars a month, or one hundred forty dollars a year, so my five hundred dollars easily covered those expenses, my tithes and offerings, and a small amount for treats, such as ice cream and soda pop.

4-H Club and Sheep

During my early-teen years at Linda Vista I had a buddy, Mervin Keeler by name, who lived on the other side of the hill from our house. There was a path through the woods connecting the Keeler farm with ours. Mervin and I did a lot of things together, including joining a 4-H Club together. Our 4-H group fostered the raising of sheep, hogs, or steers. Mervin and I both chose to raise a lamb to take to the Lane County Fair each season.

On the east end of Lawrence Road was a farmer who had a dairy herd and also a flock of Dorset sheep. Dorset's are unique in that they are one of the few breeds that have horns. I was intrigued by their horns, and Dorsets became my "breed of choice" for raising sheep. From that farmer I was gifted a "bum lamb," meaning a lamb that had no mother. Bum lambs had to be bottle fed until they could subsist on grass, hay, and grain.

My first bum lamb was a ewe which I named Bonnie. I had fun raising her on a bottle, and I was fulfilled taking her to the fall Lane County Fair where I exhibited her in the 4-H section. She was awarded a first-place blue ribbon at the fair.

I also raised a bum lamb I named Maa-Boy, which I exhibited at the fair in the Fat Lamb category. He, too, was awarded a blue ribbon. There was one aspect of exhibiting a fat lamb that was of mixed emotions. I was happy at the price received at auction, and sad for the ultimate end of that fat lamb, for at the end of the fair the local Kiwanis Club sponsored an auction wherein the fat lambs, hogs, and steers were auctioned off. The buyers were usually a business firm, such as banks, feed stores, agricultural equipment sales, etc. The Kiwanis Club auction of fat stock gained the purchasers much publicity via radio and newspapers, and the auctioned animals invariably brought a price several times higher than regular market prices. That amount of money made it very attractive for 4-H Clubbers to raise fat stock.

When I guided Maa-Boy into the auction ring, usually held on a Thursday of the fair, he auctioned at four times the market price, bringing me a tidy sum of money for my project. But the auction also brought a sad end to Maa-Boy, for I knew he would be butchered for food for humans. I had a fat lamb as my 4-H project for several years. The money from the auction padded my savings account for my SDA school tuition, books, and clothes.

Bonnie was also beginning of my flock of sheep, which reached thirty-two in number by the time I graduated college in 1956. At that time I needed a car to drive from College Place, Washington, to Bozeman, Montana, where I had my first employment after graduation. I sold the sheep for enough money to purchase a 1954 Nash Rambler.

CHAPTER VI

Loma Linda Year

1950 - 51

The Eugene Junior Academy years ended when I completed the tenth grade. My classmates were planning on taking eleven and twelfth grades at Laurelwood Academy, a Seventh-day Adventist boarding school near Gaston, Oregon. My dream was to also go to Laurelwood with my school chums. I was planning on going there, and never saw the change in plan coming, until one day in early August of 1950, when Mom causally asked me, "Which would you prefer to do: go to Loma Linda, live with Grandma Bonita, and attend Loma Linda Academy (LLA was a day school, not a boarding academy), or go to Laurelwood?"

To me that was a "no-brainer" question, for the obvious answer, to my thinking, was "I'll go to Laurelwood, of course." But Mom's question was a "set-up." Grandma had broached the idea to Mom that if I would live with her in Loma Linda and attend my junior year of academy there, she could get me a job carrying meal trays and washing dishes at the Loma Linda Sanitarium and Hospital (aka "The San"). "Curtis could earn his school expenses—tuition and books—and save some money to go to Laurelwood for his last year of Academy," was Grandma's proposal to Mom. Mom, Dad, and Grandma had already agreed on that plan, thus it was already "cut and dried." Those three connivers only vainly hoped I would jump at the chance to go live with Grandma and work at the San. Their plan was already finalized.

Came the day, late August 1950, when I boarded a Greyhound Bus in Eugene bound for the twenty-four-hour trip to downtown Los Angeles in time to catch an inter-urban train to San Bernardino and Loma Linda. I was carrying about all my worldly possessions crammed into a couple of dilapidated suitcases. I was fifteen years-old, not yet realizing I had just completed my last year of living at Linda Vista.

The bus made stops at every sizeable town or city along the way on U. S. Highway 99. To me, it was a long, slow trip into my land of exile. I remember one bus stop in some town I can't recall. The bus driver announced it would be a thirty-minute stop, in case we wanted to grab a quick snack at the bus café which was open 24/7. One of the popular songs at that time was "Good Night Irene," a love-song about some girl named Irene. As it played at the station the lyrics of that song drilled into my mind, and I can still hear it as I write these words: *Good night Irene, good night; I'll see you in my dreams!* "Ha, ha," I thought. "Fat chance that I will even dream about any girl named Irene." How wrong I was! It turned out the music teacher at Loma Linda Academy was one Irene Simpkin. I was still trying to learn how to play a trumpet that year, and Irene was my teacher. Poor music teacher, Irene. She would learn the hard way that I was, and am, a music drop-out from the rhythm band and Teach's choir of Lincoln Park School days. I'll give Irene credit, for she was always patient with me during my trumpet lessons and my playing third trumpet in the LLA Band.

I will insert here a note about that trumpet. While I attended EJA a school band was organized, with some guy from a local music store being band leader. An SDA lady in the Junction City church, by last name of Spencer, taught eighth grade in the Junction City public school system. She had two sons, Wesley and Bernard, whom she sent to EJA. For the first couple years we lived at Linda Vista, I was the only student from Junction City attending EJA, but by the time I was in ninth grade Glen Norris, an SDA back-slider, was reclaimed to church membership by my dad. Glenn had children, Bill, Anna, and Jeanie, whom he wanted to attend church school, so he purchased a WWII surplus radio vehicle that seated six to eight persons, plus driver. Glenn had our "school bus" painted bright yellow to be akin to standard school buses. The Norris kids, another girl named June, and I rode that yellow bus to the confluence of Oregon Highway 36 and U. S. 99, north of Eugene. There, the Spencer boys and Richard Withers (his father had the dairy farm on the banks of the Willamette River, where we had church picnics and baptisms) boarded the bus for EJA. Then the EJA band was formed. Mrs. Spencer found several antiquated band instruments, including a rather bulky baritone horn. She was able to procure the baritone for me to use, gratis.

Challenge to me was that I had to wrestle that monstrous horn the two miles from Linda Vista to the Norris farm on Highway 36. I had to leave my house by 6:30 a.m. in time to walk/run the two miles to be at the Norris's house by 7:00. The yellow bus had to get us to Highway 99 by 7:20, collect the kids there, and make it to EJA by around 8:00. Lugging that horn two miles, morning and evening, the two days per week we had band practice, was a real chore I didn't want.

The Greyhound Bus arrived in L. A. about 11:00 a.m., twenty-four hours after leaving Eugene. I was familiar with the downtown area, having lived in that city from age six to eleven. To catch the inter-urban train, I had to lug my two suitcases about six blocks in the heat of the August sun. The inter-urban transit arrived in San Bernardino around 3:00 where I then caught a bus to Loma Linda, arriving there late afternoon. The temperature was over 100 degrees, much hotter than the norm of Linda Vista, so I was hot and sweaty when I arrived at Grandma Bonita's apartment on Grove Street, one block from the main street through that little California town. Loma Linda means "pretty hill," but compared to the cool forested hills of the Oregon Coast Range, I did not find it pretty for I considered it to be my place of exile. Grandma made me feel very welcome, and she was a most wonderful grandma to me during the nine months I lived with her. The apartment wherein we lived was behind the larger house of her niece Beryl Hankins-Wical.

Beryl was the daughter of Grandma's older sister, Bess. My great-aunt Bess married Winfred Hankins. They were among the earliest SDA missionaries to China. In the early '40s Beryl had married Alfred Wical, a graduate of the Seventh-day Adventist College of Medical Evangelists (now known as Loma Linda University School of Medicine) which Ellen White helped found in 1905. Alfred and Beryl lived in a larger house in front of the apartments on the same tract of land.

Beryl was born in China while her parents were missionaries in the western China city of Kulangansu. Many years ago, Beryl told me a thrilling story that happened to her when her family lived in China. The Rentfros were likely one of few foreigners living in that city. When the family would walk in the streets the Chinese would call them "foreign devils" and throw garbage at them. Beryl is the little girl I talked about earlier who had the baby chick get struck by her mother's iron and who prayed that Jesus would bring her chicky back to life—and He did!

Classes at Loma Linda Academy and work at the San carrying meal trays to private rooms of patients, and washing dishes afterwards, both began the next day after my arrival. Life for me was very busy. Grandma worked in the San kitchen and her workday began very early in the morning, so she left the apartment before I was up. Uncle Ross had occupied the bedroom I now had, doing some of the same work at the San that I now did. He was a challenge to Grandma, for he did not like to get up early, so she would set two alarm clocks in his bedroom, one right by his bed and the other on the other side of the room. He could easily turn off the one by his bed, but the other necessitated him actually getting out of bed to shut it off. Ross rarely went back to bed after that. Grandma must have thought I would be difficult to arise also, for she initially set two alarm clocks for me, but I was usually up before they sounded off, so shortly thereafter she stopped setting them.

My work schedule at the San was flexible. Most days I carried breakfast trays, which meant I needed to be at the San by 6:50 a.m. to wrap breakfast rolls, working with two cohorts who also attended LLA with me. At seven sharp we began carrying trays. The food trays were tailored to the specific dietary needs for each individual patient. Diabetics needed one type of diet, while others were low-fat, etc. There were two dietitians on duty to inspect each tray prior to sliding it across the serving counter to those of us who carried the trays. Prior to carrying a tray to a patient, we had to write the room or cottage number on a chart, under our individual names. This was to be certain we each carried our share of trays, to be worthy of our high (?) salary of thirty cents an hour.

There were two trays that were equal in value to two to three ordinary trays. The tray labeled room 404 was a long-carry, for that room was far away from the main San building. I endeavored to carry that tray every time possible. The tray had no name on it, just the apartment number, 404. I was intrigued as to who the man was that received that tray. None of us ever saw him; we were instructed to never knock, but simply and quietly enter, placing the tray on a small table. I noted a portrait of a handsome gray-haired gentlemen, clad in doctoral robes with a bright red hood; I later learned a red hood stands for a Doctor of Theology. I surmised he was a very important person—VIP—in the SDA church. I now regret that never learned who that man was.

The other long-carry tray was to cottage 302, far on the other side of the San campus. Again, we entered that cottage, without knocking, and placed the tray on a small table. I never saw that person, either.

In addition to carrying meal trays, I was on the dish-washing crew numerous times during the week; during weekdays it was supper dishes; on weekends it could be breakfast, dinner, or supper dishes. Three persons were on the dish-washing crew: one to remove the trays from a cart and throw the cloth tray covers and napkins into a laundry bag; one to "scrap" the trays by scooping left-over food off the dishes and into a garbage bin (there were no automatic garbage disposals in those days), and then slide the dishes across a counter to the third person who arranged the dishes in a frame to hold them while they went through an automatic dishwasher. The water in the dishwasher was so hot the dishes and eating utensils did not need to be wiped dry, for they dried quickly from the heat. The person who removed the linens from the trays also stacked the clean dishes from the trays.

Next to the hospital kitchen was a very fancy dining room where mobile sanitarium patients ate their noon and evening meals. Several LLA girl students worked as servers. One day after carrying noon trays I was getting ready to wash dishes when one of the servers from the dining hall came into the kitchen area, screaming, "The dining room is on fire!" I stopped readying the dishwasher and ran to the dining room where I saw one large window awning blazing. On one wall of the dining room was a small cabinet with a glass door; inside was a fire hose. I quickly opened the cabinet and stretched the hose clear across the dining room to where the awning was on fire. I called to the server to turn on the fire hose valve so I could spray water on the fire, but all she could do was continue screaming, "The dining room is on fire!" I repeated to her several times, "Open the valve!" but she just continued screaming. I could do nothing but lay the hose down, run across the room, and turn on the valve. The hose came alive, writhing like a snake, water spraying everywhere. I quickly ran to the nozzle and began fighting the fire and soon had the blaze out. Hospital staff complimented me on my quickness and clear thinking, possibly preventing a potential destructive fire.

By the time I finished doing supper dishes it was often close to 9:00 p.m. I then bicycled the several blocks to the apartment I shared with Grandma. By that time, she was in her bedroom, and I often heard her weeping, calling Granddaddy Corrie by name; she was still grieving his death twelve years previously (her passed away the spring of 1938). I would think, but never said, "Grandma, why are you still weeping; it's been 12 years already; it's time you moved on?" After my wife, Rachel, passed away in April, 1996, I understood why grandma still grieved. When you lose a person close to you, you may never stop grieving.

I was, and still am, thankful for the work experience I had at the San because it was good training for the rest of my life-works.

At LLA I had the following classes: geometry, English, Spanish I, and a Bible class. Geometry was, initially, a challenge to me—math classes have always been a challenge. Geometry was my first class of the day, at 8:20 a.m., and was taught by LLA principal Perry Baden, a no-nonsense type of person. There were problems to be worked in class, usually followed by a heavy homework assignment. I was determined to earn the best grades possible, but when I received the results of the first mid-term test, for which I received a D, I was so concerned and indignant that I requested a meeting with Mr. Baden, which he granted.

I proactively began the meeting by saying, "Mr. Baden, you gave me a D grade in geometry. I have never had a D in my whole life, and I refuse to have one now."

"A D is what you earned, and a D is what you got," replied Mr. Baden.

"What do I need to do, to get that D removed? I am willing to do whatever it takes," I replied.

He thought a minute, and then said, "I will offer you this: whatever grade you earn on the final test for this semester, will be your permanent grade for the course."

I accepted his offer, then asked, "Do you have any suggestions as to how I can prepare to earn a better grade?"

Again, the principal thought, then said, "Two students received grades poorer than your D. I suggest you tutor them, for by doing so you will likely improve your own knowledge of geometry."

I learned who the other two students were—Ted Dawson and Lala Mae Davis—and I contacted them and made arrangements to tutor them every Thursday evening for one hour. In order to tutor them, I had to master the assignments myself. I studied the textbook and my class notes very thoroughly, then tutored them. As I did my own preparation, I would say to myself, "I must pound this into my head, so I can pound it into theirs." Sometimes I literally pounded my head against the wall as I prepared to tutor.

For the final exam I earned an A; Ted and Lala Mae got B's. I learned a lot by tutoring. I once read a book called *The Making of a Surgeon*. The author, a very successful surgeon, postulated this: observe one, do one, teach one. First you observe an experienced surgeon successfully perform a surgery; then you have that surgeon observe and aid you in performing that same type of surgery; then you teach another would-be surgeon how to do that same type of surgery. That was the technique of learning I used in my tutoring, and it still sounds like good advice to me.

"Two students received grades poorer than your D. I suggest you tutor them, for by doing so you will likely improve your own knowledge of geometry."

I continued on, that school year, to earn an A average. Ted and Lala Mae passed around the idea that I was *a Brain*, and that became my nickname which fellow students, and even faculty, called me, *Brain*. We all have brains, and we all need to learn how to use them!

Ted Dawson and I became very good friends. He was Black, but in those days the term was usually "Colored." I will always consider that Ted offered one of the most prized accolades I have ever received, for he said, "Curtis, you have always treated me as if you did not even see that I was 'Colored.'" He continued by saying, "You always treat me as being equal to you." Which, of course, he was!!

I have never believed in racial prejudice. The apostle Paul makes that very clear, when he declared at the Acropolis, in Athens, "God ... has made from one blood every nation of men to dwell on the face of the earth" (Acts 17:26, NKJV). I am also thankful that when I served as President of the Turkish Mission, one of the elders of the Istanbul SDA Church said to me, "Miller brother, you are the first missionary I have known who treats us as being equal with you, and not beneath you."

Back to Ted. We became very close friends that school year and made plans that when we entered college—we both planned to attend Walla Walla College (WWC, now Walla Walla University)—we would be roommates. Both of us were more than a little disappointed, and even angry, when WWC refused to admit a Black student. I have never forgotten that, but am thankful WWC now accepts all students, regardless of their ethnicity or color.

I saw Ted only one other time, after I left LLA. It was my senior year at WWC, and I was a deacon of the College Church at that time. One Sabbath morning, as I was serving as deacon, taking up the offering, I did note there was a Black man, in a U.S. Army uniform, in the balcony, but thought nothing more about it. As I sat in my home for Sabbath dinner, I saw that same man, in uniform, striding up to my front door, and then recognized it was Ted. I invited him to have dinner with us, and as we ate together, he again gave the accolade that I always treated him as an equal.

The Bible class I took that year at LLA was taught by Elder Charles Baker, who had previously been a missionary to South America. In the course of that class, each student was to give an inspirational talk to the entire group. I do not remember the precise subject of my talk, but I do remember an anecdote I related about the pitfalls of being a "permissive parent," Here's that anecdote:

A husband and wife determined they were going to raise their son "permissively" by allowing him to make all his own choices without their directions. One day as Mother was preparing lunch, she asked her son, "Bobby, what do you want for lunch?"

"I want French-fried worms," he replied. So, Father took Bobby out to the garden to dig a can of fresh worms, which Mother proceeded to deep-fry to perfection. She placed a plate of worms before Bobby as he sat at the table. He looked down at those worms but made no move to eat them.

"Bobby," said Father, "You asked for French-fried worms. I took you out to the garden to dig them, and your mother has fried them, so now it is time for you to eat them."

Bobby, looking down at the plate of worms said, "You and Mother eat one first, then I will eat one." So much for "permissive parenting," was the lesson I summed up in my talk to the class.

Evidently my class talk made a favorable impressed Elder Baker, for shortly after that he approached me, saying, "Curtis, the pastor of the Loma Linda Hill Church (this church still exists today, just below the San on Loma Linda Hill) wants a youth from LLA to be the speaker for "LLA Day" at the Hill Church. I have recommended you to give that sermon." I remember "preaching" that particular Sabbath, for it was the first sermon I ever gave, at age fifteen. The theme was based on the following quote from Ellen White: "With such an army of workers as our youth, rightly trained, might furnish, how soon the message of a crucified, risen, and soon-coming Savior might be carried to the whole world! How soon might the end come."[4]

That sermon, and the remark Elder Baker made the following Monday in Bible class, that "Curtis should become a minister of the Gospel, instead of a medical doctor" made a strong impression in my mind, as to what the future did hold for me. I had envisioned becoming a medical doctor from the time I was in the lower grades of elementary school.

---

4 *Education,* Mountain View, CA: Pacific Press Publishing Association, 1903, *p. 271.*

Prior to my odyssey to Loma Linda, my uncle Ross married his classmate from Lynwood Academy, Ree Jackson; however, he previously had, briefly, dated a young lady with the last name of Gepford; I do not remember her first name, but she had a younger sister by the name of Nancy. Nancy's mother and Grandma Bonita were friends by virtue of Ross dating her oldest daughter. Grandma mentioned to Mrs. Gepford that I would be coming to Loma Linda to live with her, and the two of them together agreed I should meet Nancy—and I did!

That year at LLA, when I was a junior, Nancy was a freshman. Keep in mind, I was only fifteen, she was fourteen, and both of us were novices as far as dating was concerned, but after being introduced, we did date. For our first date I invited her to attend a college football game with me. The Gepford home was only a few blocks away from where I lived—but way back then Loma Linda was a small town, and everything was only a few blocks away, so I walked to her home, intending to take the local transit bus from Loma Linda to nearby San Bernardino, where the game was to be played at the local college stadium. When I arrived at the Gepford home, her father volunteered to drive us to the football stadium. As we were leaving the Gepford residence her mother gave a very clear directive, "Now you kids be home by 10:00 p.m."

Kick-off for the game was 7:00 p.m., right after we all stood to sing our national anthem, the "Star-Spangled Banner." I had never been to a football game before, though as a kid I did play "touch football" in the street with my buddies. I knew a game was four fifteen-minute quarters in length but had no idea that a "quarter" was only counted when the ball was in play, and did not include all the time-outs, and other delays. About 8:30 the game was only about half-over. I became concerned that if we stayed for the whole game, we would not make it home by that 10 p.m. curfew her mother had stipulated. Reluctantly I suggested to Nancy that we'd best leave the game during the half-time band and cheerleading performance. We caught the bus to Loma Linda, arriving right at about 10. I was rewarded by Mrs. Gepford for following her request. Throughout the rest of the school year Nancy and I had occasional dates, when my San work permitted me time to socialize. It was a good year, after all, even though I had gone to Loma Linda, even though I considered it to be a year of exile before going my senior year to Laurelwood Academy.

I still chuckle over one of a series of events involving Nancy. The main hall of LLA had lockers on both side of the hall. My locker was at the very end of the hall in the middle of that tier of lockers, making my locker door open about even with my chest. I have never been a "neat-nik" when it comes to organizing my study desk, and in the case of that year at LLA, my locker was far from neat. I would just chuck my book, notebook, or other school items, helter-skelter into the locker.

One day, midway through that school year, I opened my locker door to find a carefully printed notice: THIS LOCKER HAS BEEN FOUND TO BE UNTIDY. IF IT IS NOT NEATLY ARRANGED BY TOMORROW FURTHER ACTION WILL BE TAKEN. The notice was signed as being from the FBI.

I was mystified and curious as to whom would search my locker, find it untidy, and post this notice as from the "FBI." I wrote my reply: THIS LOCKER HAS BEEN ASSIGNED BY LLA TO BE MINE FOR THE SCHOOL YEAR. IT IS MY PROPERTY, AND I WILL KEEP IT THE WAY I WANT. I DON'T KNOW WHO FBI IS BUT THINK IT COULD STAND FOR FAT BOY'S INSTITUTE.

The next day I opened my locker to find all my books, notebooks, and everything else all neatly arranged, with this note posted: THE FBI HAS ARRANGED YOUR SCHOOL BOOKS AND NOTEBOOKS. AND FBI DOES NOT STAND FOR FAT BOY'S INSTITUTE.

When I saw my locker neatly arranged, I glanced around the hall, and on the far side of the hall I spotted Nancy and a couple of her friends watching me and laughing. I knew I had spotted the "FBI." Periodically, for the rest of the school year, the FBI would neatly arrange my locker.

I queried Nancy about what "FBI" meant, but she declined to tell me. When Uncle Ross and his new bride Ree came to visit, shortly after the FBI took over, I told them about my locker, and showed them my collection of notes. Ree was attending La Sierra College, with Ross, and was taking a class called Psychology 101. She asked if she could borrow the notes to use in her class discussion group, so I loaned them to her. Later she told me, "Psychology 101 Class believes 'FBI' stands for "From Boy's Interest." I asked Nancy if that was what FBI meant, and she replied, "Ree's class is probably right."

During my year at LLA Grandma Bonita's older brother, my uncle Curt (remember, I am his name' sake), and his wife, Josie, came to visit. They hosted a dinner for Grandma, Ross and Ree, and me, at the then-famous Mission Inn, known for its fine dining. Uncle Curt had me seated between him and Aunt Josie. The waiter brought menus for each of us; Uncle Curt magnanimously said, "You each order whatever you want, for I'm paying." As host, and being a take-charge personality, he then placed his order, addressing the waiter, "I'll have a sirloin steak, medium rare."

I didn't know what "medium rare" meant, but thought, "If it's good enough for Uncle Curt, it is good enough for me," so I told the waiter, "I'll have the same." The waiter brought our plates to the table, setting them in front of Uncle Curt and me. I then learned what "medium rare" meant: the steak was browned on both sides, but the inside was solid pink. It looked raw to me. Aunt Josie saw the shocked look on my face, as I surveyed my sirloin steak, medium rare, and she signaled the waiter, instructing him to "Take this steak back to the chef and have him cook it 'well-done.'" When it came back I was able to eat it.

As we ate, Uncle Curt came to the primary reason for which he was hosting this dinner: It was to honor me, as his "Name Sake." He addressed me with a direct question: "Curtis, when you go to college, what is going to be your major and minor fields of study?"

"Uncle Curt," I replied, "You know it is a challenge to be accepted into CME (SDA College of Medical Evangelists, now known as Loma Linda School of Medicine), so I am going to take courses to fulfill the requirements for CME acceptance, and major in Religion; that way, if I am not accepted into CME, I can become a preacher." From the time I was in elementary school, my life's goal had been to be a missionary doctor. I was going to discover cures for many illnesses, become a world-renowned doctor famous for curing people of their painful diseases. I glanced at Uncle Curt, expecting to receive his smile of approval, but that didn't happen.

Instead, Uncle Curt brought his fist down on the table right by my hand, as he declared, "Curtis, don't you ever consider taking what is second-best. I want you to decide whether you are going to be a medical doctor or a preacher; don't you ever settle for anything second-best!" He then elaborated that if I should choose to become a physician, "I will help finance you through medical school and then offer you a position on my medical staff." At that time Uncle Curt had a very large, successful medical practice in Chicago.

"Curtis, don't you ever consider taking what is second-best. I want you to decide whether you are going to be a medical doctor or a preacher; don't you ever settle for anything second-best!"

That night at the Mission Inn, Uncle Curt said, "I want you to think it over the rest of your senior year in academy, then when you graduate, you can tell what your choice is: to be a medical doctor, or to be a preacher."

While I was still in my senior year at Laurelwood Academy, I wrote to Uncle Curt that I had decided to become a Seventh-day Adventist minister. I never heard from him again, nor did I ever see him again, for he passed away while I was still attending Walla Walla College, preparing for a life of ministry.

My cousin Beryl Wical's husband, Alfred, was also a medical doctor. Their house was on the street-side of the apartment Grandma Bonita rented from them the year I lived with her. They had a daughter, Patsy, attending Pacific Union College in Angwin, California, the year I was in Loma Linda. They had a son, Bobby, several years younger than I, and an adopted son, younger still. Alfred had his primary practice in Banning, California, about thirty miles from Loma Linda. He had living quarters at that office, but usually came home on weekends. He had rental apartments in Loma Linda, for which he paid me ten dollars a month to mow the lawns there.

One spring day Alfred called me to his house to make an offer to me, "Curtis I am thinking of moving my family to Banning, but I will need someone to drive my sons to Loma Linda to attend church school there. If you will stay in Loma Linda to do that, I will also pay you well to continue doing the yard work; I will also pay your tuition at LLA; if you will continue to do this when you go to college at La Sierra, I will help with your tuition; and if you decide to attend the College of Medical Evangelists (CME), I will help with your tuition then, and when you qualify as a MD, I will make you a partner in my practice." After saying this he escorted me out to his driveway, where was parked an almost new Buick sedan, and said, "And this will be your car for use in driving my sons to school, and for your own use."

I responded by saying I would consider his offer, and also seek advice from my grandma Bonita and my parents. This I did, while I also prayed for guidance. I also confided in Nancy, who urged me to accept the offer. I was concerned about Alfred "owning me" if I accepted his offer. I was concerned about his influence upon me, for I had learned he was sleeping with his office nurse/receptionist. I certainly did not want to live his lifestyle. Ultimately, I rejected his offer. I did not like living in southern California, in general, and in Loma Linda, specifically. Nancy did express disappointment, but we agreed we would write to each other occasionally.

My mother and her youngest sister, Jean, drove together to Loma Linda to bring me home to Linda Vista. Grandma Bonita came with us, for she would live with my parents from 1951–1964. That summer I worked in various farm jobs to earn money to fund my senior year at Laurelwood Academy.

CHAPTER VII

Laurelwood Year

1951 - 52

Late August of 1951 I enrolled in Laurelwood Academy (LA) for my senior year and I was very happy and thankful. It was great to be there, an answer to my prayers and dreams.

I lodged in the boys' dormitory, room 313, top floor. The EJA classmate I had planned to room with failed to come to school that year; consequently my first roommate was Jimmy Reed, but we were not compatible, so Charles Clayton became my roommate for most of the year.

The previous summer I had calculated that my saved summer earnings definitely were not sufficient to pay my school tuition, plus board and room, therefore, I would need as much income that I could generate by working at the school. Laurelwood had four financial budgets: Budget I required working twenty hours per month; Budget II forty hours; Budget III sixty hours; and Budget IV required eighty hours per month. I enrolled in the eighty hours per month plan, but even working that budget still meant I needed around $35 more per month to pay my school expenses.

Few work positions provided eighty hours per month, but either working at the Portland Sanitarium and Hospital or milking cows did. The academy had a farm, dairy, and pasteurizer, and supplied the academy with milk. I became one of the milkers, working the afternoon shift from 2:30—5:30. I reasoned my experience milking cows at Linda Vista would be an advantage for me, however, that was only partially true, for at home we milked by hand while at LA we milked by machine. The milking machines were Hindman brand, which were not the best.

The dairy manager was Frank Davis, brother-in-law to Principal Paul Limerick. Frank held that position in nepotism due to his relationship with Limerick. He may have had some experience and qualification to manage a dairy, but I do not believe he was a good manager and I still believe he was very poor at the job he held.

First of all, calves need to be adequately fed, beginning right at birth. Ideally a calf should be suckled by his mother, especially for the first few days of life, for the calf needs colostrum which is a form of milk produced by the mammary glands of mammals (including humans) in late pregnancy. Most species will generate colostrum just prior to giving birth. Colostrum contains antibodies to protect the newborn against disease. In general, protein concentration in colostrum is substantially higher than in milk.

I remember that Frank removed a calf from its mother immediately, to be fed from a milk-pail with a rubber nipple attached. He did not adequately feed calves. I remember spotting several calves that were very malnourished and I reported this to him and observed him frantically trying to get milk down a dying calf. He would even desperately break raw eggs down a calf's throat in an effort to save its life, but most of the time he was too late in that endeavor. Nor did Frank adequately feed the milk cows, but he paid me no attention when I belabored him to feed them properly. I remember the campus night watchman telling me he would often throw the cows extra alfalfa hay when he came by the dairy barn at night.

Secondly, Frank did not improve the dairy herd with cows that were producing a good quantity of milk. Most of the cows were "scrubs," producing very little milk. I remember some of them only gave a quart or two of milk per milking, though they were milked twice a day. You can't feed a cow adequately when it only produces such a scant amount of milk. Our cows at home at Linda Vista were good milk producers, giving two to three gallons morning and evening.

The dairy barn had stanchions on both sides, with thirty to thirty-five cows per side. Two of us did the milking, one on each side. Each cow had its own personality, with most of them being gentle, but there was one cow we named "Mrs. Satan" who had a foul disposition. I suspect she had been abused, perhaps even by Frank, for she invariably kicked at me when I approached her to connect her to the milking machine.

Although I worked the afternoon milking shift, I soon learned the milkers on the morning shift did not like to milk on Sabbath and Sunday mornings, so I often volunteered to milk those shifts for them, for I needed all the time I could get, to pay off as much of my school expenses as possible.

Prior to milking each cow, we had to cleanse her udder with a bleach solution, which had a strong odor that soaked into our hands. After my milking shift I would shower, trying to cleanse away that odor before going to supper at the school cafeteria which was located on the bottom floor of the girls' dorm. I particularly wanted that odor gone before skating with girls on Saturday nights.

After milking, showering, and putting on clean clothes, I was hard-pressed to reach the cafeteria before it closed, and I was often the last person to go through the line. In the cafeteria it was customary for mixed seating, three boys and three girls, per table. I wanted that Clorox odor off my hands when I had to eat at a table with girls! However, due to barely getting to the cafeteria before it closed, I often had to eat at a table by myself.

In the boys' dorm the rising bell sounded at 6:00 a.m., giving us twenty minutes to dress, groom, and be in the dorm parlor for a brief worship before arriving at the cafeteria by 6:45, eat, and then make it to our first class at 7:30.

My senior year my classes were Bible Doctrines, American History, Spanish II, and Chemistry. I had no problem with the first three, but Chemistry was a real challenge, and I never did adequately master it.

After supper and dorm worship came study period, from about 6:30—9:00 p.m., during which time we were to stay in our dorm room. A student "monitor" was quartered in the hallway to be certain we stayed in our rooms. Bedtime was 9:20 p.m. with the lights blinking one time at 9, two times at 9:15, and finally going off at 9:20.

Radios were not allowed in our dorm rooms, but my good friend Harvey Heidinger, who was one of the student electricians for the academy, had one secreted somewhere in his room on the second floor. He also had his room lights secretly wired so he could have a light to study by, even after lights were off (academies would automatically turn the lights off in the dorm so that the students would be forced to go to sleep), and he also had his light rigged so that it turned off should the boys' dean open his door to check his lights were out. Boys' Dean Wisbey suspected Harvey had a hidden radio, but was never able to find it. He also suspected Harvey's room lights, but with the same result.

A curious phenomenon occurred in the class seating, for I found myself seated next to Virginia Inman, a student from, of all places, Loma Linda. It was a given, then, that we would become acquainted, and I even considered having her as a girlfriend, but we just never seemed to "click."

Another senior girl caught my eye, Kathy Doleman. I thought she was cute and vivacious. I invited her to roller skate with me or be my partner in the Saturday night marches in the gym. In those years "dating" was not allowed at LA, or any other SDA boarding academy, therefore students, like me, did take advantage of marches and skating opportunities.

It was no secret among the students, some faculty, and even Kathy herself, that I liked her and wanted to be her boyfriend, and she did respond somewhat to the attention I paid her. I took advantage of another potential opportunity to be near her. I leaned that a senior girl, Anna Sheehan, worked in the school administration pool and made out the seating arrangements for classes, so I asked her to set up the seating for Chemistry class for me to sit by Kathy—and Anna did it for me! Chemistry was the last class before lunch. The classroom was in the ground floor basement of the gym building, and thus was the most distant classroom from the cafeteria. A few days after sitting next to Kathy in that class I offered to carry her books while walking with her to lunch, thus having another opportunity for us to know each other better.

Kathy roomed with Brooke Huntington, also a senior girl. I sat next to Brooke in Bible Doctrines class, so I asked her what my chances were of having Kathy as a girlfriend. Wow, did I ever get a surprise! I learned something many other students knew: Kathy was "going steady" with Paul Weir, who had been a student at Laurelwood but was presently in the U. S. Army in Korea. In my thinking I hoped the old adage "Out of sight, out of mind" might be true, so I continued to pursue Kathy. For Valentine's Day I posted her a large heart-shaped box of chocolates which, when she received it, did offer a brief, simple thank you, but the candy had little effect on having her become my girlfriend.

That school year LA had its first-ever, student-led Week of Prayer, and I was selected to be one of the speakers. Right after the chapel service wherein I preached, I raced back to the dorm to change out of my suit into acceptable classroom attire. In those days jeans were not acceptable classroom dress, and we were required to wear slacks and shirt. Bible Doctrines was the first class after chapel service, and I was few minutes late, entering the classroom just in time to hear Elder Peckham say to the class, "Curtis gave a very fine sermon in chapel, and I think he should become a minister."

His statement made a profound impression on me, for he was the third person, and second minister, who had made comments that I would make a good minister. It was at that point in my life that I made a conscious statement to myself, "Perhaps I should become a Gospel minister."

After hearing Elder Peckham's statement, I sat down next to Brooke, who passed me a note, on which she had written, "Curtis, don't look at Kathy now, but after your Week of Prayer sermon, I think she is thinking seriously about you."

"Maybe, just maybe, I might be able to elbow Paul Weir out of Kathy's life," I thought to myself. I continued to carry Kathy's books to the cafeteria after chemistry class.

Chemistry class, taught by Mr. White, was my last class of the day, just before lunch. One day we assembled for class, but Mr. White did not appear. We debated whether we should wait or leave. There was a vague, unwritten "rule" that if a teacher did not appear for class, we would leave after waiting five minutes. I was seated on the front row, right by the chemistry lab, just off the classroom.

Just before five minutes was up, someone glanced out the window and saw Miss Miller, the Spanish teacher, coming up the walk to the chemistry room. We knew she was probably going to substitute for Mr. White, but being a spinster and Spanish teacher, what would she know about teaching chemistry?

One of the fellows near where I was seated said in a low voice, "Let's dodge into the chem lab before Ol' Miller gets here. She won't know we are supposed to be in class." Four guys quickly went into the lab, and I impulsively followed them.

Once in the lab we began messing around, mixing up various chemical concoctions to give the impression that we were supposed to being doing our chem lab assignment. We mixed some chemicals that made smoke and others that made quite an odor. We looked busy and were having fun. One of the fellows in the lab room with me was my classmate Louie Versteeg, Senior Class President.

Miss Miller poked her head in the doorway to ask, "Aren't you young men supposed to be in the classroom?"

One of my cohorts replied, "We are supposed to be doing our chem lab experiments." Miss Miller did not reply and went back to the classroom, while we goofed around for the rest of the class period. Later we wondered if we would be counted "absent" from class.

The tardy and absent notices were posted in the dorm lobby each evening. We looked at the posting and did not see any of our names on the list, so we believed we had "gotten away with it!"

The next morning Principal Paul Limerick's office informed me that the Limerick wanted to see me in his office. "Oh, Oh!" I thought, "Maybe I didn't get away with it."

Arriving at Limerick's office, I found my four cohorts there also. Shortly Limerick opened his office door and summoned us to line up in front of his desk. By happenstance I ended up in the middle of the lineup.

Limerick looked steadily at us, then asked the Louie, the first fellow in line, "Did you cut chemistry class yesterday?"

Louie answered, "No, I didn't," and he continued to give some rambling reason why being in the lab was not "cutting class."

When he finished, he asked the next fellow, "Did you cut class?"

"No, I didn't, I was doing my chem lab assignment."

Limerick said nothing more to that fellow, and then looked at me, "Curtis, did you cut class yesterday?"

Despite what I had done in class the day before, I was raised by my parents to be honest, so I replied, "Yes sir. I cut class."

I was amazed when Limerick responded, "Curtis, you may go." I left, not knowing what the other two fellows answered to Limerick's question. I learned later that each of my cohorts were given twenty-five hours of "Free Labor" which they had to perform in addition to their regular after-class work assignments. I concluded that "Honesty is the best policy" proved true—at least it did in my case.

One of the highlights of the senior year of academy was the late spring bus trip to Walla Walla College to give students an overview of college life. This gave me another opportunity to socialize with Kathy, for we were allowed to sit on the bus with a girl and I was pleased that Kathy and I sat together both going and coming on the bus. We also socialized together while at WWC. I thought perhaps that trip had helped with encouraging Kathy to be my girlfriend. However, as time went on at Laurelwood Academy, I began to suspect Kathy was still corresponding with Paul, and I was not in the running for her affections. Soon came the day I was definitely convinced of this, and I decided I would not carry her books to the cafeteria anymore. At the conclusion of chemistry class, that day, I simply stood up, without picking up her books, and walked to the cafeteria alone. Kathy got the message I was sending her, and my pursuit of her was over.

There is a sequel to this story. When Kathy and I arrived at WWC for our freshman year, she roomed in West Hall, one of the older buildings on the WWC campus, and very near Sittner Hall, the men's dormitory, where I roomed. The sidewalk from both these dorms merged at a point halfway between them. Early on that freshman year Kathy was able to size-up Paul in comparison with other WWC students, and I heard she had now determined that Paul Weir was somewhat weird, so she dropped him. One day, as I left Sittner Hall to walk towards the administration building and the library, I spotted Kathy leaving West Hall. I slowed my steps so as not to be near the place the two walks came together when she reached that point, for I was not interested in meeting or talking with her. I was surprised to see her waiting for me where the walks converged. I continued walking and came to where she was waiting. I had heard, and sensed, that she was interested in resuming our friendship, however I was not interested. Our conversation, or lack thereof, must have given her the message I did not want a relationship with her.

While at LA Nancy Gepford and I had exchanged occasional letters. After the Student Week of Prayer, of which I was a speaker, I made my choice for my life's work: I chose to become a minister, and chose to drop my long-held dream of becoming a medical doctor. Although I was young, I had heard that when SDA conferences considered calling a man to ministry, they also wanted to know who the wife was of said minister. I meditated on that, pondering whom, of all the girls I knew, would make the best minister's wife!?

As I pondered this question, the answer soon came to me—Nancy Gepford—for the following reasons: she was very spiritual and a dedicated Seventh-day Adventist; her personality was bubbly and pleasant; she was multi-talented, being very gifted in playing the piano, violin, and singing; and we had liked each other that year I was in Loma Linda.

I wrote her a letter, asking, "Nancy, would you consider being my 'steady' (dating term commonly used in my generation) girlfriend?" I was ecstatic when she quickly replied, "Yes!" We began writing to each other at least five letters a week.

As I write this portion of my autobiography, I have open beside me the *LA Laurel*, the school yearbook of '52, and a note that Kathy wrote in it, by her picture, "Good luck, always, Kathy." Flash forward fifty years, to the golden anniversary of the LA Class of '52, which we both attended. At that class reunion I took a gel-pen that wrote in gold—in harmony with it being the "golden" anniversary—to have my LA classmates write in it. Kathy wrote, "With love from the 'has been.'" Interesting! I wonder "*What might have been*?" if I had pursued friendship with her when on our walk? I am reminded of a poem from John Greenleaf Whittier, an American poet of great renown, that includes these words: "Of all sad words of tongue or pen, the saddest are these, 'It might have been.'" And, now, I wonder *what might have been* if way back then I had pursued Kathy the fall of '52 at WWC?

Stepping back to my senior year at LA. There were seventy-eight seniors that year, most of whom had attended LA either two or four years. I was probably the only senior, that year, who had attended only one year, therefore had less opportunity to have "Offices Held" by my senior picture. In the yearbook, there are the following by my picture: *Curtis Miller, Ambition: Minister; Offices Held: Sabbath School Secretary, Ministerial Seminar Leader, Senior Class Chaplain.* My name was placed in nomination to be Senior Class President, but the vote went to someone who had been at LA several years. Like my year at LLA, '50–51, I was honored to be the Class Chaplain.

I formed a life-lasting friendship with a fellow senior at LA, Harvey Heidinger. We became prayer partners and were given special permission by Boys' Dean Wisbey to meet together for our prayer sessions after Friday evening worships and before bed time. He was my roommate at WWC, and we have maintained our friendship for more than seventy years. He visited me when I was in mission service in Istanbul, Turkey, while he was a missionary doctor in Ethiopia. We still keep in touch with each other. He has been widowed twice, and now lives in a nearby town, Silverton, Oregon.

I now look back at my senior year at Laurelwood Academy as one of the happiest years of my life.

CHAPTER VIII

Walla Walla College Years

1952 - 56

Challenge of Summer Job to Earn Funds to Go to WWC

The summer after graduating from Laurelwood Academy I sought a job to earn money with which to attend Walla Walla College (WWC). I was only seventeen years old, and most jobs in the logging and sawmilling industries required being at least eighteen years old. Nonetheless I decided to try. Every morning Mom would drive me to sawmills in our local area. I would go to the "Boss Shack" to enquire if any jobs were available. For two weeks I could find no position for anyone under age eighteen.

Finally on the third Monday of my job search Mom took me once again to the sawmill located at Cheshire, Oregon, only a few miles from where we lived. Once again I left the Boss Shack without being hired. My parents and I had been praying daily that I would find work necessary for my going to WWC. As I headed back to the car at the Cheshire Mill, a man working in the sawmill hailed me to come to him, which I did. He said, "Kid I have seen you coming here day after day, and know you are very serious about finding a job. There is a sawmill near Triangle Lake. The mill owner is a hard man to work for, and he often fires a man or else the guy quits his job. If you go there, I bet you can find a job." Triangle Lake was about twenty miles from where I lived.

Mom and I immediately headed for Triangle Lake. The name of the establishment was "Johnson Lumber Company," a Mr. Johnson being the owner. I found him at the Boss Shack and asked him if he had any job openings. He did! He said to me, "I need a man to pull on the 'Green Chain.'" There are two "chains" in sawmills; the green chain is a conveyor chain that brings lumber out to where green chainers pull the green lumber cut from a log that is still very heavy compared with lumber that has been put through the drying process, and would be on the "dry" chain. Green chain work is much harder than pulling on a dry chain.

I asked if I could have the job on the green chain, and he said "Yes, if you can begin work right now." Could I? You bet I could and would. He gave me an application form to fill out with my name, address, birth date, Social Security number, and other employment information. I filled it out and gave it back to him. The form didn't ask my age, nor did I give it to him. I simply wrote my date of birth.

I ran back to Mom, who was waiting in the car, shouting "Mom, I got a job on the green chain, and I start right now!" On days I went job hunting Mom always packed a lunch for me, in case I got a job. I grabbed my lunch box, hid it behind a bush, and rushed on to the green chain, where I pulled on a pair of leather gloves, for I came prepared for work, and began pulling lumber off the chain onto various stacks for 2x6, 2x8, and other various dimensions of lumber. I soon learned pulling on the green chain was very hard, physical work, but I pulled green lumber like crazy, for I really wanted that job. The third day of such hard labor is usually the most challenging, for by that time muscles, unused to such hard labor, are at their sorest—but after the third day it gets easier.

Mom came to pick me up at quitting time that first day. During that day I learned that the "Head Sawyer" lived in Cheshire and drove back and forth to work each day. I made arrangements to ride to work with him each day, paying him five bucks a week to help with his gas.

As I began work on the third day, Mr. Johnson came out of the Boss Shack to talk with me, saying, "Kid, you are only seventeen years old." I had a sinking feeling he was about to fire me for being underage. "Yes, I'm only seventeen; does that mean I don't have a job?"

"I have been watching how you work, and you work hard. I like that, so you can keep the job. Just don't ask me how I get around the regulation about you having to be eighteen." I never asked, and he never told me how he did it. I simply thanked my prayer-answering God for getting me a job so I could attend WWC.

One day Mr. Johnson came out of his shack, carrying a small pair of "cork-boots"—boots with spikes in the soles to aid in walking on logs, saying "I have a special job for whomever can wear these boots." I was the only one on the crew that could fit into the boots, so I got the new job, which was punching logs on the mill pond. I would send some logs downstream to the sawmill, while the others were "cold-decked" by being hauled out of the water by a huge crane and stacked on the shore until the very rainy winter months when log-trucks couldn't haul logs to the mill, due to miry roads.

My cold-decking job consisted of me using my "pike-pole," a long slender wooden rod with a spike-hook on the end that enabled me to guide a log into place or jam it into the end of a log to pull it towards me. I would select a group of logs to line up parallel to the riverbank where I could set a pair of tongs around a log so Mr. Johnson could haul it out of the water and onto the cold deck. Whenever he would lift a log out of the water I would brace myself against the rest of the logs to hold them in place, for when he lifted a log out it would create a disturbance in the water that could scatter the logs. Sometimes a log would slip out of the tongs, sending it crashing into the water. To keep myself safe under those circumstances I have an "escape log" arranged perpendicular to the logs I was pressing towards the shore. If I saw a log slipping out of the tongs I would race to the escape log—my corked boots gripping the log as I ran—to avoid the log hitting me. I remember one time a log dropped down, hitting the far end of my escape log, catapulting me way up in the air and plunging me into the pond water. I kicked to the surface, then swam to the largest a log I could find, I would then start the log rolling in the water away from me while I grasped the bark to enable the log's momentum to pull me up out of the water.

I was dunked in the water several times that summer, and worked the rest of the day soaking wet, which was fine if it was a warm day, but miserable if it was cold and rainy.

"Curtis, if you want a job next summer to earn money for college, you will always have a job with me, if you want it."

Mr. Johnson gave me benefit of several different mill jobs that summer. On my last day on the job, before setting out for WWC, he presented me with my last paycheck, as he said, "Curtis, if you want a job next summer to earn money for college, you will always have a job with me, if you want it." I appreciated his offer.

At Walla Walla College

The following Sunday I put a large trunk, packed with my bedding and what few clothes I had, to be bused to Walla Walla. I boarded a Greyhound bus to Portland, transferred to one going to Pendleton, then transferred to a third bus going to Walla Walla. Harvey Heidinger was on that same bus, which brought us to WWC together.

Freshman students, in those WWC years, by tradition were assigned to rooms on the third floor of Sittner Hall, the Men's

Dormitory. My first roommate dropped out of school, my second was drafted into the Army, so consequently I roomed alone for most of the year.

I arrived at WWC with $500 in my account, which meant I needed to get a job quickly. My uncle, Carl Heid, had his own auto repair shop in College Place. Uncle Carl also had work contacts in the area, so he referred me to a local SDA contractor who was putting in sidewalks and curbs in Walla Walla. I worked for him fall quarter, making two dollars per hour. Winter quarter saw me seeking work on campus. I first got a job sweeping the "Little Chapel" room on the second floor of the administration building, but that only gained me one hour of work, five days a week, at seventy-five cents per hour, which was hardly enough to earn the money I needed to pay my school bill.

I scouted around for more work on campus and contracted to clean and maintain the rest rooms and showers on the east end of Sittner Hall. The contract was for fifteen hours of work per week. I was a fast worker and could do the necessary work in acceptable fashion in less than ten hours per week. I decided I still had time to work more and learned that the campus elementary school needed a part time janitor to scrub, wash, and polish all the hallways every Sunday. That I could do in six hours, but I wanted yet another job.

I had a classmate who worked as one of the campus night watchmen. The shifts were 6–10, 10–2, and –-6. I learned that on weekends the night watchmen that had the 10–2 shift would welcome someone to cover for them, so they could catch up on their sleep. I was able to take that shift Friday, Saturday, and Sunday nights. I was now working forty hours per week and taking a full class load.

At the end of my freshman year I had earned all my tuition, books, plus room and board. To top it off, the college now owed me $179! I had chosen these jobs strategically: they were scattered all over the campus, making it a challenge for the business office to connect the dots of all these jobs. When the assistant business manager, Jake Mehling, learned the college owed me that money, he called me into his office and declared, "Curtis, when college classes start next school year, you will have only one job—two at the most. WWC is not supposed to owe students money at the end of a school year!"

Based on college entrance exams, freshman students were assigned to Freshman English classes. The lowest level was called "Bonehead English" —at least that's what we students called it! Based on my score I was assigned to the top echelon class taught by the head of the English Department, Kenneth "Dad" Aplington. However, there was an interesting development when first quarter grades were posted with mine being mediocre, consequently Men's dean Fabian Meier called me into his office.

"Curtis," he intoned, "I want to talk with you about your grades, which have a B/C average. Your college entrance exams indicate you are in the 93rd percentile, meaning out of 100 students, chosen at random, you placed more intelligent than 92, and less than six students. I want to discuss with you what you can do to improve your grades."

What Dean Meier told me about my percentile ranking enlightened me, for I never knew I ranked as 93rd, thus this was sufficient impetus to stir me to strive for a higher level of grades. He made suggestions on my classroom note-taking, underlining key points in textbooks, and he also coached me to "study your teacher carefully in the first few class periods. Then develop a strategy for getting the best grade possible."

He used one of my current classes, History of Western Civilization, as an example. That subject was taught by Professor Frank Meckling. Meckling always gave a quiz at the beginning of each class, and it was always an essay question, which he would write on the board. On my first quiz he gave me a "D," which I admit both shocked and puzzled me. At LA I had taken American History, for which I received an "A." In red ink Meckling wrote on my first quiz paper, "Write less and say more."

Dean Meier, who knew Meckling's style of teaching and testing, said, "Curtis, you need to 'think like Meckling.' As you study the assignment, ask yourself, 'If I were Meckling, what essay question would I ask?' then write an essay-style answer."

For example, Meckling might ask, "Compare and contrast the Hundred Years' War between England and France with the Wars of the Roses in England." The Hundred Years' War was a long struggle between England and France over succession to the French throne. It lasted from 1337 to 1453, so it might more accurately be called the "116 Years' War." The war starts off with several stunning successes on Britain's part, and the English forces dominate France for decades. The Wars of the Roses were a series of wars for control of the throne of England fought between supporters of two rival branches of the royal House of Plantagenet—the House of Lancaster, which was associated with a red rose, and the House of York, whose symbol was a white rose.

"One thing Meckling likes in an essay answer is a 'preamble' which summarizes the question, then the main body of the answer, with a final wrap-up summary of the answer."

I used that strategy after Meier's talk with me and moved up to an "A" … and that was good, considering the axiom on campus that a B from Meckling was better than an "A" from any other teacher on campus!

Nancy Again

During my freshman year I hardly dated, and the few times I did was for the sake of having someone to sit with at Saturday night functions, but my main reason for not dating was because by this time Nancy and I considered ourselves engaged, although not by a formal announcement. In our hearts, and in the thoughts we shared, we were planning to marry. We exchanged many words of endearment. We would write on the backs of the envelops of our letters "SWAK"—meaning "Sealed with A Kiss."

Even now, I remember her sending me her homemade fudge with walnuts, and I remember the time I received a letter, which had her signature, “With all my love, Nancy,” and underneath her name she had placed a “kiss” made by applying red lipstick (please know that in those days conservative SDA ladies did not wear makeup—in fact it was banned on our school campuses) and pressing her lips to the letter.

In our courtship plans we agreed that when Nancy entered college, she would be coming to WWC, where our courtship would transfer from letters to being together on the same campus. We exchanged framed color portraits, and I displayed Nancy’s on my dorm room dresser, where I would see her smile first thing in the morning and last thing at night.

Norma Beck

The summer of ‘53 I worked at the H&H Logging Company, formed by Vernon and Bob Hassell—father and son—and Earl Hutchinson, who were SDA members of the Junction City church and later of Sutherlin, Oregon. I was a “choker setter,” who placed a choker made of a steel cable of twisted stands, about 1.5” thick, around a log, which I then hooked to a Caterpillar tractor that pulled the logs to a sawmill landing to be cut into lumber. I was paid $2.25 per hour, and worked an eight hour day. During forest fire season, when the humidity reached 20%, logging was banned because of fire danger. The humidity would often go down by early afternoon, so we were early risers around 4 a.m., reaching the work site by 5, so we would have our time in by the time we had to be out of the woods for the day.

While in Sutherlin I boarded with Earl and Iva Hutchinson. I met Earl while I was in the junior Sabbath School class in the Junction City Church and he taught the junior class. Earl cared for young people in the JC church, often planning special activities for kids and the church as a whole. Not too long after I met him, he married Iva Hamstra, whom he had met while he was in the U.S. Army, stationed in Michigan. Iva readily joined with Earl in planning social activities, such as picnics to the coast, ski trips at Hoo Doo Ski Bowl near Santiam Pass, near where the Oregon

Conference of Seventh-day Adventists has a lodge and cabins for youth and family camps.

When the H&H Logging Company moved to Sutherlin, I really missed Earl and Iva, and was happy when they invited me to visit them a weekend a month. While visiting them I met a girl who lived across the road from the Hutchinson's, Norma Beck. Late one Sabbath, just before sundown, I began to wonder if I could possibly ask Norma out for a date. I kept talking about it, until Earl said, "If I get her on the phone, will you ask her for a date?"

I said, "I guess so," for I really didn't think he was serious. But he did phone the Beck residence, got Norma on the line, and grabbed me by the shoulder and put the phone in my face. I stammered, "Norma, would you want to go play miniature golf with me tonight?" She readily accepted my invitation, and Earl loaned me his Plymouth car, and I took Norma to miniature golf, then to get a hamburger and chocolate malt afterwards. Neither of us were raised vegetarian, and the standard fare was always a burger and malt to end a date.

I suppose Norma and I were "going steady" as it was called in the '50s. We dated all that summer, and when it was over, she went to one school and I another. I truly cared for Norma, and we agreed to write each other often, and see each other whenever we could. I was to write her first. I admit I wrestled with having Norma as a girlfriend while I was informally engaged to Nancy. I suppose it was because Nancy was 900 miles away in Loma Linda, while Norma lived right across the street and it was nice to have someone to fellowship with.

For some reason my mother took a strong dislike to Norma, thinking she was not good enough for me. Mom learned that Norma was boarding with a family who lived in Eugene that school year. The lady of the house turned out to be Mom's classmate from WWC, so she contacted her friend, saying, "I think my son will be writing letters to Norma, at your address. When a letter from him arrives, I want you to not give it to Norma, but give it to me." And, to my sorrow, that is what happened. Norma never got a letter from me, hence she did not write to me. We didn't meet again for many years. As the poet John Greenleaf Whittier posed, "Of all sad words of tongue or pen, the saddest are these, 'It might have been.'" When we did meet again, many years later, we were both single, and our friendship took up where we had left off a third of a century before. We married, and I called her "Rachel," and it was a most wonderful marriage. Alas, she contracted lung cancer, although she had never smoked any form of tobacco. Her oncologist said that during his thirty-two years of practice, he had only seen two cases of that type of cancer in non-smokers. The doctor predicted she would only live for another six months, but Rachel was a fighter and lived for seventeen months. We made the most of those months, and despite her having cancer those were very happy months.

And, Again, Nancy

The summer of '53 the Gepford family traveled from Loma Linda to Grants Pass, Oregon, where Nancy's mother had relatives. I hitch-hiked there from Sutherlin. We formalized our engagement during the time we visited together. It was a great weekend, sorrowed only on Sunday, late afternoon, when I had to hitch-hike back Sutherlin. Nancy's father, a prince of a fellow, wouldn't hear of me hitch-hiking and he insisted on paying my bus fare, so I rode back in comfort.

The next day, back setting chokers, I was working behind Earl's Caterpillar tractor, a D8 model, which was BIG. On the back of the Cat was a "Bull Hook" on which I would place the end-loop of a choker. Sometimes those loops become like a coiled spring, so I had to be careful to get the loop fully on the Bull Hook. That day the choker really had a coil in it, and I barely got it on the hook, when it seemed to come alive, flipping off the hook and smacking me right on my left eye. I was wearing glasses, and the choker strike drove glass right into my eye, right above the eyeball.

I was rushed to the office of an Adventist doctor, Dr. Fred Herscher, who practiced in Sutherlin. I was placed in an exam chair while Doc Herscher focused a light on my injured eye. His wife Frances, who was a nurse, assisted him. Guess they both had sharp eyesight, for I could hear them talking, "There's a shard right above the eyeball," or "See that splinter on the white of his eye." They got all the glass out, then put in ten sutures. I had one black eye for the next couple weeks, but now, almost seventy years later, the scar can scarce be found on this Ol' Man Miller's face.

September of '53 found me once more on the campus of WWC. Men's Dean, Dr. Fabian Meier, asked me to be the head janitor for Sittner Hall, the men's dormitory. I held this position for about two weeks, when Dr. Meckling asked me to be his personal assistant. His request was that I stand at the back of his classroom during each class he taught to watch carefully that no one cheated on his every-class essay question. After the quiz I was to collect all the papers and take them to his office. Over time he trained me how to grade those quiz sheets. He cautioned me to give more D's than B's and give mostly C's. As I have already written, it was a byword on campus that a B was as good as an A from any other teacher.

During the Fall Quarter at WWC, men from the SDA Theological Seminary, then located in Takoma Park, Maryland, near the SDA General Conference headquarters, came to our campus to announce that the requirements for SDA ministers were to be raised from a bachelor degree level to a master of theology degree, to be taken at the seminary. That meant that Nancy would not be joining me on the WWC Campus, but would need to come to Washington Missionary College, located very near Washington, D.C., and the SDA General Conference Office. Because this would be a major shift in our plans, I determined to phone Nancy on Christmas Eve, to wish her a Merry Christmas and tell her of the new ministerial plan. I had already sent her my Christmas present, which was quite expensive for me—a pale blue cashmere sweater, to match her beautiful blue eyes.

I dialed the Gepford phone number in Loma Linda and shortly Nancy's mother answered my call. I asked to speak with my "fiancée." Mrs. Gepford hesitated a moment before saying, "Curtis, Nancy is not at home right now."

This was a surprise to me, even a shock, for I thought "Where else would a person be on Christmas Eve, but in her own home?"

I phoned the Gepford home again, on Christmas night and this time Nancy answered the phone. After wishing her a "Merry Christmas" I explained to her the new plan for higher education for SDA ministers, and asked if she would be willing to go to Washington, D.C., with me. She hesitated before finally answering "Yes." I was bothered by her hesitation.

A few days later I received a letter from Nancy, in which she stated she wanted to break our engagement to be married, adding, however, that she had "mixed emotions" regarding her desire to end our engagement.

I was crushed, to say the least. I didn't know what to say, or how to react. I did have a hunch that since she had mixed emotions, she might change her mind; however, I had my own male image to uphold, or so I thought. Because I thought she might change her mind, I decided to write a letter, accepting her decision to end our relationship, but I did not send the letter directly to her. I calculated that if I sent it in an envelope to Earl and Iva, who were then living in Michigan, and have them forward the letter to Nancy, it might take around twelve days to reach her, during which time I might receive a letter from her indicating she still wanted to continue our marriage plans. Determining to be very formal about it, I wrote as my salutation, "Dear Miss Gepford."

Sure enough, Nancy wrote a letter stating she wanted to continue our being engaged, but alas, she received my letter the same day I received hers, and the damage was done. The engagement was ended. A couple years later I learned Nancy had married David Small, a fellow LLA student in her class. He went on the become a renowned surgeon at the Sloan-Kettering Hospital.

I still contemplate Whittier's poetic phrase, "Of all sad words of tongue or pen, the saddest are these, 'It might have been.'" For many years I had recurrent dreams about Nancy, and "what might have been." Those dreams continued until I heard a voice saying to me, "You really don't remember me, do you?"—but that will come much later in this autobiography.

Still nursing my shattered feelings about the breakup between Nancy and myself, I decided to forget about girls and dating. I threw myself into my studies and being Dr. Meckling's assistant.

Phyllis Edwards Enters My Life

Harvey Heidinger, my current roommate at WWC, and I habitually ate Sabbath morning breakfast in our room, and a fellow classmate, Bill Oaks, ate with us. One such morning Bill was lamenting that he had a date that night with a girl by name of Phyllis Edwards, of the freshman class, and he didn't have the money to take her on a date, so he asked me if I would loan him money for his date. I replied, "If anyone uses my money for a date, it will be me!" Bill moped around the room for a while, then said, "Curtis, if you won't loan me the money, would you take her on a date, so that no one else will?"

I contemplated his request, musing that I was not really wanting to date anyone at the time. Probably I, too, had "mixed emotions" about dating, as I was still recovering from the too-recent breakup with Nancy. Then I thought, *well perhaps it would be a good idea to move on with life*, for I still knew that SDA conferences wanted to know "who is the wife of a prospective minister" when they wrote a letter of invitation to become a ministerial intern in a conference.

I decided to phone the dorm where Phyllis Edwards resided, to ask her for a date that night. In those days no one had a phone in a dorm room, so you had to phone the reception desk in the dorm of choice, and ask by name the person you were calling. I phoned West Hall, the dorm where Phyllis resided, and asked for her. I waited several minutes before she reached the phone to hear me say, "This is Curtis Miller, would you please be my date for tonight?"

She responded, "I don't know who you are." I faced a dilemma, for the only way I could think of to identify myself, would be to say, "I am Dr. Meckling's assistant, the one who stands at the back of the room while you write an answer to his quiz question of the day." Few students really appreciated Meckling's classes, and his quizzes were universally unpopular and disliked, so I hesitated to use that to identify me.

I did know who Phyllis was, from her being in one of Meckling's classes. I graded those quiz questions and had noted that she usually qualified for a "B" grade in his class, and was one of the few to which I gave a B, and that, in my mind, was a mark in her favor. I took the initiative and told her I was the guy who watched the back of her head during quiz time, and in spite of that she accepted my invitation. I don't remember the Saturday night program we went to, but I did fulfill my commitment to Bill Oaks to keep her occupied so no one else would date her before he gained the money for a date. However, when I returned Phyllis to her dormitory, I asked her out for the next Saturday night. She accepted.

I wondered, however, whether she really wanted to date me, or was she waiting for Bill to ask her out again? I decided to "test the waters of dating." At the end of our second date, I did not immediately ask her out; I then told Bill to phone her on Tuesday and ask her for a date the next Saturday night. This he did, to which Phyllis replied, "I have other plans for Saturday night, sorry." When Bill relayed that message to me, I waited until Thursday to ask her for a date the next Saturday. She accepted, and I concluded I was her "other plans."

We dated regularly the rest of the school year.

Phyllis and I grew in love, and one day while on a long walk together I proposed marriage to her, just before the end of the school year, and she accepted. We did not plan to marry for at least another year, however, for she was a nursing student who would be spending the next two years of nurses' school on the Portland campus, meaning we would be separated by a couple hundred miles. Since the new plan for pastoral education called for a year or so of seminary studies, and because the SDA Seminary was at that time on the campus of Washington Missionary College, located very near our General Conference headquarters in Washington D.C., and WMC had its School of Nursing program right on campus, we decided we would both transfer to WMC so we would be on the same campus and not 200 miles distant from each other, should we both continue studies at WWC.

While on campus we endeavored to see each other as often as possible. WWC rules forbade dorm students from being together off campus, however, I had an aunt and uncle who lived just a few blocks from the campus, so we each took a round-about route to my relatives' home, and met there. One afternoon we were sitting together in their backyard, not knowing that on the other side of the fence was the home of a WWC faculty member, who spotted us and reported our clandestine meeting to the WWC President, Dr. George Bowers. The next day I attended the thrice weekly student chapel meeting, and when I exited the chapel, I was met by Rita Williams, secretary to Dr. Bowers, who informed me Dr. Bowers wanted to see me immediately in his office. I proceeded to his office, wherein he informed me I was seen with Phyllis in my relative's backyard. Dr. Bowers solemnly decreed, "Curtis, you are campus-bound for the rest of the school year. If you need to leave the campus you must first get permission to do so."

That same day Phyllis was summoned to President Bower's office, to hear the same sentence of being campus-bound. WWC rules were much more stringent in my years there than they were a generation later when my daughters attended WWC.

Phyllis' parents, John and Viola Edwards, came from their home in Sandy, Oregon, to WWC to pick up her belongings when the school year was over. I went to her dorm to help her father carry down her cedar chest from her third-floor room. As I walked into her room, her father came bounding towards me (John never did anything at a casual or normal walk; he walked like a man in a hurry!), exclaiming, "So you are the young man that is taking my daughter away from me!" Both John and Viola made me feel very welcome into their family.

The summer of '54 found me again working at a sawmill in Sutherlin, Oregon, while Phyllis worked at Portland Sanitarium and Hospital in the housekeeping department which was supervised by her mother. Thus, we were apart all summer, but thankful we had jobs to earn money before our wedding and relocating to Washington, D.C.

We celebrated our wedding on August 22, 1954. Phyllis' parents planned their annual vacation that year to visit their childhood homes in Kansas, so that Phyllis and I could ride with them that far before traveling by Greyhound Bus from Topeka, where Phyllis was born, to Washington, D.C. While in the Topeka area I met her maternal and paternal grandparents, along with some aunts, uncles, and cousins.

Travelin' to Washington, D.C., and Back to WWC

The bus trip was long, but we finally arrived in the D.C. area. We had reserved a modest apartment about a mile from the WMC campus. We did not intend to buy a car with our meager savings from our summer's earnings, and thinking we would benefit from the exercise, we planned to walk to and from our classes.

Phyllis' nursing classes began two weeks before my theology classes, so I found a part time job at an AMOCO service station, where I pumped gas and checked the oil on cars. We had agreed that we would be two years in D.C. and WMC, without going to the travel expense of journeying back home to Oregon to visit our families. I had no problem with that, for I had already spent a school year away from my parental home that year I lived with Grandma Bonita in '50–51 in Loma Linda. Phyllis, however, had never really lived away from home, for while she attended Columbia Academy and WWC, she had home-leave about every six weeks, and was also home the whole of summer vacation from school. Within two weeks of being in D.C., Phyllis became so homesick she could not bear it. She declared she wanted to return to Oregon and pestered me about returning home many hours for several days. I finally concluded we would have to return to Walla Walla College.

We purchased a four-year-old Nash Ambassador—you younger folks have likely not heard of Nash cars, for they stopped making them in the mid-1950s—into which we loaded our few worldly possessions, and hit the road home. It took about four long, long days of driving. Upon arriving once more on the WWC campus, I enrolled in my theological courses while Phyllis dropped being in nursing school and began classes in elementary education. We lived my junior year in a basement apartment on College Avenue, just a couple blocks off campus.

Initially in our marriage we had agreed we would not start a family until I graduated college, but immediately after fall quarter of '54 began, Phyllis had a strong nesting instinct and began pressing me for her to become pregnant. I preferred to wait, but finally acquiesced to her wishes. Shortly after her pregnancy was confirmed, and we awaited our first-born child, with a due date of mid-July of '55.

Selling Books to Earn a Scholarship

When school was out I needed a job to earn money for my senior year's tuition. I liked snow skiing, and went skiing in the Blue Mountains nears WWC, where a ski-accident resulted in the ligaments in my right knee and ankle being wrenched, and by summer it was apparent that because of the injury I could not do heavy work in the logging-lumbering industry. It was recommended that a theology student have experience in being a colporteur—now known as literature evangelists—so I signed on with the Oregon Conference to be a student colporteur. I soon found out I definitely did not like door-to-door sales work, but I decided I would tough it out for the rest of the summer.

We lived, that summer of '55, in a small one-room cabin my folks had built for my Grandma Bonita. She was not living there that summer, having found work as a nanny for a College Place family.

I had a partner in colporteuring, Delwin Brower, who stayed in a tent behind our cabin. The Oregon Conference assigned us sales territory in the Cottage Grove area. A colporteur trainer, by name of Charles, came to teach us the art of salesmanship, and for two weeks he worked with Delwin and me. We were selling a set of children's books, *Bible Pageant*. Charles taught us a successful technique to use at the door of the home to get us an invitation to come into the house. That was the easy part, but obtaining a sale was more elusive. Charles told us, "At the beginning of your sales experience you will make one sale out of every five to six presentations, but after a couple months experience you should be making a sale one out of three presentations." That proved to be true in our experience, but I still detested the door-to-door sales work.

Within two weeks of being in D.C., Phyllis became so homesick she could not bear it. She declared she wanted to return to Oregon and pestered me about returning home many hours for several days. I finally concluded we would have to return to Walla Walla College.

The Birth of Melody Miller

As the birthing due date approached, I still needed to continue colporteuring in Cottage Grove. Because Phyllis had an obstetrician practicing in Portland, and because she wanted to birth at the Portland Sanitarium and Hospital where her parents worked, she went to stay with John and Viola, preceding her due date of mid-July. She went into labor shortly after midnight on July 21, 1955, and she phoned me that she was being taken to the Portland San. I arrived there around 5 a.m., to learn a baby girl had been born to us. I raced to the nursery to view my daughter. She had a reddish face and a shock of dark hair that made her look like a papoose!

Phyllis and I had been choosing baby names. I think we had agreed on a boy's name, Danny, but we had not agreed on a girl's name. I favored Melody and Phyllis favored Pamela. I did not like Pamela, for my mother had a ill-tempered cat named Pamela, and I did not want a flashback to a cat when I heard the name Pamela.

In Phyllis' hospital room, we agreed I would write Melody on one slip of paper, and Pamela on the other. I would have a name-slip secreted in each of my closed hands, which I would extend toward her, and she would choose the slip in one of my hands, and that would be the name of our baby girl.

I somewhat "cheated" on that, for I wrote Melody on each paper slip, then extended my hands, and no matter which hand Phyllis chose, the name would be Melody—and that's how Melody came into our lives. I have always loved that name, and I have always loved Melody as my first-born.

My Senior Year at WWC and My Call to the Montana Conference

My senior year at WWC found us living in a tiny house on the south end of College Place. During fall quarter I was stricken by Hepatitis A, the least problematic type. There was rash of that disease going around the WWC, and it was considered to be an epidemic that school year. I missed a considerable number of my college classes and suggested that I should file a request to receive an "Incomplete" grade, then make up the classes during winter quarter. Elder Heubach, Dean of the School of Theology, advised me to complete the quarter, and take whatever grade I earned. I followed his advice, and as a result did receive the lowest grades of all my college studies.

During the month of February, each year, the WWC board met on campus. It was customary for senior theology students to have dinner with the conference presidents—key members of the board—at that time. The day before the dinner, I went to the local barber shop to get a haircut, reasoning that I needed to look the best I could for the dinner occasion. Elder Gordon Balharrie, of the theology faculty, was in the barber chair when I entered the shop. He remarked, "Curtis, it appears you are here to look your best tomorrow." I agreed with his statement, adding, "I don't think I have the best chance of receiving an internship, for I am the youngest in the class, and probably the least talented."

To this, Elder Balharrie responded, "Curtis, you should know that the theology faculty have rated you at the top of your class, and you will very probably receive a call to ministry." I did have a positive memory of a few months back, when conference presidents were on campus for a meeting and Elder Leland McKinley, president of the Montana Conference, came into one of my senior theology classes. The professor of the class invited him to say a few words. I was seated in the front row, and as he spoke to the class Elder McKinley placed his hand on my shoulder. After class, some of my fellow theology students said, "Curtis, when McKinley placed his hand on you, we think he was sending a message that he might call you to the Montana Conference." I heard what they said but was very uncertain in my mind about that happening.

The next day, at the dinner, I was seated at a table, on the left hand of Elder Heubach. As he sat down, he looked at the several students at the table, and said, "Some of you have already been chosen for an internship, but you haven't been contacted yet."

After the dinner we were to mingle with the presidents, shaking hands and talking with them. Though I really wanted a call to Montana, Elder McKinley did not come near me. My residence in earlier years was in the Oregon Conference, but the Oregon Conference president, Lloyd Biggs, did not even acknowledge me. The president of the Upper Columbia Conference, Elder C. Lester Bond, did come by me, placed his hand on my shoulder, and asked, "How old are you, Sonny?"

I inwardly gulped, and responded that I was twenty-one years old, making me the youngest of all the senior students. I was chagrined when he went on his way and thought maybe he was shaking his head at my response.

As we exited the meeting, I was walking out the door with Bud Madsen, one of my fellow seniors, to whom I remarked, "I don't think Elder Bond will give an internship to someone as young as I." Madsen was a resident of the Upper Columbia Conference. He was also the only person to whom I made the above statement.

It was customary that the North Pacific Union Conferences rotate in order, year by year, the ministerial internship calls. In 1956 it was Upper Columbia's turn to render the first call, and Montana the last. The next day after we met the conference presidents, Elder Bond called Bud Madsen to be a ministerial intern, and one by one the other conferences gave their calls, with Montana being the last. I received no call at all, and yes, I was disappointed.

Several weeks later, Elder Heubach called me to his office, saying, "Curtis the rumor is going around among the Conference Presidents that you said, 'Elder Bond does not like me.' What can you tell me about this rumor?"

His question presented a dilemma to me, for I could not remember ever saying any such thing. Then, I remembered what I had said to Bud Madsen about Elder Bond's question to me, as to my age, and related that to Elder Heubach.

Heubach thought for a moment, then said, "It was Elder Bond's intent to give you an internship, until information about your comment came to him." Heubach then concluded, "I suspect it was Bud Madsen who told Elder Bond." He continued, "All the internships for this year have been filled, but I will send a message to all the NPUC conference presidents, explaining what has happened, and we will hope and pray that eventually you will receive a call to ministry."

Because I had no ministerial internship offered, I decided I would apply to teach in an SDA parochial school, and sent letters of application to both the Oregon and Montana conferences. Shortly I received a response from the Oregon Conference, offering me a position teaching in Hood River, and also one from Montana, offering me a position teaching in Great Falls, Montana. Oregon's school was a larger, multi-teacher school, while Montana's Great Falls School had only thirty-three students in all eight grades.

I went to Elder Balharrie for counsel, and he mused, "Curtis, if you go to Oregon you will be a little frog in a great big pond, and hardly noticed, but if you go to Montana, you will be a small frog in a small pond, and you will soon be known all over the Montana Conference."

Shortly after that conversation, I was exiting the thrice-weekly chapel service at WWC to find Elder McKinley standing at the door, looking for me, and seeing me he beckoned me to him, saying, "Brother Miller, if you teach in Great Falls, I will do my best to see you receive the first ministerial internship available in Montana."

Phyllis and I accepted positions teaching in Great Falls. I was even to be principal and upper-grade teacher of that thirty-three-student school, while Phyllis would teach the lower grades. Usually the teachers would divide up the classrooms into grades 1–4 and 5–8. If that was done in Great Falls, it would mean Phyllis would have twice the number of students I would have, so it was decided I would teach grades three to eight, and Phyllis grades one and two, making our classrooms about equal. It was an exciting school year for both of us.

"Brother Miller, if you teach in Great Falls, I will do my best to see you receive the first ministerial internship available in Montana."

CHAPTER IX

The Montana Years

1956 - 1959

I graduated Walla Walla College at the end of spring quarter, 1956. My parents, along with Phyllis' parents, and her sister, attended the ceremony which conferred on me the degree of bachelor of theology (BTh) on June 3. The next day we loaded a U-Haul trailer with our few worldly possessions, hitched it to our Nash Rambler, and headed towards Bozeman, Montana.

After Elder McKinley formalized my position teaching at Great Falls, I appealed to him for help, saying, "My contract to teach in Great Falls does not commence until mid-August, leaving me without employment from my graduation date, until then." That kindly man made arrangements for me to work for the summer on the campus of Mount Ellis Academy (MEA), where my mother had graduated in 1932. I was to help build the boy's dormitory which had been demolished by fire the previous spring.

Our journey to Bozeman took pretty much all our money. We had no funds to pay for a motel during the long trip, so we pitched a tent by the side of the road along the way and slept there, arriving at the Montana Conference Office mid-afternoon of June 5. Elder McKinley had arranged for us to stay in a small house-trailer, parked behind the MEA gym. That was our home while I shoveled gravel into a cement mixer to pour the foundation for the dorm.

My shoveling was interrupted by the annual Montana Camp Meeting in early July. McKinley appointed me to be night watchman during the ten-day camp meeting. This allowed me to eat meals with the Montana Conference staff, and thus I became better acquainted with all the ministers of the conference. I also was designated as the camp "bell-ringer," ringing the bell to call the people to attend a meeting. The bell in the tower of the MEA administration building was there when my parents attended MEA in 1932. It was a joy for me to ring that bell, calling the campers to meetings all-day long.

Elder Paul Limerick, my principal at Laurelwood Academy, was now Educational and Youth Director of the conference. He was building a home in Bozeman, and for a few weeks I also helped build his house. While I worked on his house, he and his wife would often come to see how the building was progressing. One day a teenage girl came with them. She went into one of the bedrooms, peered around, and called to all nearby, "Is this going to be my bedroom?" It was a curious question to which I gave little thought, but in a few months' time I would sadly recall that girl's question.

Elder McKinley kindly made arrangements for me to do some preaching while I worked at MEA. My initial assignment was to preach at the SDA church in the nearby town of Big Timber. I appreciated that experience—the first sermon I preached in Montana.

Elder Limerick, as youth director of Montana Conference, was in charge of the yearly youth camp held at Seely Lake. The camp was near the little town of Ovando, a wide spot in the road known near Seely Lake. It was noteworthy to me, for shortly before I drove in that area, a Grizzly bear had killed a person there. I had a great time being at the Seeley Lake camp, riding herd on seven boys in a rustic cabin. One of the boys in my cabin was Phil Harris, from the Harris family, of the Choteau Seventh-day Adventist Church that is to this day a place very dear to my heart.

Late August of '56, Elder Limerick and his wife drove the Miller Family to Great Falls to introduce us to the Great Falls church and school. I preached the sermon that day, and a few days later we moved into an apartment to settle into life teaching church school.

A curious happening occurred about the apartment we rented. I attended a school board meeting in which one agenda item was the amount I was to receive for rent subsidy, as per conference policy. Some influential members of the board wanted to set a cap of twenty dollars per month. I was aghast at that small amount but felt I could say nothing. However, I didn't need to, for a gray-haired man spoke up, "Twenty dollars! You can't even rent a decent chicken house in Great Falls for that!"

In my heart, I thought "God bless that man. He must be a good member of the Great Falls church." I learned later that he was not even a member of the SDA church, but his wife was. Because of his statement the board increased the rent subsidy to an amount for which we rented a decent upstairs apartment.

As the school year began, I wondered "Why has the church not written a contract for us to teach?" Still later I learned that the teacher I replaced was about six feet tall, but had no discipline in his classroom. I was amused to learn that during the previous school year the eighth-grade girls took him down and whipped him with his own belt. The Great Falls church withheld a contract until they could be certain I could both teach and maintain discipline, and without a contract they could fire me without having to give cause. I did demonstrate I could both teach and maintain discipline, and it was a successful school year.

In October of 1956 I received what appeared to be a routine letter from Elder McKinley addressed to all pastors and teachers in the conference, simply stating, "Elder Limerick is temporarily out of the conference office. Any correspondence regarding educational matters should be addressed to the office of the president."

I remarked to Phyllis, "This is an interesting letter, and I have a hunch Limerick is in some kind of problem." Not long after I learned from Elder Lodahl, one of the departmental directors of the conference, that Limerick had been caught in an affair with a Mount Ellis Academy girl. It was the same girl that was in Limerick's house under construction that I had worked on the previous summer. The girl's mother became suspicious about letters coming to her daughter from Limerick, so she opened one of them, to learn her daughter was sexually involved with Limerick. He was shortly terminated from his position. Years later I learned he was incarcerated in California for sexual molestation of another under-aged girl.

Phyllis and I had a successful and happy year teaching the Great Falls church school.

My Appointment to Gospel Ministry

During that school year I received a letter from my draft board, informing me I would shortly be called to be in the U.S. Army. My memory harkened back to the summer after I turned eighteen years old. My then college roommate, Glenn Gingery, and I were ordered to Portland to have physicals and testing as per the draft board policies of that time. We were bussed from Eugene to Portland, lodged in the YMCA that night, and spent the next day being examined by military doctors. We ran around the exam rooms all morning, in the buff, save for a small bag dangling from our necks, into which we placed our watch, billfolds, and other miscellaneous belongings. At the end of the physicals, we were ordered to stand in a large circle, facing inward, bend over, and part our buttocks towards the docs, who proceeded to say, "You fellows are the healthiest bunch of jackasses we have ever seen." Then they all gave a hearty laugh.

That morning we also had a battery of tests. In the early afternoon we met with recruiting officers. A Navy recruiter first met with me, saying, "Curtis Miller, your intelligence and aptitude test scores qualify you to become a Navy pilot, if you would volunteer now, and not wait to be drafted."

Wow! I thought, it would sure be neat to be a Navy pilot, assigned to an aircraft carrier, taking off and landing on the flight deck. But then I replied, "I will decline your offer, for I am a conscientious objector" who does not believe in bearing arms. The term "objector" was later changed to "cooperator" by our SDA military advisors, with "cooperator" meaning we would do our best to serve our country in other ways than engaging in armed combat.

The Navy recruiter then handed both Glenn and me off to an Army recruiter, saying "These young men need to be assigned to the Medical Corps, as non-combatants." The Army recruiter proceeded to tell us that if we joined the paratroopers, as medics, we could stay together during our military service. Glenn and I were giving consideration to that offer. However, when I returned home, to talk over being a paratrooper with dad, he told me to "put a hold on that." He proceeded to contact Elder George Chambers, of the SDA National Service Organization (NSO), who guided me to file a request to my draft board to be given the draft status of conscientious Cooperator. And so, I did, thus changing my draft status from 1A—first in line for the draft—to 1AO, the designation for a person of top mental and physical status, with being a conscientious cooperator.

I contacted Elder McKinley regarding my pending draft for military service, knowing that being an elementary school teacher was not sufficient to avoid the draft. I knew the Montana Conference Committee would be meeting shortly in January 1957. Elder Ray Badgley, pastor of the Great Falls SDA Church, where I was teaching, was a member of the Montana Conference Committee and I knew he would be at that conference committee meeting. He returned on a Wednesday, in time for prayer meeting, which I attended, hoping he would be able to give me news of what the conference committee had voted regarding me and the draft, however he said nothing to me during or after the meeting, so I finally asked him, and he evasively replied, "You will be getting a letter from Elder McKinley."

I got into my car to drive home from the church, but I was so keyed-up by the suspense, I got out of my car and ran over to Elder Badgley, who was getting into his car, and said, "Elder Badgley, I won't be able to sleep, due to the suspense of not knowing what the committee voted. Can't you give me some idea of what it was?" He hesitated for a long moment—he must have enjoyed keeping me in suspense!—then said, "The committee voted to give you a ministerial internship, naming you 'acting pastor' of the Havre Church."

I went home, very excited over being accepted in the SDA church ministry. Of course I couldn't sleep that night, due to the excitement of being a minister—finally!

Although I preached numerous times in our Havre church, I did not actually "pastor" that church, for shortly after the end of the school year, when I was teaching church school in Great Falls, Elder McKinley assigned me to the Stanley Harris evangelistic team. Harris was a North Pacific Union evangelist that McKinley obtained to hold at least two series of meetings in the Montana Conference, the first in Great Falls, and the second in Missoula.

Stanley Harris was from the "Old South" of the U.S. Prior to his conversion to Christianity and the SDA church, he was a jazz musician with his own band. He played drums and led his band while he played them. His mother was a faithful SDA who prayed daily for his conversion. One evening, as he was leaving home to lead his band, he overheard hearing his mother praying for him, pleading with God to bring Stanley to Him. He continued on to his band, but during that evening's performance a strange thing happened: Stanley had to keep time with his foot-tapping. That night he could not make his foot tap, try as he might. Several times he tried to start the jazz band playing as he beat the time on his drums, but he could not move his foot. Finally, the band members stopped trying to play and looked questioningly at Stanley. He finally gave up trying to play and signaled another band member to take over leading the musicians.

Stanley returned home, to hear his mother still praying. Hearing him enter, she called "Stanley, what happened at your jazz concert? You are home early." Stanley told his mother how he had been unable to tap time with his foot, and she exclaimed, "Praise God for answering my prayers."

Stanley Harris was never able to keep time with his foot after that. He went to Madison College, a self-supporting SDA school near Nashville, Tennessee, where he received his college education to prepare for a life as a minister. My father, Lyle Miller, went to school at Madison during the time Harris was there.

A foot note to the above: Stanley Harris had a cousin, Phil Harris, who led the band featured on the Jack Benny radio and TV program. Those of the younger generation probably never heard of Jack Benny, but when I was a kid, Benny was a world-class comedian of great renown.

When I joined the Harris evangelistic team, I was put in charge of making plaster of Paris plaques. Attendees of the meetings were given a card which was punched each time they attended a meeting. When they had four punches on their card they were given a plague as an incentive to attend the meetings. I recruited local church members to come to the basement of a member's house, which we turned into a "Plaque Factory." We had rubber molds into which plaster of Paris was poured. While the plaster was still soft, we inserted a couple of hairpins on the back, so they could be hung on a wall. There were various molds, but the one I particularly remember the plaque showing Christ knocking on a cottage door.

The Harris evangelistic crusade began in the largest public auditorium in Great Falls, in September of 1957. In those years evangelistic crusades were several months in length and this series began in September and ended in February of 1958. Being a ministerial intern, I was low man on the totem pole, but I enjoyed my role in the crusade. Harris enhanced his preaching by using slides projected on a screen to illustrate his sermons. I was assigned to run the projectors—there were two of them, mounted side by side. I kept the slides in the proper order for projection. Harris had a hand-held device which when he punched the button a red light flashed on the deck of the projection booth, signaling me to change to the next slide.

Harris' very first sermon, titled "Blood and Snow on the Hills of Montana," still rings in my memory. The sermon was about Nebuchadnezzar's dream as recorded in Daniel chapter two.

Harris had a unique system to divide up the city of Great Falls into several districts, and assigned them to his crusade team, for in-home visitation. As an incentive to attend the meetings he offered free copies of his sermons for those who signed up for them. During the first few weeks the sermons were mailed to them, but beginning with the fourth week of the meetings we were to hand deliver the sermons, so that we could begin working with them on an individual basis.

One of the families on my visitation list was Matthew and Tilly Matt. Matthew was in the United States Air Force, serving at the Malmstrom Air Base near Great Falls. He had met Tilly, a German citizen, while he was serving in Germany, and married her, then brought her to the States when he was assigned to Malmstrom. Visiting the Matts, in their home, was a very interesting experience for me. The first few visits I simply gave Matthew the copy of the sermon of the week when he answered the door. On the fourth visit I invited them to ask any questions they might have, hoping to have an invitation to sit down and visit with them. Matthew, a giant of a man well over six feet tall—with a body size to match—filled the whole doorway when answering my knock at his door. He invited me in, saying, "Tilly has a couple questions for you." Their quarters were small, and their front room had only a single couch for the three of us to sit. He plunked himself down on one end, and Tilly on the other, leaving a small space between them for me to sit.

Tilly would ask a question, while Matthew appeared to be watching TV. I don't recall him ever turning it off when I visited.

Tilly would ask a question, in her broken English, and I would proceed to open my King James Bible to give her a scriptural answer. Although she had her German Bible in her lap, Tilly, in order to improve her English, would scrunch closer to me, so she could peer at my Bible. She was a buxom lady, and I was uncomfortable having her press close to me, so I would scrunch over close to him. He would give a sigh of exasperation, and scrunch over close to his end of the couch, while keeping his eye on the TV.

My impression was that he was not listening to Tilly and me as we conversed together. There were times when Tilly had difficulty understanding my English answers to her. Invariably, and loudly, Matthew would literally shout to Tilly, in German, what I was trying to say to her. She would exclaim "Ja! Ja! Ja!" and he would say to me, "Okay, preacher, she gets it now."

With Thanksgiving coming up, Tilly bought a big, smoked ham for their dinner. About that time Harris preached about clean and unclean meats, according to the dietary laws in the Pentateuch, and Tilly learned ham was "unclean." She went charging back to the supermarket where she had purchased the ham and proceeded to inform the grocer "You are guilty of selling meat the Bible declares is unclean," and she made the butcher exchange the ham for a turkey for their Thanksgiving dinner.

Harris had a large, collapsible, canvas baptistery, which he set up in the meeting hall, and "primed the pump" for baptisms by baptizing a few persons who had previously made a commitment to be baptized. By this time the evangelistic meeting site had been changed from the large civic auditorium to a local movie theatre, the "Roxie," that had closed down due to the growing use of TVs in which movies could be watched at home. When Tilly witnessed that first baptism, she declared to me, "I want to be baptized." I began baptismal studies with her, to prepare her for baptism.

When I arrived at their home to begin Tilly's baptismal studies, Matthew met me at the door, but did not immediately invite me in, but instead he blocked the doorway, saying, "So, I'm not good enough for your church to be baptized." I was taken aback by his statement, for I did not think he was even interested in religion or joining the SDA Church. I learned from that experience that I should always give everyone an invitation. Ultimately the Matts were baptized. After I left the Great Falls area, Matthew was transferred to an overseas airbase in Spain. They took with them a projector and Bible study guides, and gave Bible studies to all persons they could, at that overseas base.

A couple by the name of Holmes were on my visitation list. When Harris made an altar call, they came forward to be baptized. Because they were in my visitation area, I commenced studying with them, and in due course they were baptized in that portable baptistery. They had a teenage daughter who had attended the meetings but held back from being baptized. Just before Harris closed his series in the Roxie, to take a break for Christmas and restart them in the Great Falls SDA Church, he held what was supposed to be the last baptism in that portable baptistery.

After that baptism I received a phone call at my residence from the Holmes' teenage daughter, who declared, "Pastor Miller, I want to be baptized right away in that portable baptistery before the meetings are closed down. I want it to be kept secret from my parents, until they see me in the baptistery."

"Pastor Miller, I want to be baptized right away in that portable baptistery before the meetings are closed down. I want it to be kept secret from my parents, until they see me in the baptistery."

I contacted Elder Harris, informing him of the girl's desire for baptism. "But Curtis," Harris said, "the baptistery has been drained. I don't see how we can have a baptism there."

I knew the Roxie Theatre did not have facilities to fill the baptistery. I also knew that one of the Great Falls members, a good friend of mine by name of Dale, had a truck with a large water tank in which hauled water to houses outside the city limits, that had no water supply. Harris gave me his blessing to contact Dale to see if he could haul water to refill the baptistery. Dale was very happy to haul the water to refill the baptistery, and I helped him do it.

The surprise baptism was scheduled for the last Friday night we would have meetings in the Roxie. At the close of his sermon, Harris announced. "There will be a surprise baptism for a couple parents right now. Just wait until I can quickly change into a baptismal robe."

I had taken a seat behind Mr. and Mrs. Holmes, so I could observe their surprise when they saw their daughter in the baptistery. I could see them looking all around the Roxie, to see if their daughter might be the one to be baptized. Shortly Harris and their daughter entered the baptistery, and a spotlight was focused on them during the baptism. I was thrilled to witness the wonderful expression of happiness on the faces of her parents.

I am still thrilled by every baptism I either witness or officiate. I have a Bible my parents presented to me when I entered the ministry. I preached from it for years, even taking it with me to the Middle East Division, and to all the countries where I ministered. I recorded in a back page the names of persons I baptized. I used that Bible until it was falling apart, and have now "retired" it, using it only when I dress in top hat and coattails, of late 1800s style, to present my series of "Soliloquy of an Adventist Pioneer."

Our middle daughter, Cindy, cooperated with the evangelistic meetings. As her birthing date neared, I was concerned whether she would be born on an evening we had an evangelistic meeting. The meetings were five nights per week, and Thursdays were one of the two nights with no meeting. Midafternoon, Thursday, November 11, 1957, Phyllis went into labor. We gathered up the suitcase she had prepared, and we headed, I thought, to the Great Falls Deaconess Hospital. But Phyllis was in no rush to go to the hospital, instead she wanted to drive around for a while. Finally she agreed to proceed to the hospital, for by that time her birthing pains were coming often. Arriving at the hospital, delivery room nurses hustled her into the maternity section, while I checked Phyllis in. When check-in was complete, I hurried to the maternity ward, thinking I could hold her hand until she was ready for the delivery room, but by the time I got there she was not in her bed, for Cindy decided she wanted to be born ASAP, and within a few minutes a nurse informed me I was the father of baby girl!

I was hoping our second child would be a boy, to carry on the family name, but that was not to be, and I am, alas, the last of the Millers on my branch of the family tree.

I Am Appointed Pastor of the Conrad and Choteau Churches

I learned much from working with Stanley Harris in Great Falls, and wanted to learn more, so I asked Stanley if I could join his team at the next crusade that was to be held in Missoula, Montana, where I was born. He said he would request Elder McKinley to assign me to the team, and I was excited by the prospect of joining the Harris team, but it was not to be. One Monday afternoon Elder McKinley knocked at my door, saying, "Curtis, I want you to be in Conrad, Montana, at 9:00 a.m. tomorrow, to receive the keys to our church there, from the out-going pastor. He does not yet know he is being relieved of his pastorate, but he will by the time you arrive there."

That pastor, whom I choose not to identify, had been pastor of the Conrad-Choteau-Cut Bank district for less than a year. He lived in Conrad for about a year, and attendance had radically dropped. In fact, the group of forty persons attending church at Conrad had disintegrated to no one attending at all.

We moved to a residence in Conrad, and I began calling on those who had formerly attended our church there, in an effort to reclaim as many as possible. During my intensive visiting I learned somewhat about my predecessor. On his first pastoral visit he would ask the person or family, "How much money do you earn? Do you pay tithe? Do you eat meat?" Such questions were offensive, and members shied away from him. I pastored that district for eighteen months, during which time I was able to reclaim eighteen members, and church services were commenced again in Conrad. We met in the local Latter-day Saints church, and I established good rapport with the local bishop there, who was also the banker of that small town.

I loved that district, covering 10,000 square miles of north-central Montana. It even included Glacier National Park in the northwest portion of my pastoral territory. Whenever we had a chance, the Miller family drove up to Glacier to camp. Although the district was vast, I never tired of driving the long distances involved—in fact, I thrived on it. It was a beautiful area, with the Rocky Mountains bordering on the west, and the open plains of wheat, cattle, and sheep bounding it on the east. I loved every day I pastored the churches of my parish.

The first Sabbath after being assigned to my new pastorate, I was driving to the small cattle and wheat town of Choteau. The sky was clear and sunny, which should have made for a good, safe drive, but it was not. Montana can be a very cold place in winter, and the falling snow is often not wet and flaky, but dry, with very small flakes. It was not snowing that day, but I experienced a "ground blizzard" with the wind blowing sufficiently hard to blow snow from the nearby fields, across the roadway. I was driving through such a blizzard, with the blowing snow so thick you could hardly see through it. That day the blizzard was slightly higher than the hood of my car. I had clear vision higher than the hood, but had only fleeting glimpses of the highway, and consequently I was driving slowly and carefully, causing me to arrive late for the preaching service.

At that time the Choteau congregation had no building of their own, but rented out a hall belonging to the ODD Fellows Lodge (a fraternal order of laboring men begun in England in the 1700s). The hall was rather stark, lighted by a few bare light bulbs hanging from the high ceiling. The local church elders, Dick and Vern Harris, were proceeding with the service by having the congregation sing hymns. I then stepped into the pulpit, introduced myself to my new flock consisting of thirty-five persons, including children. I declared to them, "I will visit each of you within the next month," and I proceeded with my sermon.

At the end of the church service, as I was shaking hands with those good folks, Millie McCann challenged my statement that I would visit them all within the next month, by saying, "Curtis Miller, my family has never been visited by an SDA pastor, and we live 100 miles from where you live." I met her challenge and the McCann's were the very first pastoral visit I made.

Max, the Marlboro Man

Millie, with her husband Max, lived on large cattle ranch a few miles from the very small town of Augusta, Montana. Max was the foreman of that ranch. The ranch house was made of logs, with several upstairs bedrooms that served as the "bunk house" for ranch hands. There was also a very large, three-story barn. The top floor was for hay storage, second floor for grain bins, and ground floor was for cattle and horse stalls. It was a very famous and noteworthy barn. One day I began describing it to my father, Lyle, and as I did so, suddenly Dad took over the description of that barn. I was amazed, for he described in accurately. "How," I asked him, "can you describe that barn, when you don't even know where it is?"

"I know that barn, very well. That ranch used to belong to your great-grandfather, John Mathison."

I wanted more proof of that, so I countered, "Okay, if you think you know that barn, and have been there, what is the date of the building of the barn that is branded onto one of the main beams on the ground floor?"

"The brand on the beam is 1888!" he replied, and it was. He had been there, and I was thrilled to know that the 60,000-acre ranch, known as the "Soap Creek Cattle Company," used to belong to my family. To this day, I wished the family still owned that ranch.

When I arrived at the ranch, Max was just setting out to round up some cattle and he invited me to ride with him. He chose an interesting horse for me to ride, a Quarter Horse that was well-trained as a "cutting horse," skilled in cutting a cow from the rest of the herd. The cutting horse was rather comical, as I sat in the saddle. It was born a "ketch-colt" on a cold winter night that was so cold the colt's ears literally were frozen to the degree they fell off, so sitting in the saddle I looked down on this earless horse.

That cutting horse was very well-trained. All I had to do was guide him towards the cow that needed to be cut from the herd, and he did the rest. He was fast and very agile—he could turn a square corner on a dime! I knew that a good rider didn't grab the saddle horn for support in staying in the saddle, and I tried not to do so. But while the horse and I were cutting a cow from the herd, he turned sharply to the left, and I, not grabbing for the saddle horn, continued going straight, and I hit the ground rather hard. As I got up, dusted myself off, I glanced at Max, who was too polite to laugh at my face, so I saw him looking the other way, but I knew he was chuckling at my leaving the saddle so ignominiously, for his shoulders were shaking with laughter.

I got back in the saddle, and Max and I continued working the cattle.

Max and I had a yearly custom, way back in those days—fishing together the first day of Trout season on a small stream that flowed through the ranch. I would arrive at the ranch on Saturday night, then Max and I would get up early and hit the stream at dawn. The fishing was great, and we would soon catch our limit, which in those days was twenty-one pounds plus one fish. One year we knew the limit had been changed, but neither of us knew what the change was. As we were fishing, we met another fellow fishing, and Max casually asked him, "Do you know what the trout limit is this year?"

"Fifteen fish," the man replied. Max thanked him and continued to fish until that man was out of sight, then he said, "Curtis, let's get out of here, for I already have twenty-one trout." We left speedily.

Max was a "Jack-Mormon" as a "back-sliding" Mormon was called. While Millie very regularly attended the Choteau Church where I pastored, Max did not. I never did learn why the McCanns were unable to have children, but they adopted two, a boy named Randy, and a girl named Janelle. Janelle had "special-needs," having been born with a congenital defect in her hips which needed a couple corrective surgeries. She was spunky gal and braved those surgeries.

Came the day Millie wanted me to dedicate Janelle to the Lord in a special service. Through the years, Max has maintained he was present for that dedication, but I have a clear memory of Millie came to the front of the church, alone, holding Janelle in her arms. Janelle's dedication was one of my last services before I left my pastorate to attend the SDA Theological Seminary in Berrien Springs, Michigan, the fall of 1959.

Fast-forward ten years, when I returned from mission service. The Millers stayed with the McCann family for a weekend. I was scheduled to preach in Choteau. Janelle, on Friday evening, said to me, "Elder Miller, you dedicated me before you went to Turkey; now I want you to baptize me." I baptized her the next day in the Choteau Church.

Max, again, insisted he was present for the baptism, but my distinct memory is that he was not present. We rode to church, that Sabbath morning, in the McCann's Buick. Millie was driving, and I was seated in the back seat, from which I looked out the back window, to see Max, riding his horse to do ranch work.

Fast forward again, to when I was pastoring the Wenatchee, Washington, SDA Church. I was seated in my study, when the phone rang, and across 600 miles of phone wire, I heard Janelle say, "Elder Miller, you dedicated me to the Lord, you baptized me, and now you must come to Montana and perform my wedding!"

"Elder Miller, you dedicated me to the Lord, you baptized me, and now you must come to Montana and perform my wedding!"

Shortly I traveled to the McCann residence in Augusta, where we stayed in their home. We arrived Friday eve, just before sundown. Millie was serving supper, when Max came in from his ranch work, and sat down to eat with us. It was a warm and satisfying experience for me. I preached in Choteau the next day, and Max was present and t'was the first time I had ever seen him in church.

The wedding was to be held in the Great Falls SDA Church, seventy-five miles away from Augusta. I rode with Max in his pickup to the wedding practice. After the practice, as we were driving home, Max still driving, and me rather sleepy after a long day, I dozed, but Max was in a talkative mood, and I, sleepily, sort of half-listened to his rambling, but suddenly I came awake, as I heard Max say, "Curtis, the Marlboro Company came to the ranch last summer, stayed for two weeks, and took 7,000 pictures."

"Max, are you saying you will be in the Marlboro cigarette ads," I asked?

This was back in the days before the U.S Surgeon General had declared cigarettes were a health hazard that could cause cancer. Cigarette ads were still allowed, often appearing on the backs of popular magazines of that day, such as *Time*, *Newsweek*, and *U.S. News and World Report*.

Max said nothing, but when we arrived at the ranch, he went to his study, and returned to with several of those magazines, and there, on prominent pages I saw pictures featuring Marlboro cigarette ads. The one I remember best features Max standing up in a wagon pulled by a team of horses. Another showed a picture of a cowboy, on horseback, dragging a Christmas Tree at the end of his lariat. I am pleased to have one of Max's lariats, which he gifted me

"Max," I asked, "How does it feel to have your picture plastered all over America?"

"Curtis," he replied, "When I first say my picture in those ads, I felt great. On I-90 I saw myself on a large billboard. At some ad on a baseball stadium, I stand ninety feet tall. But when I realized I had given my face over to advertise cigarettes, it made me so ashamed I quit smoking."

The next day we were all at the Great Falls Church. Janelle had her wedding well organized, with as many wedding pictures as possible being taken before the service. One of the first pictures to be taken was the father with the bride. I chuckled to see Max in a tuxedo, with cummerbund, and black patent leather shoes. That was the first time I had ever seen him sans his cowboy boots—he always wore Justin boots made in Texas, and a cowboy hat, not a Stetson, but a Resistol, a very famous western brand.

After having his picture taken with the bride, there was nothing more for Max to do, but appear briefly walking Janelle up the aisle, then be seated by Millie, and pay for the wedding reception.

I was standing at the rear of the Great Falls Church, while Max was seated in the second row on the right. I saw his chiseled face, with a strong jaw. It was now more than twenty-five years that I had known Max, and he was still not baptized into the SDA Church. I remembered back to the days Max and I used to ride the range together, and I would half-joking and half-serious, say, "Max, if I ever catch you at an unguarded moment by the horse trough, I'm going to baptize you." And Max would reply, "Any day you think you are man enough, go ahead at try it."

I never tried it. But as I watched him that day, in the Great Falls Church, I had an almost overwhelming feeling that I should go sit by him, and say, "Max, it is time for you to be baptized."

But how could I do that, say that? He was the Marlboro Cowboy. I decided to find Millie to tell her about my conviction. I found her at the rear of the Great Falls Church, doing whatever mothers of a bride do. I said, "Millie, see Max sitting there, all by himself. I strongly feel I should go sit by him and invite him to be baptized."

I was shocked to hear Millie say, "Curtis Miller, I wrote you a letter, a few days ago, stating I think Max is ready to be baptized, and I have wondered all weekend why you have not spoken to him about being baptized."

I had not gotten that letter, before I left Wenatchee, but it was waiting for me when I returned from the wedding. I needed no further urging. I quickly went to that second pew of the Great Falls Church, where sat Max. I placed my hand on his shoulder, and said, "Max, it's time, and past, that you should have been baptized." Then I studied the face of the Marlboro Man, Max S (for Simpson) McCann. How would he react?

I saw the Marlboro Man's jaw tighten, as I tried to read his body language. I had once read a book entitled *How to Read a Person by His Look*. I watched for a clenching of the jaw which can be a negative sign. Next, I saw the Marlboro Man swallow hard as his prominent Adam's apple bobbled. A positive sign?

Then I saw something you never saw in a Marlboro cigarette ad: I saw a tear well in his eye and trickle down his cheek. "Curtis," he said, "I have felt for a long time I should be baptized, but I guess I have just been waiting to be asked." I mentally kicked myself for waiting so many years to ask Max to give his heart to the Lord and be baptized. There was no time or place for a baptism that wedding weekend, but I promised Max, "I will come as soon as I can work it into my pastoral schedule to come back to Montana and baptize you." But months went by, and I never found time to baptize Max, something I had been waiting twenty-five years to do.

Finally, Millie wrote, "Curtis, if you can't find time to come to Montana, we will come to you in Wenatchee, for Max to be baptized." Max and Millie came to Wenatchee, where I baptized him the last Sabbath of my pastorate there. I wrote his name in the Bible my parents gave me, when I entered the SDA ministry. Max passed away, Christmas time of 2000. Joy and I traveled back to Augusta, Montana, where I presided over his funeral.

I will always cherish the years I pastored in Montana, for those years are a most precious memory. Now, I can only cry "Maranatha" which means, "Even so come, Lord."

Now it is time to take up the story of Chapter I, "Turkey Calling."

CHAPTER X

The Voyage to Turkey

1960

After accepting the mission call to Turkey, I took the final exams for the courses I was taking the fall quarter at the seminary. The General Conference transportation office sent a van to collect our few belongings we had with us in Berrien Springs to transport them to our New York travel office in Brooklyn. When that was complete the Miller family drove on wintery roads to the Dick Harris ranch near Choteau, Montana, where we had stored our household belongings in the basement of their home for while we were at the SDA seminary on the Andrews University campus. Those goods also needed to be crated for shipment to Turkey. We were allowed to ship 6,000 pounds of our household goods. Prior to going to the seminary, we believed we would be returning to the Montana Conference, but the appointment to be missionaries in Turkey completely changed those plans!

We were allowed a month to visit our families prior to sailing for Turkey. We also visited many of our parishioners to bid them farewell. We arrived in Oregon in late January to visit our families before proceeding to New York where we were scheduled to sail out of Pier 44, Brooklyn, New York, on the S.S. Hellas, in early

March. We had a good visit with my parents and with Phyllis' family. On the one hand our families were proud to be parents to missionaries to Turkey, but on the other hand it was sad to say goodbye, for a mission term, in those years, was six years until a year's furlough home was allowed.

At that time we had a new 1959 Chevrolet station wagon. The SDA travel bureau had informed us that the import tax on vehicles was about five times the value of the car, way more than we would be able to pay. We decided we would look for an older car and finally chose a '53 Chevrolet sedan. I wanted it to be in top condition, so we took it to my uncle Carl Heid, who had a car repair shop in College Place, Washington, to have him do a complete overhaul. We still had the Chevy wagon, which we had sold to Max and Millie McCann, and we would deliver that car to them on our way to New York.

After leaving the McCann ranch, we stopped at a ranch near Helena, Montana, to say goodbye to my Grandma Miller, who was working as cook for the ranch hands. As we were driving away from that goodbye, Grandma received a phone call from my parents, seeking to tell us the GC travel office in Brooklyn informed them that the sailing date for the S.S. Hellas was being delayed another two weeks, set to sail in mid-March. But the phone call from my parents came after we were driving on the mile-long drive to the main highway. Grandma went racing to the front porch of the ranch house, we later learned, to wave us to return, but we were looking ahead, and not in the rear-view mirror, and didn't see her.

Knowing we planned to stop by Berrien Springs on our way to New York, my folks phoned Earl and Iva Hutchinson of the delayed sailing, so we spent those two extra weeks with them, and once again proceeded to New York. We arrived in New York, only to be informed that the S.S. Hellas was going to be delayed another two weeks and would sail on April 8. Keeping us in a hotel in the heart of New York was very expensive, so the GC under-treasurer in charge of our travel to Turkey advised us to drive to our GC headquarters in Washington D.C., where we could stay in a guest apartment for missionaries traveling in the area. We decided to drive the 225 miles to DC the next day.

That night both Phyllis and I were stricken with strep throat, which was very painful. While we drove from New York to D.C., neither of us felt like driving, so we would change drivers every half-hour. We arrived at the GC headquarters late in the afternoon, checked into the guest apartment, then proceeded to the SDA hospital there, where we were seen by an emergency room doctor. He would have hospitalized both of us, but we had no one to watch Melody and Cindy, so he provided medication for us, and we returned to the guest apartment, and alternated caring for the girls an hour at a time.

After getting over our strep throat, I was called to our GC building, where I met several of our world leaders. As I left the office of some, I would hear them say, "One more thing, brother Miller, when you get to Turkey, above all else make certain you learn the language, for if you don't there will always be a curtain between you and the people." When I arrived in Turkey, for the first few months I was quite immersed in studying Turkish, to the degree that I now am one of the few non-Turkish persons who can preach a sermon in Turkish.

One of the men I visited at the GC was the head of our Health and Temperance Department, a Pastor Scharffenberg. He had met with many government leaders in the Middle East, and he provided me with several letters of introduction to influential persons in Istanbul and Ankara. I packed those letters in my suitcase bound for Istanbul. One of those letters was the key to opening the door for me to enter Turkey. Elder Roenfelt, the GC leader who gave me the call to go to Turkey, told me, "Brother Miller, we can book your passage to Turkey; we can provide you with funds to go to Turkey, but we can't get you into Turkey. You will have to figure that out for yourself."

Conard Rasmussen and his family were missionaries in Turkey during the '50s. He was aware we were on our way to Turkey, and invited us to his residence in Perth Amboy, New Jersey, just across the river from NYC. We arrived at his home on Thursday, April 7. Knowing we had no family or friends to see us off when we sailed from Brooklyn Pier 44, Rasmussen offered to be there when we sailed.

After supper at his home, he got me in one corner of the room, and his wife talked with Phyllis in another corner. Each of them regaled us with horror stories of their years in Turkey, including this account:

On September 6–7, 1956, a pogrom occurred, primarily in Istanbul. Orchestrated mobs rampaged down one of the main streets of the city, about a half mile from our Turkish mission building. At least thirty persons were killed and many more wounded. Greek and Armenian priests were among the slain. Some were scalped and burned alive. Rape was rampant. Rioters entered Christian-owned shops and threw merchandise into the streets, until they were about knee-deep in some places. 5,317 properties were damaged or destroyed, along with 4,214 homes, and 1,004 businesses. That day seventy-three churches were heavily damaged or destroyed, along with two monasteries, one synagogue, twenty-six schools, and twenty-one factories.

Pastor Rasmussen was away from home when the pogrom started. He made his way through the mobs until he was on the far side of Taksim Square, a few hundred yards from our mission building. A police line had been formed there. He told me, "I always carried a very small American flag on me. I held it up to a police officer, who guided me through the police cordon. I made my way quickly to the mission, let myself in, then waited by the door. It was not long until a mob of men tried to break the door down. I prayed to God to deliver my family and our building, as I braced myself against the door. The Lord gave me strength, and I was able to keep them from battering down the door."

Conard Rasmussen, in the environs around the SDA mission, was known as the "Buyuk Papaz," meaning the Big Priest. I was later known as the "Kucuk Papaz," or the Little Priest!

Turkey, newly admitted to NATO, was embarrassed in the eyes of the western nations. Rasmussen and our Middle East Division leaders recognized that this presented a golden opportunity to apply for permission to build a church, for we had no church building of our own in Turkey at that time. Prior to WWI and the Armenian genocide by the Turks, we had twenty-three churches scattered around Turkey, with about five hundred members. One by one those congregations disappeared, until the time of that pogrom, when we had only eighty-three members left in Istanbul.

Quickly our Middle East leadership applied for permission to build a church and the Turkish government granted permission. Rasmussen rapidly built a Seventh-day Adventist church that still stands at 14 Saray Arkasi, Ayazpasha, Taksim, Istanbul, Turkey. I preached in that church from 1960–70. One of the construction workers was an Armenian by the name of Hayk. Hayk stayed on with our Turkish mission, after the church was built, to become the mission building's Kapici—Kapi, in Turkish, means door—so he became the keeper of the door and janitorial services. He was very faithful in his work. When I was ordained as a minister, in the Istanbul Church, Hayk came to me, offering his congratulations, and declared he wanted to be the first person I baptized. I felt most honored to baptize Hayk. I purchased the material for his suit and Hagop Tulgar, a tailor in our Istanbul Church, made the suit. It was the last place I preached in prior to returning home to the USA. I will always love that church, for I left a part of my heart there.

Hayk and I After His Baptism

By the time Conard Rasmussen and his wife finished telling me of the long history, and current history, of persecutions of Christians in Turkey, and particularly of that pogrom just four years earlier, I confessed that I, and my family, might even become martyrs. I thank my Lord that I felt no fear in going to Turkey.

Friday, April 8, 1960, found us at Pier 44, Brooklyn, New York, finally ready to board the S.S. Hellas, an old freighter owned by Aristotle Onassis. A Mr. Vacquer was the SDA travel agent in NYC at that time. He arranged for our '53 Chevrolet to be taken to the ship prior to our arrival. Herein is an interesting anecdote: James Russell, that long-term missionary in the Middle East, had given us several bits of counsel for our trip to Turkey. "First, know that the meals on the freighter will not be vegetarian, so obtain a number of cans of vegetarian food to supplement your diet while sailing to Turkey. Second, bring a few books you will want to read during those long days aboard ship. And don't forget your children. I suggest you buy them each some simple toys, wrap them in paper, so they can have the joy of opening their 'gift' each day."

This we did, placing all these things in a large box, instructing Vacquer to have it placed in our cabin, on board the Hellas. Alas! That box stayed in the car, which was placed in the lowest hold in the ship, to be disembarked in Istanbul, and was not available to us at all during the voyage.

We boarded the Hellas, a small ship which didn't look too small while at dock, but on the North Atlantic, during a storm, she looked and felt too small for our liking! Conard Rasmussen came to see us off, mid-afternoon that Friday. The ship's cabin boy guided us to our cabin. Vacquer had told us we would have a cabin large enough for all of us to be together during the voyage, which was to take thirty-one days, from Pier 44 to Istanbul. There was not a single cabin on that ship that could sleep more than two persons, but we did have two cabins, side by side, on the first deck. Each had a single-person bunk bed, a small table, small closet, and a porthole. We decided Phyllis would occupy one cabin, I the other, and Melody and Cindy would rotate, night by night, from one parent to the other.

Around sunset two towing barges hooked onto the Hellas to pull the ship out of the harbor and into the lower Hudson River. We went up on deck to watch the departure, and after catching a last glimpse of the Statue of Liberty we went to our cabins.

There was little to do aboard ship, except rise in the morning, go to breakfast, then walk the deck, which was small, look out to sea, while away the time, eat lunch, take a nap, walk the deck, read to the girls, eat supper, walk the deck, put the girls to bed, and then in the evenings Phyllis and I played board games. By the end of the voyage I never wanted to see those games again!

There were several other interesting passengers aboard with us: a very charming older Greek lady returning to her homeland; a middle-aged lady traveling just because she loved to travel; a young American man, of Greek ethnicity, newly graduated from college, was aboard to visit his ancestral land; a young doctor who had recently finished his residency in psychiatry and his wife and baby were returning to his home in Greece; and lastly, two Muslim Turks who were being deported after having their visas expire.

The Muslim men were not happy about being deported. I still remember their names, the younger was Nureddin—Nuri, for short—and the older was Ahmet. I probably made a tactical error by letting Nuri and Ahmet know that we were a missionary family, bound for Istanbul. They belligerently let me know that Turkey was for Muslims, and Christian missionaries were illegal in their country.

An ominous event occurred during the latter part of our voyage. Our cabins were about seventy-five feet away from the restrooms and showers, and directly opposite the Turks' cabin. Late one night Cindy, who was bunking with me that night, needed a trip to the restroom. When she was finished, I backed out of the restroom, with Cindy tucked under my left arm. As I turned to walk to our cabin a knife flew past my shoulder, striking the wall behind me, then hitting the floor at my feet. I was both surprised and shocked. I saw no one at all in the hallway, but the knife came at me as I stood right in front of the Turks' cabin. I left the knife where it fell.

I stopped by the cabin where Phyllis and Melody bunked, saying to Phyllis, "Look down the hallway. What do you see on the floor?"

She looked, then exclaimed, "I see a knife. What is it doing there?"

"I don't know, but someone threw that knife at me. It is right in front of the Turks' cabin."

By 6:00 a.m. the next morning the knife was gone. I wondered where it was.

Our cabins were at the end of the first below deck floor, right next to the dining salon. The dining steward was a jovial young Greek by name of Spiro. He kindly endeavored to serve our dietary needs. There was no vegetarian menu, which posed a challenge for Melody and Cindy, for they had never ever eaten meat. The little elderly Greek lady, a fellow passenger, was concerned about the girls, and talked Spiro into allowing her to go to the kitchen, where she prepared food the girls would eat.

A few days after leaving port, we headed into rough seas in the north Atlantic. Many of the passengers came down with sea sickness. Phyllis became very ill. Many times, Melody, Cindy, and I were the only passengers to show up for meals. I tipped Spiro to provide fresh fruits for Phyllis.

After ten days at sea, the Hellas put into port at Funchal, in the Madeira Islands. We docked there for several days, for one of the holds held a large shipment of wheat to be off-loaded there. Stevedores shoveled the wheat into gunny sacks,

As I turned to walk to our cabin a knife flew past my shoulder, striking the wall behind me, then hitting the floor at my feet.

which were placed on a sling for a crane to lift the sacks to trucks on the dock.

Knowing we would be docked in Funchal several days, we looked up the local SDA church. I was amazed to learn that the pastor's wife had been the translator for my uncle Clarence Rentfro, the first SDA missionary to Portugal, in 1904. This lady was only a teenager when she translated for Uncle Clarence. The pastor drove us on a grand tour of the island. He invited me to preach to Funchal Church, giving me my first experience in speaking through a translator. The pastor's wife was my translator, almost half-century after she translated for my uncle.

We sailed on, and on, and on. I was thrilled when we sailed through the Strait of Gibraltar, where we could see Europe on the port-side and Africa on starboard side, and into the Mediterranean. After a week we docked at Genoa, Italy, then onto Naples, and then Palermo, on the Island of Sicily.

After leaving Italy, the Hellas now sailed to its home port of Piraeus, the port for nearby Athens. Our ship docked there several days while routine maintenance was done for our vessel. We found the office of our SDA Greek mission, where Nicolas Germanis was president of the mission. Germanis was an American citizen but also of Greek ethnicity. He helped us tour Athens, a very historic city, where we saw the Acropolis, the Parthenon, and Mars Hill, where the apostle Paul visited two millenniums prior. He saw altars to the many gods the Greeks worshiped, including one ascribed to the "unknown god," for the Greeks did not want to omit any god. Paul preached to the Athenians about the "Unknown God." It was a powerful sermon.

It was while we were in Athens we heard about demonstrations against the government of the Prime Minister of Turkey, Adnan Menderes. This news was ominous, as we found out about a month later.

Sailing from Athens, the Hellas headed for its last stop before Istanbul, and docked in Thessaloniki. We went ashore to do some sightseeing, and in that city another unfortunate event occurred, this time it directly targeted ME! I had $200 in traveler's checks which I carried in a side pocket of my jacket. To my dismay, I found those traveler's checks missing when I was back aboard the Hellas.

We sailed on from Thessaloniki towards Istanbul.

CHAPTER XI

My Mission Work in Turkey

1960 - 66

Arrival in Istanbul

As the S.S. Hellas approached the Dardanelles, the forty-mile-long, one to five miles wide strait between European and Asian Turkey which connected the Aegean Sea with the Sea of Marmara, I went to the portal window in my cabin. I was holding several communications from the General Conference giving me the name and address of our Turkish mission, along with the names of our mission and church staff. I was directed to memorize the information, then destroy it before entering the strait. I tore those communications into little pieces then threw them out the portal. I remembered those instructions stating, "We can book and fund your passage to Turkey, but we cannot provide you with the means to enter Turkey. You will have to work that out for yourself."

After disposing of that information, I went up on deck, as the Hellas entered the strait. A small Turkish naval vessel put out from the eastern tip of the strait and pulled along the starboard side of the Hellas. A naval officer came on deck, was met by the first mate, who gave him the sailing papers for the ship. Finding all was in order, the officer debarked and sailed back to shore, as the Hellas continued up the strait, and into the Sea of Marmara, the Marble Sea.

Shortly after dawn, May 6, the Hellas dropped anchor a few hundred feet from Kadikoy, the port area of Istanbul. I anticipated the ship would anchor by the dock, but later learned there were no facilities dockside, to offload the cargo. Instead, a large barge with a small crane came out to the Hellas for that purpose.

I asked the first mate, "How will we and our luggage be able to reach the dock, if we are anchored so far away?"

Pointing to a small rowboat that was approaching the Hellas, he replied, "You will take that boat to shore. You will pay the boatman for rowing you to the dock." Deck hands carried our luggage down a ramp that was gently swaying and placed it in the boat for us. A gentle rain was falling when the Millers stepped into that boat.

"How," I wondered, "will I be able to pay the man? My pocket was picked in Thessaloniki, and I have no money." Moreover, the GC instructed our Turkish staff to make no contact with us until we had cleared emigration and customs control, so I expected no one to meet us.

"We can book and fund your passage to Turkey, but we cannot provide you with the means to enter Turkey. You will have to work that out for yourself."

Pastors Benjamin Mondics, an American, and Manuk Benzatyan, an Armenian Turk, were also counseled to not make contact with me until I had cleared emigration and customs control. However, as the hymnist Cowper has wisely said, "God moves in mysterious ways His wonders to perform." This was to prove true time and again during my sojourn in the Middle

East. It proved true when I stepped ashore that day. The Hellas sailing had been delayed several times, prior to sailing from Pier 44; it was further delayed while enroute; consequently, the two pastors had been looking for our arrival for a couple weeks. They enquired at the Greek shipping line about the arrival of the Hellas, and finally learned it would be May 6. Early that morning they used binoculars to spot the Hellas anchored offshore, and contrary to their instructions they decided to chance going to the dock at Kadikoy.

As our small boat docked, I noticed Ben Mondics and Manuk Benzatyan, standing on our route to the emigration/customs office which passed right by them, and I intuitively knew who they were. We greeted each other simultaneously and shook hands. They assured us they would be waiting for us when we cleared the customs and emigration check points.

Unbeknownst to us, a Turkish secret police officer saw our handshake, and when we stepped into the emigration office he approached me, saying, "Sir, if you are a priest like the man we saw you greet, you will never be allowed to stay in Turkey."

We submitted our passports to the authorities, and the barriers to our being able to stay in Turkey began to go up. In those years, passports required a notation as to a person's occupation. For some reason, of which I was never able to figure out, the GC, in helping me obtain a United States passport, had me state I was a "Missionary Teacher." The immigration officer spotted that immediately, and informed me, "Sir, Americans are allowed to stay in Turkey up to three months as a tourist. After that you will need a residence visa, which I tell you now, the Turkish government will never allow you to have."

We therefore entered Turkey on a temporary status as tourists. Then, after clearing emigration and customs, we met Ben Mondics and Manuk outside; they took us to the Park Hotel, which was about three blocks from our Turkish mission building. It was Friday, May 6, 1960, and we were finally in Turkey, where we served as missionaries for the next six years. Finally! The Millers were thrilled. We were happy. We were excited.

The next day, Sabbath, I preached my first sermon in our Istanbul Church, with Ara Kahraman as my translator.

American and Turkish flags near our SDA mission; Istanbul near where our ship anchored

On Monday I registered our family at the U.S. Consulate, and then proceeded with obtaining our household goods, and that '53 Chevrolet, from customs. It appeared that there would be a long, full-of-red-tape, process to have our goods released. It had taken Mondics close to a year to have his household goods released from customs, and even then a huge tax was levied.

I remembered the packet of letters of introduction provided me by W.A. Scharffenberg, prior to our leaving D.C. At random, I chose the letter at the top. It was addressed to Vechihi Divitci, Director of Yeshilay. Manuk told me Yeshilay was the "Green Crescent," the organization combating alcohol in Turkey. This now made sense for me, for one recommendation the GC gave me was that I could be a representative of the Seventh-day Adventist International Temperance Association, headed by Scharffenberg. Manuk accompanied me to the office address of Mr. Divitchi, which was on the far side of the Golden Horn, a thumb of water jutting out from the Bosporus. The Bosporus Strait, twenty miles in length, connects the Black Sea to the Sea of Marmara. It bisects Istanbul, making it a unique city that sits astride the two continents, Europe and Asia.

The building where Yeshilay was quartered was very old. The letter was addressed to Divitci and endorsed me as being an educator for temperance education. Divitci read the letter, then extended a warm welcome handshake. He then said, "Mr. Miller, it will be a pleasure to work together with you to combat the evils of alcoholic beverages. Is there anything I, as director of Yeshilay, can do, to aid you in your work?"

"Yes, there is," I replied, through Manuk, who translated. "I have come to live in Istanbul, which will be my headquarters. My household goods are being held in the customs building, and I am seeking a way to have them released."

"Very well, I believe I can help you with that." He pressed a button that buzzed the office next to him, summoning a man who came immediately, and was introduced to me as "Tajutin Bey." In Turkey, the custom is to address a man by his first name, followed by the term "Bey"—a title of respect. During the years of my sojourn in Turkey, I was known as "Curtis Bey," and Manuk was "Manuk Bey."

Divitci Bey read my letter of introduction to Tajutin Bey, then said, "Mr. Miller needs assistance to clear his household goods from customs. Will you please help him?"

"I surely shall," replied Tajutin Bey, as he handed Manuk his business card, which indicated his full name and business address. "Please come to my office tomorrow at 9:00 a.m. Have your passport and bill of lading (shipping papers from the S.S. Hellas) with you."

The next morning found Manuk and I, passport and bill of lading in hand, at Tajutin Bey's office. It was the customs building. We proceeded to his office, on which were the words, "Chief of Customs!" We entered Tajutin Bey's office. He asked for my passport and bill of lading, affixed his stamp on one of the pages, then he said, "Curtis Bey, take your passport and bill of lading to the port building where the Hellas was off-loaded, and your household goods will be released to you."

And that is just what happened! My entire shipment of household goods was released without me paying even one cent tax, and within two weeks of my arrival in Istanbul! When the

U.S. Consul General of Istanbul learned of this, he marveled, saying, "Not even I could get my goods through Turkish customs in that short of time."

I admit I was impressed that my Lord worked a miracle for me then, and He continued to work miracle after miracle during the ten years I spent in the Middle East.

By the third week of May 1960, the Millers were at home in an apartment on Ihlamur Yolu—Linden Lane. We had come a long way from the seminary in Berrien Springs, in October of 1959, where I sat in my first seminary class and heard the lady from the registrar's office call out, "Curtis Miller has a long-distance phone call." I still remember the thrill in my heart when I heard the voice of the Montana Conference president, George Taylor, say, "Curtis, the General Conference has appointed you to be a missionary to Turkey."

The miracles God worked for me actually began prior to my arrival in Istanbul. Let me tell you a most thrilling miraculous story about the origins of the SDA Church in Turkey.

A Brief History of the Seventh-day Adventist Church in Turkey

The first SDA to enter Turkey was a layman, a Greek shoemaker named Theodore Anthony, who had migrated from Turkey to the USA, where he became a Seventh-day Adventist. The Lord laid upon him that he must take the message of his new-found faith to his homeland. In February 1889 he returned to Turkey as a self-supporting missionary. His arrival in Turkey marked the beginning of permanent SDA work in the Middle East, and the Turkish Mission of SDA is the oldest in all the Middle East.

Anthony began to work among the Christian people of Constantinople (this city was called "Istanbul" after WWI and the overthrow of the Sultan of Turkey). When his money gave out, he took up cobbling to support himself. Among his first converts was a young Armenian, Zadour Baharian, who was convinced of the seventh-day Sabbath and the SDA Church being God's church to take the Gospel to all the world. Baharian was baptized in 1890, went to Basel, Switzerland, and after two years of study and translating returned to Turkey in 1892 as an SDA missionary.

After WWI Seventh-day Adventist work in Turkey progressed slowly. I would call Baharian the "Apostle to Turkey," for he traveled far and wide throughout the land, raising up churches; he was quite like the ancient apostle Paul who labored much in Asia Minor—modern Turkey. By WWI, there were twenty-three SDA churches scattered around Turkey, with around 500 members.

On one occasion Baharian wanted to have all the SDA workers in Turkey to have a council meeting; this was during the time of WWI and the Ottoman genocide of Armenians when they were not allowed to gather or move unless given government permission. About that time the Turkish government arrested all SDA workers they could find and placed them in the prison cell. While jailed together Baharian conducted the worker's meeting, after which all of them were released. Baharian declared that the Turkish government supplied room and board for that workers' meeting!

For those readers of my autobiography who may be interested in the history of SDA work in Turkey I strongly urge you to read the book *Diamondola* authored by Mildred Olson, who, with her husband Wayne, were my fellow missionaries in Lebanon. She also wrote a sequel to this book, *Diamondola and Aram*. Both of these books will thrill and fascinate you.

Shortly after I arrived in Istanbul I learned (I wonder if *Diamondola* told me this story?) of an intriguing story of a faithful SDA peddler of Bibles who once packed his suitcase full of Bibles and took a train from Istanbul close to 600 miles to Trabzon a city on the Black Sea coast of northeastern Turkey and the capital of Trabzon Province. Trabzon, located on the historical Silk Road, became a melting pot of religions, languages, and culture for centuries and a trade gateway to Persia in the southeast and the Caucasus to the northeast.

Arriving in Trabzon on a Monday, the Bible peddler wandered up and down the residential streets of old Trabzon, selling a Bible where he could. Now, a suitcase full of Bibles is heavy, so the peddler was bent over, initially, as he carried the suitcase from door to door. He was clothed in old Turkish costume that included baggy trousers with a long band of cloth, folded in half, and wound around his waist. When he sold a Bible, he would tuck the money into that waistband. As he wandered the streets, he noticed a strange man who seemed to be following him, day after day, and wondered, "Why is this man following me?"

By Thursday morning the peddler had sold all the Bibles, so he hastened to the train station. His suitcase, now quite empty, was held loosely in his hand. On the way to the station the peddler noted that man was still following him and still wondered why. After purchasing his train ticket, the Bible peddler took a seat on a bench at the train station to wait. The man sat down nearby.

Shortly the train pulled into the station and the peddler got ready to board. He saw that man standing very nearby him. By now the peddler had concluded that this man was a definite threat to him, so instead of immediately boarding the train, he waited until the train whistle sounded and the porter called, "All aboard!" He waited until the train barely started to pull out of the station then he jumped aboard the train car right behind the engine, hoping to thus elude that man. The peddler proceeded to run through each train car until he came to the very last. He made his way to the last compartment, opened the door, found the compartment empty of passengers, then sat down, praying he had at last eluded that man.

And the train went clickety-clack along the track towards Istanbul.

Shortly the peddler heard footsteps in the corridor. The steps came closer and closer. Then the door to the compartment slowly opened. The stranger peered inside, saw the peddler, came into the compartment, closed the door behind him, and sat down facing the peddler, fixing his eyes ominously upon him.

Finally, the stranger spoke, "I saw that you spent several days in Trabzon, going from home to home."

Slowly and cautiously the peddler responded, "Yes, I did."

"You were carrying a suitcase that was very heavy at first and became lighter through the week."

"That's true," admitted the peddler.

"And your waist band seemed fuller and fuller each day," continued the stranger. The peddler was silent.

"You have a waist band full of money, don't you," declared the stranger. The peddler remained silent. Suddenly the stranger drew a pistol which he aimed at the peddler then commanded, "Give me your money!"

The peddler, very sad and distraught, certainly did not want to give up the precious money he had gained from selling all those Bible, but eyeing that pistol he slowly started to put his hand in his waist band.

Suddenly the robber became very cautious, for he wondered if, in addition to money, the peddler also had a pistol in his waist band. "Stop! Don't make a move," he ordered, then asked, "Do you have a gun in your waist band?"

Realizing the robber feared that he, too, was armed, the Peddler exclaimed, "Yes! I have a gun," and he quickly drew a small Bible from his waist band. The robber looked at that small black book and laughed, "You don't have a pistol; that is just a harmless book."

"Ah," said the peddler, "but this is a book that is very special. It is a Kitabi Mukkades [Turkish words for "Holy Book," or Bible] which can shoot you right in your heart."

Incredulously the robber asked, "What do you mean? How can that Bible shoot me in the heart?"

Turning to the Ten Commandments in Exodus 20, the Peddler opened the Word of God, explaining that "stealing"—which was what the robber was attempting—was a sin, a transgression of God's law, and "those who break God's law will be judged by God, and if found guilty will ultimately be put to death."

The peddler, sensing the robber was so intently listening and the pistol was in the man's lap, continued telling him of God's wonderful plan of salvation. By this time the train was beginning to slow down for the station in the next city. The would-be robber now declared, "I was going to rob you, and I still am," then once more picking up his pistol he said, "But I am going to rob you of your Kitabi Mukkades. Give it to me!"

Calmly the peddler replied, "You cannot rob me of my Kitabi Mukkades because I am going to give it to you as a gift," and he gave the robber his Bible. Taking the Bible, the repentant robber left the train at that station.

Only in heaven will he, and we, learn the outcome of the robber and the Kitabi Mukkades. Hopefully the arrows of truth struck him in his heart and he will be in heaven, too.

As the train traveled on the peddler prayed, "Thank You, Father, for Your protection, for saving the Bible money, and for giving me opportunity to witness for You. Bless that stranger as he reads Your Holy Word."

The peddler never saw the stranger again. Only in heaven will he, and we, learn the outcome of the robber and the Kitabi Mukkades. Hopefully the arrows of truth struck him in his heart and he will be in heaven, too.

During WWI, the Muslim Turks so persecuted the Armenian Christians, that many were killed or exiled. Zadour Baharian was a martyr for his Christian faith. One by one twenty-two of those churches winked out, until our only SDA congregation was a few score members in Istanbul. Our church had no building of its own; they met in homes and fields. By the mid '50s they were allowed to hold services in an Armenian Gregorian Church, because an SDA member had been a boyhood friend with the Armenian pastor, who showed his friend kindness and allowed our members to meet in his church.

In 1955 there was a tragedy in Istanbul that God used as a means for the SDA church to be built in Istanbul. Adnan Menderes, Prime Minister of Turkey during the decade of 1950–60, orchestrated the Istanbul Pogrom, which targeted the city's substantial Greek ethnic minority. In September 1955 a bomb exploded close to the Turkish consulate in Greece's second-largest city, Thessaloniki, also damaging the Atatürk Museum, site of Atatürk's birthplace. The damage to the house was minimal, with only some broken windows. In retaliation, in Istanbul thousands of shops, houses, churches, and even graves belonging to members of the ethnic Greek minority were destroyed within a few hours; over a dozen people were killed and many more injured during these riots.

The ongoing struggle between Turkey and Greece over control of Cyprus, and Cypriot intercommunal violence, formed part of the backdrop to the pogrom. The United Kingdom invited Turkey and Greece to a conference in London, which started on August 26, 1955. The day before the Tripartite London Conference (29 August–7 September 1955) began, Menderes claimed that Greek Cypriots were planning a massacre of Turkish Cypriots. Seeing the opportunity to extricate Britain, Prime Minister Anthony Eden advised the Turkish delegates that they should be stern. Foreign minister Fatin Rü tü Zorlu paid heed to Macmillan and launched a harsh opening salvo, stating that Turkey would not reconsider its commitment to the Treaty of Lausanne unless Greece reconsidered its position on Cyprus. The Greek delegates, surprised by harshness of the speech, blamed the British.

Deflecting domestic attention to Cyprus was politically convenient for the Menderes government, which was suffering from an ailing economy. Although a minority, the Greek population played a prominent role in the city's business life, making it a convenient scapegoat during the economic crisis in the mid-50s. The DP responded first with inflationary policies, then when that failed, with authoritarianism and populism. DP's policies also introduced rural-urban mobility, which exposed some of the rural population to the lifestyles of the urban minorities. The three chief destinations were the largest three cities: Istanbul, Ankara, and Izmir. Between 1945 and 1955, the population of Istanbul increased from 1 million to about 1.6 million. Many of these new residents found themselves in shantytowns (Turkish: gecekondus) and constituted a prime target for populist policies.

The Istanbul pogrom, also known as the Istanbul riots were organized mob attacks directed primarily at Istanbul's Greek minority on September 6–7,1955. The events were triggered by the false news that the Turkish consulate in Thessaloniki, in northern Greece—the house where Mustafa Kemal Atatürk had been born in 1881—had been bombed the day before. A bomb planted by a Turkish usher at the consulate, who was later arrested and confessed, incited the events. The Turkish press, conveying the news in Turkey, was silent about the arrest and instead insinuated that Greeks had set off the bomb.

A Turkish mob, most of which had been trucked into the city in advance, assaulted Istanbul's Greek community. Armenians were also harmed. The police remained mostly ineffective. During the riot, and the violence continued until the government declared martial law in stanbul and called in the army to put down the riots.

The pogrom greatly accelerated emigration of ethnic Greeks from Turkey, and the Istanbul region in particular. The Greek population of Turkey declined from 119,822 persons in 1927, to about 7,000 in 1978. In Istanbul alone, the Greek population decreased from 65,108 to 49,081 between 1955 and 1960. The 2008 figures released by the Turkish Foreign Ministry placed the number of Turkish citizens of Greek descent at 3,000–4,000; while according to the Human Rights Watch (2006) their number was estimated to be 2,500. Some see the attacks as a continuation of a process of Turkification that started with the decline of the Ottoman Empire, rather than being a contemporary, bilateral issue. To back this claim they adduce the fact that roughly 40% of the properties attacked belonged to other minorities. The pogrom has been compared in some media to the Kristallnacht, the 1938 pogrom against Jews throughout Nazi Germany. Historian Alfred-Maurice de Zayas has written that in his view, despite the small number of deaths in the pogrom, the riots met the "intent to destroy in whole or in part" criterion of the Genocide Convention.

Finally, the conference fell apart on 6 September, the first day the subject of Cyprus would be broached at the conference, when news broke of the bombing in Thessaloniki. The 1961 Yassıada Trial after the 1960 coup d'état accused Menderes and Foreign Minister Fatin Rü tü Zorlu of planning the riots, finding that the supposed assault was in fact a provocation organized by the Menderes government, which planted the bomb in Thessaloniki and also bussed infuriated villagers from Anatolia into Istanbul with the aim of "punishing" Greeks. Menderes subsequently apologized and offered compensation to those affected.

During pogrom, in Istanbul, there was a riot against Armenian and Greek Christians. Both Greek and Armenian Christians were killed, along with other atrocities. Mobs took to Istikal Caddesi (Independence Avenue) in the heart of Istanbul, where many Christian-owned shops were located. Merchandise in their shops were destroyed, with the streets, reportedly, knee-high with goods.

The minister of the interior, Namık Gedik, committed suicide while he was detained in the Turkish Military Academy. President Celal Bayar, prime minister Adnan Menderes and several other members of the administration were put on trial before a court appointed by the junta on the island Yassıada in the Sea of Marmara. The politicians were charged with high treason, misuse of public funds and abrogation of the constitution.

The tribunals ended with the execution of Adnan Menderes, Minister of Foreign Affairs Fatin Rü tü Zorlu and Minister of Finance Hasan Polatkan on mralı island on 16 September 1961.

A month after the execution of Menderes and other members of the Turkish government, general elections were held on 15 October 1961. The administrative authority was returned to civilians, but the military continued to dominate the political scene until October 1965. General Ismet nönü held the office of Prime Minister for the third time from 1961 to 1965. Turkish Army Colonel Talat Aydemir organized two failed coups d'etat in February 1962 and May 1963. In the first free elections after the coup, in 1965, Süleyman Demirel was elected and held the office until 1971, when he was removed by another coup.

Our Church in Istanbul

The Istanbul Church was a three-storied structure, with a basement. The basement had a furnace room for a coal furnace, a small apartment (Manuk and his wife, Anahid, occupied that apartment for the first two years we were in Istanbul), and a third room named "Rasmussen Hall," in honor of the man who organized the building of the church. The middle floor consisted of two children's classrooms, and a larger fellowship room where members gathered to talk and eat after church services. Many members came a long distance to church services and enjoyed socializing and sharing food. The top floor had a small narthex, opening into the largest room in the church—the sanctuary.

The sanctuary had a small balcony, for extra seating, and a baptistry, behind the pulpit. It is possible that our church had the only baptistery for immersion in all Turkey.

One unique feature of the sanctuary was the words inscribed on the wall behind the pulpit, and above the baptistery, "Iste Tez Geliyorum," — "Behold I Come Quickly" (Rev. 22:12). I am comforted by those words of promise above the pulpit where I often preached from 1960–70.

I have a precious memory of worshipping in our Istanbul sanctuary. A tiny Armenian widow often worshipped with us. In harmony with her widowhood, she always dressed in black. She would come into the sanctuary, go to the fourth pew on the right side, then stand with her arms outstretched, with palms up, her eyes looking upwards, while she silently prayed. Melody, then about six years old, was seated with me, across the aisle from the faithful and pious widow. Melody watcher her carefully, then asked, "Daddy, what is that lady doing?" I explained to Melody that the lady was praying to God, prior to sitting in her pew. Melody, very quickly, went to the lady's side, put out her arms, palms up, then looked upwards, as did the lady, and I was gratified and proud of my eldest daughter following the modeling of a very godly woman.

Our mission building and church were just a few blocks from one of the main landmarks in Istanbul: Taksim Square. To reach the mission you take a street leading down the hill to the Bosporus—Gumusuyu Sokak, the Street of Silver Water. I used to walk down that street to our mission, and along the way would pass a small silversmith's shop. Now and again, I would stop to watch the silversmith at his work; once I even purchased a silver vase he had made. He used to collect silver coins, which he would melt in a pot over a fire that he would use bellows to fan to a high heat. As the silver coins melted, the silversmith would skim the dross off the molten silver. I once asked him, "How do you know when you have melted all the

Our Church in Istanbul, Taken from Fourth Floor of the Mission Building

Sanctuary of the Istanbul Church

dross away?" to which he replied, "I melt the silver and skim the dross until I can see my face clearly in the molten silver, then I know the silver is pure."

I have thought since then that is the way God works with us: He places us in the crucible of this world, where He allows us to be heated until He can behold His face in us—then He knows we are ready for Him to fashion us into a fit vessel to bear His name, and be ready for heaven when our Lord comes again to take us to heaven.

My prayer is that each of my family will reproduce the image of our Lord so that He will take us home to heaven—and may He come soon!

The Mondics Family

Ben and Margaret Mondics were in Istanbul as missionaries when the Millers arrived in Turkey. They had adopted twin boys, who were twelve years old when we arrived in Istanbul. Mrs. Mondics was an elementary school teacher at the Robert College, which was originally founded by American missionaries in the mid-1850s.

Ben was a complex person, whom I believe had an obsessive-compulsive personality disorder (OCD). During the first year or so of my tenure, he functioned in a fairly normal fashion. We shared the Sabbath pulpit. He conducted a mission staff meeting on Monday mornings. I was puzzled by these meetings, for he would lead us in making plans, but seldom implemented them. Because I was busy studying Turkish and traveling with Yeshilay

> *"I melt the silver and skim the dross until I can see my face clearly in the molten silver, then I know the silver is pure."*

staff, showing films and speaking about the dangerous effects of alcohol and tobacco, I did not think too much about what Mondics did. Finally, I took note that Mondics was often staying in bed. He would arise, dress, and conduct or staff meetings, then return to bed. He was vague in his answers to my questions regarding his health, as was his wife. I also noted that he would only get out of bed whenever staff from the Middle East Division (MED) or the GC would come to Istanbul.

Toward the end of my second year in Istanbul, I was requested by Middle East College, in Beirut, to conduct a Week of Prayer on campus. I was also to attend staff meetings at the MED. Prior to flying to Beirut, I went to Mondics' residence. He was in bed, as usual; nonetheless I went to his bedroom, to find him, as per usual, in bed. I informed him I had been directed by the MED to proceed to Beirut, for he was not aware of my assignment.

I decided to be frank and direct, saying, "Ben, I am flying to Beirut, today. I will be meeting with the MED Executive Committee, and I intend to tell them about you being mostly in bed, unable to function in your mission work."

He reared up in bed, and declared, "I forbid you to say one word to the committee about me." At that I departed, saying, "I am going to inform the committee about you."

During that meeting I told Elder Roger Wilcox, MED president, and the rest of the committee members, what I was observing about Ben. The MED medical director was dispatched to Istanbul. As a medical doctor, he examined Mondics, and suspected he had cancer. The MED acted quickly, directing Ben to return to the U.S. immediately, where he was diagnosed with stomach cancer; sadly, he died a few months later. Margaret Mondics stayed a couple months longer at the mission to finish her term of teaching.

I was appointed to be President of the Turkish Mission, and Manuk was designated pastor of the Istanbul church. Together we forged one of the best relationships as co-workers that I have ever had. We traveled to many places in Turkey, showing temperance films and giving lectures. During our tenure together, we traveled more than any other SDA workers since the days of Zadour Baharian during WWI.

Manuk Benzatyan

In the early 1930s there lived near Istanbul an Armenian lady, whose last name was Benzatyan; she longed to have a child, but, alas, she was barren, like unto Hannah in Biblical times. She went to a local Armenian priest who directed her to go to the pillar in St. Sophia, the church built by the Byzantine Emperor Justinian in A.D. 532. In its day it had the world's largest unsupported dome, held by four massive marble pillars. One of the pillars is called the Weeping Column which ancient Christian believers alleged had the blessing of St. Gregory and has led many to rub the column in search of divine blessings or miracles, creating a large hollow in the marble. The lady followed those instructions, and a year later she bore a son whom she named Manuk. His parents were very loving and caring. He has a younger sister who married a German and migrated to Germany.

Manuk lived his early years in the village of Bakirkoy (Copper Village) on the edge of Istanbul. A mischievous boy he was. For example, when he was an early teen, he watched for foreign tourists who needed to change their money into Turkish Lira. Manuk would say to a tourist, "If you like, I will take your money to have it exchanged for Lira, giving you the best exchange price better than you can receive at a bank

Manuk placing his finger in hollow of marble

or marketplace." Manuk looked like a boy who was honest and trustworthy, so tourists often accepted his offer and gave him money to exchange. He would scurry away as though he was going to the "Cambio" where he would exchange their money, but, alas, he would disappear around a corner and never come back! The tourist was scammed.

From the time of WWI and the emergence of Mustafa Kemal Ataturk, who was the major force in the founding of the Turkish Republic, the SDA Church in Turkey produced no new ministers and by the early '50s the only Adventist ministers in Turkey were missionaries from other countries. Mischievous Manuk was the only prospective person we could send to become a minister, so the SDA Turkish Mission sponsored him as a student at Middle East College (MEC).

Manuk agreed to attend MEC, taking advantage of much financial help from the mission, although he would also be required to do student labor at college to earn funds for his education. MEC had a slogan, "Middle East College Where Students Earn to Learn." Thus, Manuk journeyed to Beirut, attended MEC, but he thought to himself, "I will take the Mission's money for my education, but I will take business courses so I can become a rich business man; I will not become a minister."

At MEC Manuk continued his comic, mischievous ways. First, it was the custom in those countries to not wear shoes inside your residence; consequently in both the men's and women's dormitories the students would leave their shoes just outside the door to their dorm room. One morning the young ladies could not find their shoes in the hall. They were mystified, until someone spotted the toes of many shoes showing over the edge of the dormitory roof. Manuk was the guilty culprit who snuck into the dorm, gathered the shoes, and placed them neatly in a row on the edge of the roof! His second mischief was in the men's dorm. One night at bedtime none of the residents in the men's dorm could find their pajamas. The next morning the pajamas were found flying from the flagpole in the middle of the campus. Again, Manuk was the practical joker!

Manuk was of keen intelligence, a quick learner, and soon became an accomplished electrician for MEC. During the latter part of the time Manuk was a MEC student a second floor was added to the administration building. One day Manuk was connecting a new mainline electric cable to the new addition. That morning he stretched the cable to the building, then went to lunch in the college cafeteria, planning to connect the cable to insulators on a power pole after lunch.

When he finished eating, he went to the college maintenance building and turned off the main electric switch, thus cutting off all the electric power on the campus buildings while he connected that mainline that would carry 240 volts of electricity. After throwing that switch he proceeded to the power pole, donned his climbing spurs to aid in ascending the pole, put on a safety belt that would keep him safe while he climbed, and also put on the belt that held the equipment necessary for him to do his work. Two fellow students, Hovic and Arsen, would be his helpers on the ground, aiding him while he worked.

Manuk proceeded to climb the pole, reached the top, then took hold of a metal spar with his left hand and with his right hand he grasped the main electric line, thus completing an electrical circuit that shot 240 volts into him. After he had turned off the main electric switch in the maintenance building, the girls who worked in the college laundry had proceeded from the cafeteria to the laundry to iron clothes. But the laundry room lights were off and their irons would not get hot. The laundry manager sent a girl to the maintenance building to request the electricity be turned back on. The student on duty there, unaware that Manuk had turned off the electricity while he connected the mainline, turned the switch on. That mainline was now pulsing with high voltage electricity when Manuk grasped it. 240 volts surged through him. He sought to cry out for help, but he could only make a gurgling sound.

On the ground, Hovic and Arsen heard Manuk, but believed Manuk was once again up to his old tricks. Hovic exclaimed,

"There goes Manuk again; he is trying to make us believe he is being electrocuted." But as they looked up at Manuk suspended by his safety belt as he grasped the metal cross beam in one hand and the electric mainline, they suddenly realized Manuk was not joking—he *was* being electrocuted!

Hovic and Arsen raced to the maintenance building, a long block away, where Hovic shut the mainline electric switch. They were winded from their fast running and sat on the floor to catch their breath. As they rested, Hovic remembered Manuk on that power pole. With the electricity turned off, the 240 volts no longer shooting through him, he might be in danger of falling. They raced back to the power pole to behold Manuk hanging upside down from his safety belt. He appeared dead!

Summoning help, a ladder was brought and rescuers lowered Manuk to the ground. He appeared lifeless; nonetheless those who came to Manuk's aid gathered around him and prayed. Shortly Manuk regained consciousness and was helped to his bed in the dorm. As he rested there, he thanked God for saving his life, for he could have been fatally electrocuted that day. That evening, during worship in the dormitory, Manuk thought about the Turkish Mission that funded him to come to MEC, praying he would become a minister of the Gospel and return to Turkey to preach the Adventist message of Jesus' promise to return a second time to take His faithful to their heavenly home.

Manuk proceeded to become a minister of the SDA Church. While studying theology as MEC, he met Anahid; they courted, and shortly after his graduation from MEC they married. Manuk and Anahid came to Istanbul, where I met them, becoming close friends, not

As they looked up at Manuk suspended by his safety belt as he grasped the metal cross beam in one hand and the electric mainline, they suddenly realized Manuk was not joking—he was being electrocuted!

just while we labored together in ministry on this earth—we pledged we would also live next door to each other in heaven. During all the years Manuk and I worked together we never had an argument or disagreement; we worked in wonderful harmony between us.

Our Temperance Work in Turkey

Joining with Yeshilay to further utilize my being connected to the GC's International Temperance Association was a boon to our work in Turkey. The very first mission journey I took after assuming my position with the Turkish Mission was traveling to Izmir, the biblical Smyrna. It was a thrilling trip for me, for I made the first airplane flight of my life. Mondics, Manuk, Yeshilay Director Divitchi, and I flew with Turk Hava Yollari (THY) — the airline motto was "Fly With THY." Americans in Turkey modified that motto to say "Fly and Die with THY." During my tenure in Turkey THY had numerous plane crashes.

We traveled by taxi from Izmir to the small town of Tire, where I lectured in a school and held a community meeting in a public hall about the dangers from use of alcoholic beverages. After the evening lecture we were entertained in the home of a local community leader who was also a medical doctor. The man in Tire who headed Yeshilay's work in the area presented me with a copy of the local newspaper with the headline: "Doktor Miller Tire'ye Geldi" — Doctor Miller Comes to Tire!

It was through Yeshilay that I met Nureddin Terciolu (Nurredin Bey), who worked for the Turkish government. He obtained permission for me to visit any school in Turkey to show our films and give our lectures. The International Temperance Association had given me a projector and numerous films that Manuk and I could show at schools. Nureddin Bey often traveled with us, for he, being a government employee, facilitated our being readily accepted wherever we traveled. Often we had a full schedule, showing films and giving lectures in three to four schools a day, so we set a goal to have our program to at least 1,000 students daily.

While lecturing at an elite high school in Izmir, I noticed some Turkish Army officers sitting in the back of the auditorium. At the close of our program, Nureddin Bey talked with the officers, then beckoned Manuk and I to meet the officers. Colonel Hallil was the ranking officer, and as we shook hands, he enthusiastically invited us to come to his army base where he was the commanding officer of 16,000 Turkish Army troops. He wanted us to come right away, but we already had appointments for all afternoon. We agreed that we would come back to Izmir, where his base was, the following week.

A week later we landed at the Izmir airport, to be met by Col. Hallil's chief of staff, a captain. He had with him two jeeps, with drivers, and one was to carry our equipment. Manuk, Nureddin Bey, and I usually wrestled with our equipment and luggage, but the captain assured us his soldiers would care for our baggage.

We were speedily transported to the army base, to be greeted by the colonel. He escorted us to two Quonset huts, each seating 400. While a motion picture was shown in one Quonset hut, I lectured in the other, then the projector and film and I switched huts, to carry on the program. Thus, were able to render our program to 8,000 troops a day, for two days, to reach all 16,000 of them.

The first day, the colonel entertained us at the Officer's Mess. It was a pleasant day, so the colonel had a table set up outside, in a courtyard. He sat at one end of table, and I at the other, which indicated he was treating me as his equal in rank. Manuk and Nureddin Bey sat on one side, and two of the colonel's aides sat on the other. As the meal was being served, Nureddin informed the colonel that Mr. Miller always prayed at the beginning of the meal. The colonel graciously bade me pray, and he and his aides bowed their heads.

At the conclusion of the meal, Colonel Hallil, with a gracious smile, said, "Mr. Miller, I always pray at the end of my meal." We all bowed our heads as he prayed.

On another trip, the three of us were traveling south from Ankara, to Konya (the biblical Iconium of the apostle Paul's day; he and Barnabas preached there). I was driving a small German-made Opel on that trip.

I will interrupt my story, here, to explain what I faced having an automobile in Turkey. I shipped a '53 Chevrolet to Turkey in 1960. It was a challenge to have it released from Turkish Customs, because I did not have a "Triptik" — a document like unto a passport, for an automobile, issued by a recognized automobile organization, like AAA in America. I had never heard of a Triptik before, and never even dreamed I would need such a document; hence I had no such thing. It took several months, but eventually our SDA travel bureau in New York was able to provide me with one. But I was not allowed to import the car into Turkey. The first year in Turkey, I was on a temporary tourist visa, which allowed me to stay in Turkey for three months at a time; then I would have to drive out of the country, then re-enter for another three months stay — a lot of red tape, to me. Eventually the Turkish customs figured out what I was doing and would not let me bring the Chevrolet in again. I drove it to Beirut, but I didn't want to pay the import tax there, because I could not use the car in Turkey. Eventually I gave the Chevy to Fakry Neguib, one of our Egyptian pastors. I even had to pay the $300 to ship it to Egypt. Because it was a "gift" to Fakry, he was able to obtain permission to import it. I was car-less many times while in Turkey. I did purchase the Opel in Beirut, obtained a Lebanese Triptik, and was allowed to keep

Meal with Colonel Hallil

it in Turkey, driving it out every three months. Eventually I was again refused by Turkey to continue having the Opel in Turkey. I sold it in Beirut.

Now, back to driving the Opel towards Konya. The weather was fine, the road stretched out over the high Anatolian plain, and we were making good time, hoping to reach Konya by early afternoon. But it was not to be, for suddenly the Opel coughed, sputtered, and the engine died; the timing belt had broken, stranding us by the side of the road, about twenty-five miles north of Konya.

Nureddin flagged down a truck going south, bargained with the driver, and for a few hundred Turkish Lira, arranged for us and the Opel to be towed to Konya. The truck could not maneuver the narrow streets of the town, so we unhooked from the truck, and Nureddin Bey bargained for a donkey to pull the Opel into town. There were no auto repair shops in Konya, but we did find a mechanic that worked on tractors. The mechanic assured us he could replace the timing belt, but it could be a day or so before he could receive one from Ankara.

It was late on a Friday afternoon. The three of us found a modest hotel for the weekend. We ate a simple meal at a nearby ristorante (Turkish for restaurant), then returned to our hotel. Around sundown, Manuk and I read our Bibles; Nureddin Bey, noting our reading, felt his own need of worship, especially since we heard the Muslim call to prayer resonating from the minaret of a nearby camii (Turkish for mosque). Devout Muslims hear the call to prayer five times a day; it is a strong tenet of the Muslim belief. Nureddin phoned the hotel desk, asking which direction Mecca was from the hotel. Mecca is a city in Arabia that is sacred to Muslims around the world, due to it being the place where Mohammed — the founder of Islam (that word means "surrender") had his awakening to Allah (God). Muslims always face toward Mecca when they pray.

Upon receiving his bearing as to which direction Mecca was, Nureddin Bey commenced his prayers, to be congruent with

Manuk and I reading Scripture. Nureddin paused his prayer, saying to me, "Curtis Bey, is it true that Seventh-day Adventists do not drink alcoholic beverages?"

I assured him SDAs do not drink alcoholic beverages.

I will digress to explain that Muslims also believe it is "haram" — sin — to drink alcoholic beverages; the Koran emphatically proclaims, "Thou shalt not drink a drop of wine." It is a fact that many Muslims drink wine, but before doing so, they flick a drop of wine from the glass; that is the "drop" they don't drink, thus by casuistry — getting around the "letter of the law," that Jews often use — and they can continue to drink the rest of the glass of an alcoholic beverage.

After I assured him SDA's do not drink alcoholic beverages, Nureddin Bey continued his prayers, only to pause again, as he asked, "Curtis Bey, is it true SDAs do not eat 'domuz' [pork]?"

I assured him that, along with Muslims and Jews, SDAs abstain from eating pork, for it is an unclean animal, forbidden by God to be eaten. Nureddin Bey continued his prayers, then suddenly he paused again, to solemnly declare, "Curtis Bey, that means that I, a Muslim, can worship with you in your church, for it is a 'clean' place."

Manuk, foreground, with Nureddin

I was pleased to hear his declaration. Here, I have only barely begun to tell you about my association with Nureddin Bey, which lasted many years; I will tell you the "rest of the story" about him, in later portions of my book.

Sunday found the needed timing belt for the Opel arrive from Ankara, and we continued our journey to Sivas.

The Millers and Benzatyans Achieve Many "Firsts" in Turkey

At the time I went to Turkey, it was against the law to preach anywhere, unless it was in a church duly recognized by the Turkish government. It was also against the law to pass out religious literature—books, pamphlets, tracts, etc. It was against the law to have Bible studies with anyone under age eighteen. It was a penal offense to baptize a Muslim into Christianity.

I learned that from the time SDA work commenced in Turkey in the mid-1880s until the time I began working in that country, there had been only a single Muslim baptized into the SDA Church. I determined I would change that and baptize a Muslim. I commenced praying God would lead me to such a Muslim, which He did; I will tell that thrilling story later in this book.

We preached the first public SDA evangelistic meetings since WWI. Announcement of our meetings was mostly by word of mouth, and it brought results, for our church was packed for many of our meetings.

Ben Mondics had been very cautious in his approach to working in Turkey, which was a puzzle to me, for God had worked several "miracles" for him, some of which I will relate still later. Nonetheless, when Mondics departed the Millers and the Benzatyans began praying God would guide us in endeavoring new missionary projects we could launch. God answered our earnest prayers.

I now introduce Miss Yebraksi Gomigyan, the daughter of one of the earliest converts to Adventism in Turkey. She was a very devout and faithful Seventh-day Adventist, and functioned as a Bible worker for many decades in Turkey. Because her family had been harshly persecuted during the Turkish pogrom of Christians, especially towards Armenians, such as her family, Yebraksi was, like Mondics, very cautious, not wanting to being the Turkish government down upon her. She became aware that Manuk and I were contemplating starting projects of an evangelistic nature, such as holding a Vacation Bible School (VBS), which had never before been held in Turkey. She very sternly admonished us, "Don't hold a VBS!"

Miss Yebraksi, in 1962, was sent as a delegate from the Middle East to the General Conference quadrennial session, which was held in San Francisco that year. She had only traveled to Lebanon, thus far in her life, so it was the experience of a lifetime for her to visit America. I endeavored to give her travel tips for touring the U.S. Miss Yebraksi was fluent in Armenian, her mother language, and Turkish. She was fairly conversant in English.

Like many foreign visitors to the U.S., she had heard of "Cowboys and Indians," and believed they should be avoided, for certain. In those years, the Greyhound Bus system offered tourists a special bus ticket "$99 for 99 days" — for $99 they could purchase unlimited travel, anywhere in the U.S., for 99 days. Miss Yebraksi obtained one of those tickets, and enthusiastically began seeing many touristic places as she traveled across the States.

I had told her, that by all means, she must see Yellowstone National Park, instructing her that at Rock Springs, Wyoming, she should take a side trip to visit that park. At Rock Springs, as she exited the bus, she saw a pickup truck pull to a stop just a few feet from her. She could see saddles in the bed of the truck. She saw two men, with 10-gallon hats, clad in jeans and cowboy boots, step out of the truck and walk towards the bus. From all she had learned about cowboys and Indians, she was very frightened, and instead of boarding a bus for Yellowstone, she got right back on the cross-country bus she had been on, and didn't get off until she reached San Francisco!

The main thing she brought from the GC session, back to Turkey, was the theme song for that session, "We Have This Hope" (which is in the current SDA Hymnal).

The First Vacation Bible School in Turkey

As soon as Miss Yebraksi left for the States, the Millers and Benzatyans began planning the first VBS! We had no access to VBS materials, but I did remember some VBS activities from my previous ministry in the Montana Conference. I knew we would have a theme, stories, songs, and choruses. We chose the theme: Know Your Bible. I have always been a storyteller (even unto this day, as I write my autobiography!) and was able to remember many stories we could use. We also designed crafts the children could do. And refreshments? Cookies and lemonade, the good ol' standby, were easy to do.

Selma Yeshil, wife of our head elder, Kevork Yeshil (literal translation is George Green), spoke very fluent English and had a gift of translating English hymns and choruses into Turkish, such as "Slizleri Insan Avcisi" (Fishers of Men), "Ufk Otesinde" (Way Beyond the Blue), "Isa Tekrar Geliyour" (Jesus Is Coming Again), and many others. She even translated one of my favorite hymns, "How Great Thou Art."

We estimated we might have perhaps fifteen children attending, with most of them our own church children, and perhaps a few others. Advertising our VBS was mostly by word of mouth. We were surprised to have over twenty attend the first day, with some of them having to walk a considerable distance to attend. Manuk and I decided we could use my '53 Chevy to pick some of them up. This VBS was before the Turkish government forbade me to have it in the country. We instructed those children who were walking a long way to gather at certain street corners for us to collect.

At the first pick-up corner, we expected three children, but there were five; we bundled them into the car. At subsequent stops there were often more than we expected, but we packed them in. How many kids can you pack into a '53 Chevy? We really stacked them in, both in front and back seats, until we had fifteen of us in the car!

Attendance grew and grew at our first VBS, until we had over fifty attending. We truly believed God blessed our VBS evangelism.

There was a further blessing: We had a very kind maid (maids were quite inexpensive in Turkey, at that time), Araksi, by name. During the VBS, which lasted two weeks, we requested her to come to our house earlier than usual, to care for Valerie, who was still in babyhood. She became curious as to what VBS was; when we explained it to her, she sent her daughters, Mayram (Turkish for name Mary), and Luiz, who enjoyed VBS so much that they wanted to attend Sabbath services in our church. Shortly, Araksi began attending church with them, and we gave Araksi Bible studies which ultimately brought about her baptism into our church in Istanbul. Still later, after my departure from Turkey, Mayram and Luiz were baptized.

The First Pathfinder Club in Turkey

With a growing number of youth attending our Istanbul Church, Manuk and I decided to organize a Pathfinder Club (Izji Kulubu in Turkish). We held regular meetings, taught various honors classes, including those which helped our Pathfinders become "Friends, Guides, and Master Guides." An SDA Istanbul member, Hagop Tulgar, who was a tailor by occupation, made Pathfinder uniforms for Manuk, some of the Pathfinders, and me. We enjoyed much fellowship with our Pathfinders; I especially remember one special trip we made, to the Sultan's Forest, near Istanbul.

The Pathfinder Club served as a stepping-stone to our next "first" in Turkey.

The First Youth Camp in Turkey

After holding that first VBS, the Millers and the Benzatyans took a short vacation together at Lake Abant, on a side-road about 175 miles from Istanbul, about midway between Istanbul and Ankara.

Lake Abant (Turkish: Abant Gölü) is a freshwater lake in Turkey's Bolu Province in northwest Anatolia, formed as a result of a great landslide. The lake lies at an altitude of 4,357 feet at a distance of twenty miles from the provincial seat of Bolu city. A Turkish tourist folder described Lake Abant as like "a drop of mercury in the delicate hand of a beautiful girl." Compared with many lakes in the U.S., Abant did not quite measure up to their beauty, however, it was a nice, peaceful place. We camped about midway on the eastern side of the lake. While camping there, it dawned on us that Lake Abant would be an ideal place to hold a youth camp for our Pathfinders.

I remembered my own youth camping years, around ages nine to eleven, at Cedar Falls Camp in the San Gabriel Mountains west of Los Angeles in the mid-1940s. I had a great time at Cedar Falls; the only event that marred it was my second year there, when a classmate and buddy of mine, Alfonso Luna, drowned at the camp.

Manuk and I began planning for our first youth camp, which was held the summer of 1963. We made a list of all the things we would need to conduct a camp: tents, sleeping mats, primus stoves, meal trays, cutlery, pots and pans.

During the many years Manuk and I worked together in Turkey from 1960–70, and later when the Benzatyans emigrated to the U.S., we planned many activities with never a difference of opinion coming between us. We were very blessed to have such co-workers and friends!

We designed the tents ourselves and hired a professional tentmaker to construct them. Our design fully met the purpose we intended.

Several days prior to the camp, Manuk, Hayk (our church janitor), and I went to Lake Abant to set the camp up: erecting the sleeping tents, each of which held ten campers and setting up the cook tent, and other facilities. The campsite had on it a spring that yielded good, cold water, and adequate outdoor toilets. About half-mile away was a quaint village lokantisi—café—where we took our meals while we worked.

We hired a bus to carry the campers from Istanbul to Lake Abant. We had around forty campers that first year. Araksi and a couple of her sisters-in-law were our camp cooks, and they were terrific cooks, in spite of having to cook on several primus stoves. We needed to acquire everything fresh daily, for we had no refrigeration. Camp provisions were purchased at the small mountain town of Bolu, about fifteen miles away.

We erected a flagpole in the midst of the camp, from which we hoisted the Turkish flag, which has a red field, with a white crescent and star — symbols many Muslim nations have on their flags. The camp day began at 7:00 a.m. with my blowing a whistle to rouse the campers. They had twenty minutes to dress, groom themselves, and make their tent and themselves ready for inspection, after which we raised the flag and the campers sang the Turkish National Anthem.

The highlight of a day at camp was the evening campfire, and the campers always wanted a big one. Behind the campsite were hills, and over one hill was a small village. We hired a villager to haul firewood for us. He used a donkey to carry the wood. Around the campfire we sang choruses, which Selma Yeshil translated from English to Turkish. It was around the campfire that I honed my skills of storytelling; I have developed s favorable reputation of being a storyteller, and I thank God for that gift. The campers especially liked my telling a continued story that took most of the nights to finish. I endeavored to close each segment on a point of high suspense; when I did so, the campers would beg me to tell just a bit more of the story, but I believe I heightened their interest at stopping at a climatic point. Campers particularly liked stories about Native Americans, and I told several stories about them. One year each tent of youth chose to name themselves by the name of a Native American tribe: Sioux, Comanche, Apache, Blackfeet, Arapaho, and others.

Two other Sabbath activities were popular with the campers. The first Sabbath was a nature hunt, where each tent group was given a list of things to collect during a hike in the hills such as leaves from certain trees, wildflowers, rocks, insects, etc. The second Sabbath was "Bible Story Charades," wherein each tent of campers would act out a Bible story, such as David and Goliath or Daniel in the Lion's Den. The groups secretly planned their charade, and while they were performing it, the rest of the campers would try to guess what the charade was. This became a very popular event during the several years I was involved with Manuk in leading the camp.

The many youth camps that I conducted with Manuk are stored in my most precious memories of my life. The following event is one I will never forget, and always cherish. It happened thusly:

Late one afternoon during the week, a bus load of male university students, Muslims all, pulled into our camp area. They spread out their blankets for a picnic, all the while eying the campers, particularly the teenage girls in our camp. They were overheard remarking what they would sexually do to the girls, after dark. Many of the Christian campers were terrified, for they all remembered the stories their parents and grandparents told them about the persecution and genocide of Armenians by the Turks before and during WWI. The campers rushed to their tents, barricading them with their blankets and sleeping mats.

As darkness drew on, Mauuk and I talked together as to how we could protect our campers. We knew that on the far side of Lake Abant was a camp for rest and recreation for Turkish Army officers and their families. We decided Manuk would quietly evacuate the tents, one by one, and send them up the trail of the hillside, to keep them as far away as possible. I would drive around the lake to the Army camp.

Arriving at the camp, I approached the two sentries on duty, stating I wished to speak to the camp commander. I was escorted to the colonel's headquarter. I spoke to him in Turkish, asking if he spoke English; to this he replied that he found my Turkish adequate, then asked how he might be of service. I identified myself as an American citizen, in charge of the youth camp on the other side of the lake. I described the situation taking place, the threats of the Muslim students, and added, "Although many of our campers were Christians, there are some who are Muslim, and the Turkish students will not be able to tell Christian from Muslim."

I will never forget the reply I received from that Turkish colonel, for he said, "Mr. Miller, I do not care what nationality you are; I do not care what nationality your campers are; I do not care what the religious beliefs of your campers are. You shall have the protection of my Turkish Army." With that he began issuing orders for a truckload of Turkish soldiers to proceed to our camp to protect us.

The Turkish troops, with rifles and bayonets, quickly assembled into a military truck. I raced my car ahead of that truck, for I wanted to reach our camp first, so that I could welcome the troops. I arrived at our camp just as the truck pulled to a stop, and the first trooper jumped to the ground. In the darkness I extended my hand to shake his, but I felt the sharp tip of a bayonet pressed against me; those troops were ready to protect us!

Upon hearing the roar of the truck approaching them, the university students quickly boarded their bus, seeking to drive away. The troops were enthusiastically spoiling for a fight and yelled derisively as the bus roared away. The Turkish officer in charge of those troops said that we would be safe, under their protection.

The next day a truckload of officers, their wives, and children came to visit our camp. They entertained our campers with Turkish folk dances.

Came the Sunday camp ended, we were striking our tents and loading a truck with our camp gear, and the campers were readying to board their bus to return to Istanbul, when an army truck came into our campsite, with troops aboard. They had been watching our camp via binoculars, daily, since the incident with the university students. Seeing us striking tents, they thought we were leaving because we were again endangered. When I informed them the camp was over for that year, they left, assuring us we would be protected.

Close to midway through my ninth decade this ol' man often reflects on life-events of long, long, and long ago, such as this one:

Way back in the 60s, when I was an SDA missionary to the Middle East, living in Istanbul, Turkey, Manuk and I joined together to hold the first Vacation Bible School and first youth camp in our Turkish Mission.

As we prepared for the second youth camp, during our annual VBS, we decided to have any VBS attendees who wanted to go to camp to put their name on a slip, place it in a large jar, and then on the last day of VBS, we would draw a name out of that jar and that person would receive a free trip to youth camp that summer.

Many youngsters wrote their names on slips of paper and put them in the jar. On the last day of VBS, as we prepared to draw a name, Aysha, a twelve-year-old girl, excitedly said, "Last night I had a dream. In my dream I saw a hand reaching into the jar, draw out a name, and it was my name! I believe it will be my name that is going to be drawn right now."

I reached into the jar, drew out a slip of paper — after Manuk thoroughly stirred the jar of names—and to my amazement and the amazement of everyone present — except Aysha, I read the name on the slip of paper: AYSHA!

Aysha clapped her hands with joy as she exclaimed, "My dream has come true!" She enjoyed a free time at the ten-day youth camp that year!

My beloved readers, at this time the Ruler of our universe is in the midst of judging us, to decide whom of us is "Safe to Save" in His kingdom. From His heavenly record He is drawing out names of those to be saved.

I have a dream, but it is more than a dream for I determine to make it a reality. I see my Lord drawing my name to be saved in His everlasting kingdom. I claim His promises, particularly John 3:16, "For God so loved the world, that he gave his only begotten Son, that whosoever believeth in him should not perish, but have everlasting life."

Our Second Youth Camp

Kevork Yeshil (George Green) was one of our very faithful elders of our Istanbul Church, and each year he was on the camp staff, thus he witnessed the events of our first camp. Kevork had a unique experience that I regard as a miracle, or divine intervention.

Kevork loved swimming. He even liked swimming in the Bosporus, the strait of water leading from the Black Sea to the Sea of Marmara, that also divides European Istanbul, on the west, from Asiatic Istanbul to the east. Kevork and Manuk both swam in the Bosporus, and they both were progressing into baldness. I, in contrast, do not like to swim in cold water (my not liking cold water harks back to my birth, when it was -28 degrees below zero, outside, when I was born), and I am not growing bald. So, I make my case of swimming in cold water causes baldness.

But back to Kevork and swimming. He was teaching his two daughters to swim, at a place in the Sea of Marmara. Nearby was a Turkish man trying to teach his two daughters to swim, but the girls were reticent. The Turk father was a retired Turkish Air Force officer, trained in the U.S., Colonel Gulseren. Kevork helped Col. Gulseren to teach his daughters, Fisun and Julide, to swim. This resulted in the two fathers forming a friendship.

I have a dream, but it is more than a dream for I determine to make it a reality. I see my Lord drawing my name to be saved in His everlasting kingdom.

After the crisis at our first camp, Kevork related to Col. Gulseren what happened at Lake Abant. The Colonel declared, "I am going to send my daughters to your next camp, and I will direct my nephew, who is the provincial governor of that area, to make certain the camp is protected.

Fisun and Julide attended our camp the summer of 1964. Kevork had described our camp program, which included each tent of campers having a "Prayer Circle" in connection with morning worship. "That will be no problem for my girls," stated the colonel, "I will instruct Fisun and Julide, to politely turn their backs to the prayer circle."

Julide, that year, was in Anahid Benzatyan's tent. Several days into that year's camp, Anahid came to me, saying, "Curtis, I am excited; Julide did not turn her back during our prayer circle this morning. She even offered a prayer, ending it with 'Isanin ismine, amen'" ("In Jesus' name, amen").

The last youth camp I directed, the summer of 1965, prior to our furlough in '66, brought visitors who asked a lot of questions about our camp; they must have learned about it being a Christian-based camp, directed by an American — me.

The next summer, while I was on furlough, the camp was directed by Kevork Yeshil and Nebil Koyagsi. During the camp, Turkish police came, stating, "We want to see the American who is directing this camp." Kevork assured them no American was in the camp or directing it.

After returning to the MED, after furlough, I directed camps the summers of 1967 and '68. During the latter camp, I was leading a hike on a mountain trail. A small rock rolled under my right foot, causing me to twist the ligaments in my right ankle. I could not walk on that ankle, so Hirant Tulgar slung me over his shoulder and carried me back to camp. His wife, Hermine — the nurse I had baptized, put a tight elastic bandage around my ankle. We debated about my crippled condition, and I wondered if I could continue directing the camp. Then I remembered a donkey a villager used to bring wood for our evening campfires. The villager let Valerie ride the donkey, and one day, as she was riding, the donkey stopped, refused to walk, and shortly gave birth to a foal, which the villager named "Izci" — Pathfinder.

I sent word to the villager, asking if I could rent Izci for the rest of the camp. Izci was brought to the camp, and for the remainder of the camp I directed the camp from the back of Izci. I rode him everywhere during camp, even leading hikes as I rode that donkey.

One day during our second youth camp I was standing by the flagpole ready to blow my bugle to call the campers to lower the flag when suddenly the ground around me began to heave from an earthquake. I was knocked off my feet. I turned to look at the lake behind me; it appeared as though a giant hand had whipped it into a froth. The next day Manuk and I drove to the nearest large town, where we saw the damage wrought by the earthquake.

Me on Izci

Pictures of our Youth Camp at Lake Abant—

Earthquake Damage

Colonel Gulseren and Fisun

As I am writing about Col. Gulseren, I have before me the headlines of the leading Turkish newspaper, *Hürriyet* (Freedom) dated Sunday, October 22, 1967. Dr. Herschel Lamp, MED Medical Director, Manuk, and I, are conducting another "First." During this era of the International Temperance Association, a popular public service was the "Five-day Plan to Stop Smoking," a series of five evening seminars teaching techniques to break the tobacco smoking habit."

To prepare for our holding a stop smoking series of lectures, we had sent Manuk to Ankara to work on some preliminary projects: placing posters about the program in public places, placing banners across main streets in Ankara, and newspaper publicity. When Lamp and I arrived in Ankara, Manuk had completed only the posters. I asked him why he had not put banners across key streets, and he replied that it was "too expensive," as were newspaper ads. I replied to Manuk, "The cost of flying Lamp and myself from Beirut to Ankara; the cost of our hotel while there, plus our daily food allowance, is far more than a newspaper ad."

I appealed to Manuk to go with me to the *Hürriyet* newspaper office, where I began to dictate and ad to the news agent. As I was dictating and came to the part of a person being able to break the tobacco habit in five days, the newspaper agent said, "If your program really works, you don't need to buy an ad; we will do a news story for you for free."

Lamp and I, directed by the newsman, posed for a picture of us standing in front of a visual aid of the human brain and heart, showing adverse effects of tobacco on those vital organs. However, I had some doubt as to whether the news article would really be in the newspaper, and even if it was, I was concerned that it would be relegated to a small column on a back page of the paper, so I insisted on placing an ad as a precaution.

Sunday morning, October 22, we sent Manuk to buy us several copies of *Hürriyet*, which we began to scan in the back pages of the paper. We searched in vain, in the back pages, and found not article. We did see the ad I placed. Suddenly Manuk exclaimed, "Look at the front paper headline, which featured "Bir Adet Sigara Omru 14.5 Dakika Kisaltiyor!" — "One Cigarette Cuts 14.5 Minutes from Life" — and there was a large picture of Lamp and myself, splashed across the front of that newspaper!

That night, in the amphitheatre of a large public building, we had the room full, with people standing in the aisles, as we kicked off one of the most successful Five-Day Plan To Stop Smoking I have ever conducted.

The day after our opening meeting, headlined in *Hürriyet*, I received a phone call from Col. Gulseren; he had seen the *Hürriyet* headlines, with my picture on the front page. He invited me to his home, and as I sat talking with him, I sensed his daughter, Fisun, standing by my side, holding a tray with two shot glasses of what looked like wine to me. Knowing that Gulseren, a Muslim, was not a drinker of alcoholic beverages, I queried him as to what the beverage was, to which he replied, "Oh, this is just a cherry cordial; we even let our girls drink cordials."

With that assurance, I drank the shot glass in one swallow. It burned all the way down! Please know that I am a life-long teetotaler, and that small shot glass of cherry cordial is the only time I have drank an alcoholic beverage.

As my visit with Col. Gulseren continued, he, knowing I was an SDA missionary, asked about my work in the Middle East, and particularly what church facilities we had in Beirut. I told him about Middle East College (MEC), which was located further up the hill, known as "Septia Hill" — Seventh-day Hill — on the outskirts of Beirut. He became very interested in MEC and proceeded to ask many questions about our college of Septia Hill, so I went into greater detail about the school, in answer to his questions.

Suddenly, he called for Fisun to come into the room, again. He proceeded to say, "Fisun, I am going to send you to Beirut to go to Mr. Miller's college there. I am directing him to be as your father while you are at MEC."

"As you say, Father," replied Fisun, responding in fashion as a good Muslim daughter was trained.

I glanced at Fisun, who was wearing a short skirt, for this was the style of the time, known as the "mini-skirt," and upper-class Turks often took up with the latest fashions. I said to the colonel, "At MEC short skirts are not allowed."

"Fisun," directed Col. Gulseren, "You will follow the dress code, and Mr. Miller will approve which dresses you will wear."

"As you say, Father," she responded.

And so it went, while Fisun attended MEC. She followed the colonel's direction that I would be as her father while she was at MEC.

Fisun was at MEC two years, during which time she attended morning and evening worship in the girl's dorm, Sabbath services, and the Fall/Spring Weeks of Prayer, one of which I was the speaker at morning and evening services.

Came the time when Fisun wrote her parents that she desired to become a Seventh-day Adventist! This was something the colonel had not foreseen, and he directed Fisun to "wait awhile, to determine this is something you truly want; but know that you will be a Muslim as long as you live in my house."

I do not know whether Fisun ever became an SDA, for shortly after that the Miller family returned to the U.S. on "permanent return," for a reason I will address in another chapter of my autobiography.

Nebil Koyagisi

As I have said, when I began my ministry in Turkey, I learned that from the time the Seventh-day Adventist Church was formed there, in the mid-1880s, until my arrival in Istanbul, there had never been a Muslim Turk baptized as an SDA. Even though I learned it was a penal offense to baptize a Muslim, I now began to regularly pray that I would have the privilege of baptizing the first Muslim as an SDA.

When the Turkish government decreed I could not have my own vehicle, I concluded that the Turkish Mission would need to engage a taxi for our exclusive use. Since very few Turks, in those days, owned their own cars, most persons utilized the trolley, bus, and train systems. It was common practice for taxi drivers to establish a taxi stand at key corners or intersections in Istanbul. Such a taxi area was only about 100 feet from the Mission House. There about three taxi drivers would park as they waited for persons needing a taxi. The taxis all had meters which calculated the price of the fare; however, drivers all expected a "tip" from a customer, and often they wanted a sizable amount, especially from "rich Americans." I noted one driver, who parked near the Mission, never tried to exhort me to give an exorbitant amount; his name was Nebil (Noble) Koyagasi (Village Chief). And true to his name, Nebil was a very noble man, always kind and dependable. I asked him if he would let me hire him exclusively, and he agreed.

Manuk and I gave a lot of Bible studies as we went about our ministerial work. Nebil, after he became my exclusive driver, was the one who drove me from home to home; he would dutifully wait in his taxi, a 1941 Mercury sedan, while I was in a home conducting a Bible study. Came the day when Nebil asked, "Curtis Bey, what do you do in all these houses you go to?"

"Nebil Bey, why don't you come in with me to the next home, and learn for yourself what I do?" And he did! He began attending every Bible study I gave. He listened, and carefully!

Came a day when I had laryngitis, and talking became more difficult, so I directed Nebil, "Please take me home, my voice is about gone."

"But Curtis Bey," he replied. "We are not done giving Bible studies for today," and he emphasized "we," as though he was an integral part of the Bible study team. And I soon learned he was, indeed, part of the team, for he asked, "What is the next house you were going to?" and I informed him of the home. "And what is the subject of the study for that home?" I told him of the topic, to which he replied, "Oh, I can give that study for you," and he did!

As the time of our second youth camp drew near, we faced a dilemma: I no longer had a car, and one was needed. I decided to ask Nebil if he would come to camp to be our purchaser by bringing daily needed food items for our camp. Nebil accepted, and our second camp was also a success.

During camp we often had rain showers, which put a real "damper" on the camp. If it showered at mealtime, the campers had to scurry to the serving table, then head for their tents, to keep dry as they ate. One evening I called the campers together to have prayer circles asking God to give us fair weather, and no rain, for the rest of our days in camp.

Nebil expressed skepticism, wondering if "Allah would really listen to youth who prayed for good weather?" As he drove us home, when camp was over, Nebil said, "I have learned that Allah does hear our sincere prayers; I am going now to begin praying, 'in Jesus' name, amen,' too."

Arriving home that evening, Nebil found his wife, Irkiye, with an upset stomach. He quickly squeezed a lemon into a glass of water, with no sugar, then taking it to Irkiye, he said, "Drink this, and you will feel better."

"What is it?" she asked.

"Don't question me, just drink it," and while she drank the lemon water, Nebil silently prayed, "In Jesus' name make Irkiye well."

As Nebil told me about her drinking, he admitted he was not quite ready to admit to his Muslim wife that he was now praying, "In Jesus' name."

And I wonder, did Irkiye drink lemon water thereafter, whenever she had an upset stomach?

Nebil drove us to and from church each Sabbath. One Sabbath day he asked, "What do you do when you go to church?"

I replied, "Please come into church with us and see what we do." Nebil began attending church with us. I thought, *God is leading Nebil step by step*, and I rejoiced.

Early fall of 1964, Nebil was one day driving me to the Istanbul international airport, about a thirty-minute drive from our home. On the way he asked me where I was traveling on this trip. I replied, "I am flying to Tehran via Beirut, where I will hold the Fall Week of Prayer at our SDA academy, then I will fly to Baghdad for a few days, and then I will travel on the Beirut to attend the MED Fall Council."

"How long will you be gone?" he queried.

"I will be gone a little over a month," I replied.

"What if you don't come back?" asked Nebil, to which I replied, "Nebil, I am going on a journey for God. Each time I fly in a plane, as it taxis on the runway for takeoff, I always pray, 'Father in heaven, I am going on a mission for You, and commit myself to You, praying that You keep me safe.' I believe my God will keep me safe, but if He determines that I have fulfilled my life for Him, and He sees fit for my life to end, until the great resurrection morn, I accept His will."

Nebil seemed deep in thought at my reply, but shortly he said, "Curtis Bey, I am not referring to what happens to you, should you not come back. I want to know what will happen to me, because I have not been baptized!"

This was a new thought to me; I had not even thought Nebil was considering being baptized. I pondered this, and as we approached the airport, I made a promise to Nebil, "My good friend, I now truly believe God is going to bring me safely back to Istanbul, and the first Sabbath after my return, I will baptize you." I was thrilled beyond words that God was answering my prayer of more than four years—I will have the privilege to baptize the first Muslim Turk into the SDA Church.

It was in November when I returned to Istanbul. Manuk and I prayed together was we considered Nebil's baptism. We knew it was a penal offense to baptize a Muslim, but that was not what we feared. Our greater concern was that we do nothing to jeopardize our Istanbul congregation. We did not want our church closed down, after waiting from the years from WWI to 1958 for an SDA church to be built—the first church of any denomination to be built during all that time.

We decided we could not baptize Nebil in our own church's baptistery. We further decided we should not jeopardize our own congregation, therefore we must keep his baptism a secret from the congregation. As we prayed, we sensed God's guidance, and ultimately decided we would hold the baptism at a lonely place on the shore of the Black Sea, north of Istanbul.

It was a very cold day when the Miller family and the Benzatyan family journeyed with Nebil to the place of baptism. While our families waited on shore, wearing warm coats, Nebil and I waded out from the shore to a place where the water was deep enough for Nebil to be immersed. Just prior to my baptizing him, Nebil called to those on shore, "You are all witnesses to my baptism, for which I thank God."

I then realized that waves were hitting me from my back and told Nebil that we would time his baptism between waves. I then had him grasp my right hand and wrist with his hands. I raised my left hand above and joyfully said, in Turkish, "My dearly beloved brother Nebil, because you have taken Jesus Christ as your Savior, I now baptize in the name of the Father, and of the Son, Jesus Christ, and in the name of the Holy Spirit."

We decided we could not baptize Nebil in our own church's baptistery. We further decided we should not jeopardize our own congregation, therefore we must keep his baptism a secret from the congregation.

I then immersed him. I had previously instructed him that when I began to lift him up, he would aid me by standing up

Nebil's baptism

himself. My timing was a tad off, for when I struggled to raise him up, a wave hit me and bowled me over, and I went down to the bottom! Nebil had to lift me up, for which I was grateful.

Nebil's baptism is surely one of the high points of my mission service, and of my whole life. I am thankful for the privilege of baptizing Nebil (Noble) Koyagasi (Village Chief)!

Nebil drove Manuk, Nurredin Bey, and I to many places, as we lectured on the dangers of alcohol and tobacco and showed our temperance films. On one trip, we decided to also tour the seven churches of Revelation, clustered around the large city of Izmir — Biblical Smyrna. As we arrived at each site, I would read to Nebil the story of that church, as recorded in the book of Revelation.

Arriving at the site of Laodicea, the last of the seven churches — we are now living in the "Laodicean" period of time — we stayed in a motel located right on the edge of the famous "Lukewarm Pool." As I read that the last-day church would be lukewarm, spiritually, neither hot nor cold, and that Christ would spew Laodiceans out of His mouth, Nebil was shocked. He exclaimed, "Don't tell me the SDA Church, that I have just joined is lukewarm! Why you and I are not lukewarm; we are red hot to do the Lord's work."

I tried to explain to him that the church of the last days, like to lukewarm pools, would grow comfortable and wish to simply stay "lukewarm."

Very early the next morning — it was late in October, when we were there — we went swimming in the lukewarm pool. As we waded in, I reminded Nebil that we could stay in the water for only a short time, for we had an appointment at 9:00 a.m. to lecture and show films in Denizli, the closest town to the ruins of Laodicea. The air was brisk, and to be comfortable, we settled down with only our heads above water. It was very comfortable, for that lukewarm pool was just about 100 degrees Fahrenheit.

When it was time to leave the pool, I braced myself when that cold mountain air hit my chest. I called to Nebil, "Come out, we need to be on our way to the school."

Nebil stood up, the cold air hit his chest, and he went back down into the water, till only his head was out. "Curtis Bey, it's too cold out there to come out! Let me stay just a few more minutes."

"Nebil, now you can understand how some Christians today get to feeling so comfortable they just want to relax in this old world," I said over my shoulder, as I walked to our pool-side room. Nebil lost no more time staying in that lukewarm pool.

Nebil was very fervent in witnessing for Christ; thankfully, he was also discreet. On one trip, in a small town, he and I decided to go to a Hamam — a Turkish bath. When we entered the men's section of the hamam, the attendant gave each of us a towel, which we wore around our waist in the steaming hot room of the Turkish bath. We seated ourselves on the warm central stone in the room.

After being comfortably seated, Nebil said to me, in a voice to be heard by everyone in the room, "Mr. Miller, you say you are a Christian?" He and I had been conversing in Turkish, and I was thankful I was now quite fluent in Turkish.

I was startled by his question, for I was probably the only Christian within a hundred miles. "Yes, I am a Christian," I replied, wondering why he would single me out as a Christian.

Nebil continued his line of questions, with "But Mr. Miller, Christians are known for drinking wine, beer, vodka, and whisky, but you don't drink those things. Why?"

"As a Christian, I consider my body to be the temple of God, and I don't want to weaken it by using any alcoholic beverage. Nebil, you know that the Koran condemns drinking alcoholic beverages," I replied. As we talked, I noticed the Muslim men had grown quiet, and were listening intently to our conversation. It stuck me that this was Nebil's inspired way to tell those listening Muslims about the Gospel of Christ. And the men around us nodded their heads in agreement.

Nebil continued, "Christians eat pork, don't they?"

"Most Christians do eat pork, but not my church. Like Muslims and Jews, we abstain from eating pork, for the pig is a most unclean animal," I responded. Then I continued to explain the Biblical differences between "clean" and "unclean" animals. The Muslims began nodding their heads in agreement.

Finally, Nebil asked his key question, "Christians all worship on Sunday, but you worship on Saturday. Why are you different from all the rest of Christians?"

I proceeded to quote the fourth of the Ten Commandments God has given mankind — the commandment mandating the keeping of the seventh-day Sabbath. This was something completely new to just about every Muslim in the hamam. I went on to explain more about the seventh-day Sabbath, which brought Nebil to his last question: "Mr. Miller, what is the name of the church you belong to?"

"My church is called 'The Yedinci-gun Advent Kilesi.' My church is one of the very few Christian churches in the world that worship and keep holy the seventh-day Sabbath—the only true Sabbath."

There was in the hamam that day a Muslim Hoca — a priest. When I spoke about the seventh day being the Sabbath, the Hoca said, "It is taught in the Holy Koran, that if we want to know 'the true people of the book' (meaning the Bible) we should seek

Some of the persons I baptized while in Turkey. Hermine Tulgar, the nurse who was prominent in the story about Valerie is second from the right

someone who keeps the seventh day of the week as Sabbath. This man, by keeping the seventh day, is a true Christian, unlike the Catholics of Rome, who have tried to change the Sabbath to Sunday." As he said these last few words, his face showed his disgust. "What this Christian, who is a guest in our country, has told you is the truth!"

I thanked God, that day, for Nebil — noble Nebil — the first Muslim to become a Seventh-day Adventist.

First Trip from Istanbul to Beirut and Jerusalem

One of the great benefits of overseas mission service is the opportunity to travel and see the world. Mission service enabled me to travel in Portugal, France, England, Denmark, Sweden, Norway, Holland, Germany (during those Cold War years, East and West Germany were two separate nations), Austria, Switzerland, Italy, Sicily, Yugoslavia, Bulgaria, Greece, Turkey, Iran, Syria, Lebanon, Jordan, Iraq, Kuwait, Qatar, Egypt, Libya, Cyprus, Mexico, and Canada — twenty-eight countries, total.

The fall of 1960 I was a delegate to the quadrennial session of the Middle East Division in Beirut. We decided to drive the '53 Chevy the thousand miles from Istanbul to Beirut. Although I had driven that road many times, the first trip was an adventure. Ben Mondics, also a delegate, rode with us. The first day of the journey we reached Ankara, where we stayed in the Park Oteli, a very comfortable hotel.

The next day we drove south, from Ankara, over the high Anatolian plateau. From the highway we could see small villages, far off the road. We also saw many flocks of sheep and goats, guarded by large Anatolian Shepherd Dogs; they wore spiked collars around their necks, to protect them from wolves. These dogs are highly intelligent, always guarding the sheep. They constantly ran between the highway and the flocks they were protecting.

Late in the afternoon we passed through the Taurus Mountains. There is one very narrow place in the road, called the Cilician

Gates, so narrow that a small force of soldiers could hold off a much larger force from coming through that narrow notch. After passing through the mountain pass, the road quickly descends to the Mediterranean coast, and arriving in the small city of Adana, near the Biblical town of Tarsus, birthplace of the apostle Paul.

In Adana there were no high-class hotels, so we stayed that night in a humble lodging, then continued on to Beirut. It was a long drive, from Adana to Beirut, but we always endeavored to do it in one day. Close to the Turkish-Syrian border, the road goes through the ancient town of Antioch, where followers of Jesus were first called Christians. Sometimes, if it was still early in the day, we would press on to the smaller town of Iskenderun, named after Alexander the Great — Iskender in Turkish.

Cilician Gate picture

The last village before the border is Yayladag (Meadow Village). The road to Yayladag is narrow and winding. If it is dark or foggy, it is a challenge to see the very edge of the road. On one trip to Beirut, we left Iskenderun very, very early in the morning, while it was still dark. Phyllis was driving and having a hard time seeing the edge of the road, in the fog and darkness. At a critical point she ran off the side of the road, near a steep drop-off. The tires on the right side of the car were teetering on the edge. We needed to safely exit the car, but not on the downhill side of it. It was a challenge to open the doors on the left side, due to the steep angle of the car, but we finally made it out.

I determined there was no way we could get that car safely on the road, by ourselves, so I left the family — Phyllis and our three girls — huddled by the side of the road, while I went to Yayladag to find a truck that could pull the car back onto the road. It was so early that there were no vehicles coming from either way, so I started walking fast and jogging, when I could, towards the village, which was several miles away. The road was very winding, so I could cut across fields, in some places, to save time and distance. Just as I reached Yayladag, I met a truck pulling out of the village; I flagged it down, explained my predicament to the driver, who responded, "Giren, ve ben seni kurtaricaum" (Get in and I will save you).

Arriving at the site, he carefully studied the situation, then hooked a chain to the front of my car, as he explained that he was concerned that as he pulled on the car, it might twist upside down as he did so. I decided we had no choice but to try. I prayed as he pulled, and the Millers were thankful the car stayed upright, and was soon safely on the road. We reached Beirut safely that afternoon.

After the MED meetings were over, we decided to take some vacation time to drive through Syria and Jordan, to visit Jerusalem and Bethlehem, which meant driving east over the Lebanese mountains, through the Bekaa Valley, then into Syria. In those years Syria was subject to periodic revolutions, but nowhere near the turmoil, battles, and mass killings that are the mode at the time I write this (2018), and visas were easily obtained. Jordan welcomed tourists, for they brought good income to their country.

The first city we came to was Damascus, where we saw the street called Straight where the apostle Paul was taken after being blinded on his journey to Damascus in his quest to take captive Christians back to Jerusalem. A stone marker, by the city gate, identified Damascus, as the oldest city in the Middle East. South of Damascus we passed through the area where Jesus confronted Paul.

It was dark when we passed through Amman, Jordan, home of the ancient Ammonites that harried the children of Israel. The Moabites and Ammonites are descended from the same line. After Sodom and Gomorrah were destroyed, Lot, the nephew of

Abraham, fled with his daughters to the caves around the Dead Sea. His daughters, afraid of dying without any sons, schemed together and tricked their father into sleeping with them. The incestuous relationship produced two male children. The oldest daughter bore Moab, the progenitor of the Moabites, and the younger bore Benammi, the ancestor of the Ammonites. The Amalekites were descendants of Esau. Esau was the eldest son of Isaac, and had a younger brother named Jacob.

Following the map of the area, I knew we should turn west to head to Jerusalem, but not being familiar with the area, nor seeing signposts to guide me, I was lost. I came upon a Bedouin encampment, and with hand gestures, I asked which way was "Jerusalem." The Bedouins did not understand that word, for, as I learned later, the Arabic name is al-Quds, "The Holy One."

I continued on the road, until by chance — or luck? — I came to the famous "Allenby Bridge" spanning the Jordan River, which I recognized from pictures I had seen of it. Field Marshal Edmund Henry Allenby, First Viscount Allenby, was an English soldier and British Imperial Governor. He fought in the Second Boer War and also in the First World War, in which he led the British Empire's Egyptian Expeditionary Force, during the Sinai and Palestine Campaign against the Ottoman (Turkish) Empire in the conquest of Palestine. Upon seeing that bridge, I knew I was on the right road.

After crossing the Jordan, in the darkness we saw Jericho, another ancient city. Jericho is located 846 feet below sea level in an oasis in Wadi Quron in the Jordan Valley, which makes it the lowest city in the world. Jerusalem, about eighteen miles away by road, is 2,474 feet above sea level — quite a rapid drop in altitude in those few short miles. These statistics are among those I use to illustrate the accuracy of the Bible, which says, in Luke 10, "Jesus said: A man was going down from Jerusalem to Jericho, when he was attacked by robbers." I remember seeing the sign on the Jericho Road that says, "Sea Level."

In the Holy Land there are signs and inscriptions for any place of Biblical reference; for example, along the right side of the road, going toward Jericho, there is a natural formation of reddish-colored rocks, with the sign claiming it was the place where the Samaritan found the wounded man that he aided; the rocks were alleged to be that color from the wounded man's blood!

The Millers enjoyed, and were benefited by, our tour of Jerusalem and its environs. I have visited Jerusalem several times, and will tell of some of my experiences there, in another chapter of this autobiography.

One of the ancient sites that I had long wanted to see was the "Rose-red City of Petra," which was built possibly as early as the fifth century B.C. To reach Petra we had to drive 140 miles south of Amman. The magnificent ruins of ancient Petra occupy a high plateau that rises out of Wadi Mousa, the Valley of Moses, in southwestern Jordan. In 300 B.C., Nabataean invaders captured the city of Petra, which had been the capital of the Edomite kingdom, securing their hold on the region. The site is hidden amidst nearly impenetrable mountains to the east of the valley connecting the Gulf of Aqaba and the Dead Sea. On December 6, 1985, Petra was designated a World Heritage Site. In a popular poll in 2007, it was also named one of the New Seven Wonders of the World.

That rose-colored city was carved 2,600 years ago from sandstone drenched in an array of red hues. The first major attraction for Petra is the Siq, roughly translated "the shaft," which is an impressive 200-feet-high, red sandstone canyon that leads you into Petra. Jagged cracks and peaks, mixed with multiple hues of red sandstone, come together to make this a gorgeous half-mile long introduction to Petra. Alas, the return journey as you leave Petra gives you a much deeper insight into why it's called the "Siq." The path is uphill on the return, and although gradual, is the killer at the end of a long day of walking, leading most people to feel cramped, frustrated, and most definitely "Siq."

The Millers each rode a horse through the Siq. At places it was so narrow I could almost touch both sides with my out-stretched arms.

Here is a picture of the first building you see as you come to the end of the Siq; it is of the Treasury, where taxes were paid by caravans that passed through the city.

View of Petra's Treasury, taken from the end of the 2-mile Siq

Many buildings and homes are carved out of the rose-colored sandstone. They are truly magnificent to see. Even now, I wish I could travel to see Petra again.

Journey from Istanbul to Amsterdam

The MED Executive Committee authorized me to attend a meeting of the International Temperance Association, that was held in Amsterdam, the summer of 1962. We decided my family would accompany me, so we drove the '53 Chevy on a round trip of about 3,400 miles. The journey proved to be quite an adventure for us.

We carefully planned our trip, and I sought counsel from Anees Haddad, Youth Director of the MED, who had previously driven from Beirut to Western Europe to attend a similar meeting. I also sought counsel from Ben Mondics, who had driven to Istanbul from Europe.

It was strongly recommended that I obtain currency for several of the countries through which we would travel. Beirut, in the land of the ancient Phoenicians, who were famous for their marketing skills, was one of the best places in the world to purchase currency for just about any nation on earth. Money changers seemed to have shops on every street corner. Trading currency was very advantageous in Beirut. I will use Turkish currency as an example. If I would purchase Turkish lira, using U.S. dollars, the legal rate in Turkey was nine liras for one dollar, but in Beirut I could obtain eighteen liras for a dollar. While in Beirut, preparing for the trip, I purchased currency for Bulgaria, Yugoslavia, and a few other European countries.

At the Turkish-Bulgarian border, exiting Turkey was easily accomplished, but entering Bulgaria, at that time one of the most Stalinist of the Communist countries behind the "Iron Curtain," as Winston Churchill dubbed the Communist bloc, was quite a challenge. In those post WWII years, many countries required you to declare all the monies you had in your possession, so when a most belligerent Bulgarian customs official asked me to declare my various currencies, he promptly confiscated my Bulgarian lev, as that country's currency is called. That meant I would have to now obtain Bulgarian lev at the official government rate, which was very high.

Bulgarian inspectors probed every nook and cranny of our car: inside the spare tire, looking into the gas tank, and everywhere else. They found nothing more to confiscate, and we finally entered Bulgaria. We had intended to stay the night in the capitol city, Sofia, but we felt quite unwelcome, as Americans, in Bulgaria.

Shortly after entering Bulgaria, we were harassed by another problem. Prior to leaving Istanbul on this trip, the front license plate of the car was stolen. I had no way of obtaining another license plate, for the plates were from Oregon. Now, with no front plate, we had a further challenge. There were very few vehicles on Bulgarian roads, for the people were very poor and few could afford a car. On the roads we saw mainly wagons and trucks, along with a few buses. And during the whole drive through Bulgaria, I did not see another American made car, so our Chevy really stuck out on the road.

Every few miles were stationed police officers, standing by the side of the road; each held a stop sign, and the first one we met flipped his stop sign at me. I stopped. He came to the driver's window and beckoned me to get out, which I did. He proceeded to direct me to the front of the car and pointed to the empty front license frame. I could not understand his Bulgarian, and he could not understand my English. I took him to the back of the car, to show him the Oregon plate; he took me to the front and gestured to where the front plate should be. He kept us there for twenty minutes, before throwing up his hands in surrender to the missing plate, and finally waved me on.

The problem continued, with every police I came to flicking out his stop sign, and the dialog of the missing plate went on and on, consuming an inordinate amount of time. Upon entering Sofia, we found there was a police officer at about every corner, and the stops became more numerous and taking a lot of time. I thought about transferring the back plate to the front of the car but believed it would be even more problematic to stop to do that now that I was right in Sofia, for it could easily attract a crowd, which would likely then attract police.

I hit on a new strategy: as I approached a police officer, I stuck my head out the window and shouted "Belgrade, Belgrade," and waved a hand indicating I wanted to know the route to Belgrade, Yugoslavia. That worked, time after time; each officer would promptly snap to attention, then gesture with his stop sign and shout "Prauo, Prauo," and direct me to continue straight ahead (I already know that!)

Picture of street in Sofia

The strategy worked very well, until we reached the northern edge of Sofia, where I failed to spot the police officer in time to use my strategy. That last officer quickly stopped me, and the process of his gesturing to the missing front plate and me taking him to the rear plate, went on, and on, and on. It must have gone on for more than thirty or forty minutes, and the afternoon was on the wane as dusk drew on. At that point there was a growing number of people forming a crowd around the car, as they observed the situation, and beginning to block traffic; I was relieved when the frustrated police finally waved me on.

The Bulgarian-Yugoslavian border was only a few miles away, and I decided we definitely did not want to stay in a hotel in Sofia; we would drive into Yugoslavia as fast as possible. By this time, the gas gauge showed we were close to empty. I knew that in many of the countries in which I traveled gasoline was called "benzine." I had not seen a single gas station thus far, in Bulgaria, so I asked the next police who stopped us where I could find benzene. I was directed to the nearest train station, where there was a 50-gallon drum of benzene, from which I was able to purchase a few gallons at $3 per gallon. This was exorbitant. Gas in Turkey was about twenty-eight cents a gallon, with even Syria being only a few cents more. $3 per gallon, in 1961, was truly a very high price, indeed!

A few miles out of Sofia we were met by a large troop of Bulgarian soldiers, marching on the highway, accompanied by their commander, who was riding a horse. He called his troops to halt and rode his horse to our car. Surprisingly, he spoke some English. He gestured to me to get out of the car, then he pointed to the missing plate. I explained the situation to him, stressing how I had been stopped by police after police. When he understood my dilemma, he assured me that I would not be stopped again, and I wasn't stopped again. I do not know how

The Bulgarian-Yugoslavian border was only a few miles away, and I decided we definitely did not want to stay in a hotel in Sofia; we would drive into Yugoslavia as fast as possible.

that Bulgarian commander was able to send the message, but from then on, as we met police, he would snap to attention, wave his stop sign for me to proceed, as he shouted "Prou! Prou!" and waved us on.

Entering Yugoslavian was easily accomplished. (The former Yugoslavia is now divided into several countries: Slovenia, Croatia, Serbia, Bosnia, Montenegro, and Macedonia.) It was now too late to drive to the city of Skopje, where we would have spent the night, if we had not been so delayed in Bulgaria. We reluctantly decided to sleep by the side of the road, with Melody and Cindy sleeping in the car, while Phyllis and I slept on the ground — I should say we tried to sleep. Although it was late at night, a constant procession of farm wagons drove by us, making so much noise that sleep was nigh on impossible. We decided to give up on sleep and continue driving.

By mid-afternoon it became apparent that we were getting low on gas, which was complicated by my not having any more Yugoslavian currency, and banks where I could exchange dollars for Yugoslavian dinars were closed. I very carefully studied a map of the region. We were traveling on the main highway (a red line on the map), through Yugoslavia that would take us into either Italy or southwest Austria, which chosen route, prior to facing being low on gas. I noted a small blue line branching off the red line. This secondary highway connected Ljubljana, Yugoslavia, with Klagenfurt, Austria. On the map, that blue line looked much shorter, to Klagenfurt, than the red line was to Italy or southwestern Austria.

At Ljubljana I made a right turn to travel north to Klagenfurt. What I did not realize was that the blue line also took us through the Carnic Alps of southern Austria, and within a few miles of driving that blue line, the road began to climb up and up, and still further up, and the road got steeper and steeper.

At the steep angle we were climbing through the Carnic Alps, I saw the gas gauge registering close to empty. I clutched the steering wheel so tightly, my knuckles turned white. I suppose I thought if I squeezed the wheel hard enough, I could squeeze more gas into the engine. I also thought the steep angle of the road is causing the gas in the tank to be the further away from the pipe from the tank to the engine. For once, my conclusion was on target! My theory was, that if I could reach the top of the pass, before running out of gas, I could coast all the way down to Klagenfurt.

Picture of Carnic Alps—the road we traveled is in the upper left of picture

But it was not to be; about 300 feet from the top of the pass, the engine died for lack of fuel. I could see the border post just up the road, so I hiked up to the Yugoslavian side of the border and asked the guards there if they had any "benzene" I could purchase to have enough fuel to drive over the pass; they had none. They gave me permission to cross the border to the Austrian side, where I asked the guards there, if they had any benzene. They had none. I learned that no cars had been over that road for several hours.

I silently prayed for deliverance, and shortly a car came up the Austrian side; it was driven by a Yugoslavian. The border guard explained my dilemma to him, and the Yugoslavian agreed to siphon a liter (somewhat more than a U.S. quart) of benzene into a bottle for me — for the sum of a $10, which was the smallest currency I had. $10 for a liter was probably the most expensive gas I have ever purchased.

I knew one liter would not be sufficient to put directly into the tank so that gas could be pumped from the tank to the engine, so I opened the hood, sat on the front fender, and dribbled gas into the carburetor while Phyllis drove the Chevy over the top of the pass. We were then able to coast all the way to Klagenfurt.

We entered Germany near Munich, drove on to Stuttgart, planning to continue on to Frankfurt. In Stuttgart I needed directions to Frankfurt, so I drove up to a policeman that was directing traffic, and with a wave of my arm said, "Frankfurt." The policeman answered in German, with hand gestures of where to turn, etc. Seeing a blank look on my face, he realized I did not understand German, so he asked if I understood Italian, to which I said no. He asked if I spoke French, and I said no. Finally, he asked if I spoke English, to which I could say *Yes!* So, he proceeded to give me very adequate directions in English, and we arrived in Frankfort, where we spent the weekend.

Our journey through Germany was only a few years after WWII, when parts of the country were heavily bombed by Allied planes. We saw many buildings that were reduced to rubble that still had not been cleaned up. We Americans can be thankful that our country has been spared the destructive forces of war, except for the Japanese raid on Pearl Harbor in '41, and the several planes hitting key buildings in New York City and Washington D.C. on 9/11.

My experience with the Stuttgart policeman impressed me that in many European countries, many people know more than just the language of their own country — often two or three other languages. This is in sharp contrast to Americans, who often know only English, although there are some who live in areas closer to the southwest where states border Mexico, and they may know some Spanish.

Prior to starting this trip to Amsterdam, an SDA military chaplain, serving in the U.S. Army, passed through Istanbul; he was guiding a group of SDA military personnel, traveling by train, through the Holy Land. I informed him that the Millers would be driving to Amsterdam, and we would pass through Frankfurt. He invited us to stay in an SDA guest house in Frankfurt. While there we attended church at the U.S. military base.

Arriving in Amsterdam, we initially stayed in a modest hotel; however, that was a challenge for Phyllis and our girls, for they had nothing worthwhile to do while I was in meetings all day.

From tourist literature we received at the Dutch border, we learned there was a nearby campground that had a play area and swimming pool, so we purchased a tent large enough to hold the five Millers, and we set up camp. We enjoyed touring Holland, seeing windmills, visiting tulip gardens — the Dutch are famous for their tulips. Interestingly, Holland is not the origin of tulips — Turkey is. We also visited a couple cheese factories, for in addition to tulips, Holland is also famous for cheese. I also followed the advice of the Dutch Auto Club to have a replica of my Oregon license plate made at a sheet metal shop; having plates both front and back should avoid any more stops by police.

When the meetings in Amsterdam were over, we drove south through Germany to Switzerland. From boyhood I had always wanted to visit Switzerland, particularly the small town of Zermatt, to see the famous Matterhorn. We drove through the length of that beautiful and mountainous country. To reach Zermatt, we traveled on a cog-railroad. It was a trip of a lifetime. We drove the length of Switzerland, through St. Moritz, Interlaken, Zurich, and Lucerne. One day we watched a cowherder driving his herd up to mountain pastures; several of the cattle wore cowbells, and one carried the largest cowbell I had ever seen — it was about the size of a gallon container.

Leaving Switzerland, we drove through northern Italy. One night we camped in the courtyard of an ancient castle. It rained hard during that night, a real cloudburst that proved the weatherproofing of the sleeping compartment of the tent. This compartment was large enough for the five of us to sleep. The bottom of the compartment was coated to make it waterproof; this coating extended about eight inches up the sides of the compartment. In morning, we woke to the water lapping several inches up the waterproof sides. Had it not been waterproof, we would have been sleeping in a pool of water.

Our last sightseeing in Italy took us to Venice, famed for its canals instead of paved streets. It is situated across a group of 118 small islands that are separated by canals and linked by bridges, of which there are 400. Parts of Venice are renowned for the beauty of their settings, architecture, and artwork. It is listed as a World Heritage site. We took a motor launch into the city, spending the day roaming about. Melody and Cindy really liked feeding the flocks of pigeons at Piazza San Marco.

Leaving Italy, we once again drove the length of Yugoslavia. That portion of our journey was unremarkable, except for two incidents. The first occurred as I came upon a truck carrying a load of spindly logs. Suddenly the top log broke loose, striking the pavement just ahead of the Chevy. Its first point of contact was on the end of the log; I swerved left to miss it, but the log then bounced on its other end, falling right in front of where I swerved. God surely had His hand on the wheel, for I turned the car sharply to the right, and missed the log by a very few inches.

The next event was more humorous. The roads in southern Yugoslavia were often unpaved for long stretches. One portion of the unpaved road was so rough, it took eight hours to travel 100 miles. A few miles from the southern border we passed through a small village, where we encountered a railroad crossing. By the side of the track was a small wooden booth, manned by the railroad crossing guard. He had just lowered the gate, barring any traffic crossing the tracks. The guard spoke no English, and I didn't speak his language, but with hand gestures I got the idea a train was expected at any minute. We waited, and we waited, and we waited. There was not much vehicle traffic in that area, but after an hour of waiting, there were a few vehicles, mostly small trucks, waiting on either side of the track. And still no train came. The faithful guard was certainly not going to take

God surely had His hand on the wheel, for I turned the car sharply to the right, and missed the log by a very few inches.

a chance that any vehicle would be struck by a train on his watch! I finally learned from a driver that spoke a little English, that a train was scheduled to be on the track "about this time, every few days." With no train in sight, with no train being heard, the vehicle drivers began shouting at the guard to raise the gate, but he steadfastly refused. Finally, one burly driver pushed the guard aside, raised the gate, and we all drove through.

The wait at the railroad crossing consumed some travel time; we were already behind schedule and now had no hope of crossing the border into Greece that day.

Because of the previous experience we had transiting Bulgaria, I certainly didn't want to return to Turkey via the shortest route through that country, opting instead to take a longer route through Greece. That night we slept in the car, by the side of the road, and drove into Thessaloniki the next day, Friday. We found a campground on the edge of town, pitched our tent, and spent a quiet Sabbath, planning to depart for Istanbul early Sunday morning.

On that Sunday morning we drove from the campground to the main highway leading to Turkey, at the border town of Edirne, on the Greek-Turkish border. To reach that highway, we drove on a narrow stone side street. Arriving at the corner, I saw a bus, whose driver indicated he wanted to enter that narrow side street, from my left; there was not sufficient room for both the bus and our car to be in that narrow space at the same time. Evidently, seeing my turn left turn signal was blinking, the bus driver motioned me to pull into the intersection, so that he could drive into the side street. I could not see if there was any more traffic coming from the left; however, I could see that none was coming from the right. The bus driver motioned again for me to pull into the intersection, to clear the road. I was hesitant, because I did not have a clear view to my left, but I slowly drove into the intersection. The front of the Chevy was barely past the bus, when I heard the sound of something coming from behind the bus, then, suddenly, a young man, on a motor scooter, traveling at a high speed, came along the side of the bus. I came to a complete stop, as the scooter driver smashed into the left front fender of my car. I was horrified to see him careen several feet into the air, then crashing down on the cobbled roadway.

I jumped out of my car, and ran to the young man's side. I saw his left leg had several huge cuts and he was bleeding profusely. Shortly, a Greek police officer was on the scene. He sent the young man to the nearest hospital, then proceeded to investigate the accident, taking statements from the bus driver, myself, a young Greek lady, and a couple other persons who were present.

I told the policeman about the accident from my perspective, maintaining that I had not crashed into the young man, for I had come to a complete stop when I heard the motor scooter coming around the side of the bus. He asked for my estimate of the scooter's speed, to which I stated I thought he was going twenty to forty miles per hour. It was a serious situation, for I was a foreigner, and an American; I was soon to learn that Greeks often assumed all Americans were rich.

The policeman counseled me to contact the American Consulate as soon as possible, which I did. The Consul arranged for my Chev to be impounded at the Consulate, and for the Miller family to stay in a local youth hostel, for I was now low on funds, and staying in even a modest hotel was beyond what little cash I had. I was issued a traffic ticket, with court on my case set for the next Thursday. It was a long wait, from Sunday till Thursday.

On Monday, I was able to contact the Adventist pastor of the Thessalonica Church; his name was Christiforides, and I learned he was a relative to one of the Greek families in our Istanbul Church. He helped me send a cablegram to Ben Mondics, explaining the reason for our delay in returning to Istanbul.

Pastor Christiforides showed me the Monday edition of the local newspaper; right on the front page, in large letters, was the headline that "An American Apostolos (apostle) struck a local Greek citizen, who sustained a serious injury." Pastor Christoforides was of the opinion that I was already believed guilty of "assault with a motor vehicle." My situation certainly did not look good, and I was concerned about having to serve time in a Greek jail.

The American Consul obtained the services of a Greek lawyer, who was also fluent in English. The lawyer advised me to visit the young man in the hospital, and he even accompanied me when I made that visit. The young man seemed to be certain that I would be found guilty, and that I would have to pay him a goodly sum of money, as compensation for my having assaulted him with a vehicle. You can be certain the Millers were earnestly praying every day from Sunday to Thursday.

On Thursday the young man was still hospitalized. I learned, later, that he assumed I would not be able to leave Greece, at least not before I served time in jail.

Arriving at the court on Thursday, with my lawyer, I found I would be tried before a court of three judges. The arresting officer was present, the prosecuting attorney was present, as were a couple of young male witnesses, and the young lady, who also was a witness.

The prosecuting attorney presented the legal charges against me. I was the first to give testimony about the accident, stating "I was on the side street, seeking to turn left, as the bus was in the intersection waiting to turn left. The bus driver gestured to me to pull into the intersection, to make room for the bus to turn into the side street. I hesitated to do so, for I could not see if other traffic was coming from the left, but, finally, I started into the intersection, at the insistence of the bus driver. The man on the scooter came careening around the bus and struck my car while I was at a complete stop."

The prosecutor then put the police officer on the witness stand; the officer gave a summary of his investigation. The prosecutor then put the two young men on the stand; when it was time for my attorney to cross-examine the young men, he succeeded in having one of them admit he did not actually see the accident, for he was not facing the street; he only saw the aftermath of the crash.

My lawyer, by cross examination, had the second man admit he did not see the accident, either; he arrived on scene after it had happened.

There remained the young lady, who testified that she "saw the whole of the accident occur right in front of me." She described the position of the bus and of my vehicle. She stated that the bus driver was not gesturing for me to enter the intersection, but, to the contrary, he was signaling me to back up so that he could drive into the narrow side street."

When my lawyer had opportunity to cross-examine the young lady, he asked, "Was there room, in the side street, for both the bus and the American's car to be there at the same time?" To this question, she replied, "Yes, there was room for both the bus and the car."

My lawyer, himself having seen that intersection, then asked her, "How could their bus enter the side street, if it was only wide enough for one vehicle?" to which she replied, "All the American had to do was drive his car up on the pedestrian sidewalk."

When she made that statement, the three judges laughed, as did the prosecuting attorney! It would have been illegal for me to drive on the sidewalk.

The prosecuting attorney then made motion that my case be dismissed, to which the three judges readily accepted.

I was now a free man. The brief trial, which began at 9:00 a.m., was over, and we still had ample time to drive to Istanbul that day. The only other incident, as we proceeded towards home, occurred on the road between Edirne and Istanbul. It was late at night, with no moonlight. I knew that oxcarts could be

"How could their bus enter the side street, if it was only wide enough for one vehicle?" to which she replied, "All the American had to do was drive his car up on the pedestrian sidewalk."

expected on the highway, even at night, for it was harvest time. Such animal-powered farm vehicles were supposed to display a lighted lantern at the rear of the wagon. I had just remarked that I should be very watchful for them. Just then I was blinded by the bright headlights of an oncoming car; just as it flashed by me, I saw the black silhouette of a farm wagon, loaded with hay, directly in front of us. There was no lantern at the back. I slammed on my brakes, and was going only a few miles per hour, when I hit the rear of the wagon. The impact, thankfully, was cushioned by much hay hanging over the rear of the wagon.

No one was hurt, nor was the Chevy or the wagon damaged. I did hear the screeching sounds of persons riding atop the wagon, and likely the oxen did travel a few feet at a much faster speed than was their wont.

We were very thankful to once more be safe at home.

Thanksgivings and Christmas Holidays

During those years in Istanbul we often had our mission staff to our home for Thanksgiving and Christmas. I remember Thanksgiving in 1963; I attended the annual Fall Council of the MED Executive Committee, which due to a long agenda went into overtime sessions that lasted until late Wednesday afternoon prior to the holiday; therefore, I was unable to catch any flights from Beirut to Istanbul that day. I sent a cablegram to my family telling them I would be on the morning flight home, Thanksgiving Day, and should therefore be home in time for Thanksgiving dinner.

I was at the Beirut airport early that morning, not wanting to miss that flight. The call to board the Pan Am flight came, and along with the other passengers I boarded the plane. In due time the plane left the boarding gate and taxied to the runway to take off. Once there the plane sat there an inordinate amount of time. Along with other passengers I wondered why the delay. Finally, the pilot spoke over the loudspeaker, informing us that there was a crack in the windshield and he deemed it too risky to take off. The plane returned to the terminal and the passengers were allowed to leave the plane. We were told that a replacement windshield was being flown in from Karachi, and, hopefully, the flight would leave late afternoon; in the meantime we would be taken by bus to the best hotel in Beirut, where we would be given a room in which we could rest, along with a noon meal. I ate the meal, then went to the very sumptuous room provided me, where I had nothing to do but wait; hotels in the Middle East, in those years, had no TV, so it was a very boring afternoon. Finally we were bussed back to the airport and our Pan Am flight to Istanbul was uneventful; however by the time I arrived home everyone else had already enjoyed Thanksgiving dinner and I had the leftovers!

For Christmas each year I would use mission funds to provide a food basket for several needy church families. Brother Avram and his wife (I have forgotten her name) were Armenian refugees who had escaped from Bulgaria. They were as poor as proverbial church mice. I had great respect for brother Avram; whenever I visited him, I would ask how he and his wife were doing; he would always hold his hands heavenward and state, "God has been so good to us, providing for our needs." I would look around their second floor, one-room apartment which had no running water or toilet facilities. He and his wife would use the communal kitchen and toilet facilities. Often, I would see little evidence of food. I was always blessed by taking food to Avram and his wife.

One day I received the message that Avram's wife had undergone gallbladder surgery. Due to their abject poverty, they had no money for the surgery to be done in a hospital, so their physician elected to do the surgery in his office; unfortunately, she did not survive the surgery. When I received this news, Manuk and I went to visit Avram in his bare apartment; we found him seated at a small table, with his Bible open to 1 Thessalonians 4:13–18:

> *But I would not have you to be ignorant, brethren, concerning them which are asleep, that ye sorrow not, even as others which have no hope.*

For if we believe that Jesus died and rose again, even so them also which sleep in Jesus will God bring with him.

For this we say unto you by the word of the Lord, that we which are alive and remain unto the coming of the Lord shall not prevent them which are asleep.

For the Lord himself shall descend from heaven with a shout, with the voice of the archangel, and with the trump of God: and the dead in Christ shall rise first:

Then we which are alive and remain shall be caught up together with them in the clouds, to meet the Lord in the air: and so shall we ever be with the Lord.

Wherefore comfort one another with these words.

Avram, along with Manuk and myself, found comfort in this beautiful promise.

Osman Bey

As an SDA missionary in Turkey, I was running an "underground" mission, and the Turkish Secret Police were often on my tail. One day I arrived at our Mission Building and was met by Anahid, Manuk's wife, who informed me a police officer had just been there, looking for me. I immediately left, and went home, where Phyllis told me a police officer had been there a few minutes ago, looking for me. I left home and went to our church building, where our janitor informed me a police officer had been there about a half-hour ago, looking for me.

As an SDA missionary in Turkey, I was running an "underground" mission, and the Turkish Secret Police were often on my tail.

I was puzzled as to why the police were looking for me, so I decided to go the headquarters of Yeshilay, the organization that I worked with in Turkish schools where I showed films on the dangerous effects of alcohol and tobacco. Vechihi Divitchi, the head of that organization, had been very helpful in getting our household goods out of Turkish customs when we first arrived in Istanbul. When I arrived at that office I was told the police had just been there, looking for me. Vechihi suggested he and I travel to Izmir for a few days to avoid the police, which we did. While in Izmir we saw a Turkish newspaper with a front-page article declaring that for several days the police had been searching for a man suspected of engaging in illegal Christian missionary activities. The article went on to say that the police had arrested an American Jehovah's Witness who had been engaged in illegal missionary work and that he was being deported from Turkey.

When the Millers first arrived in Turkey, an American could obtain a tourist visa for six months. Because my first year of mission service was to be devoted to learning the Turkish language, I was able to stay in Turkey as a student. Phyllis and the girls were on their own U.S. passport, together, and they were allowed a visa based on mine.

At the end of two years I no longer qualified for a tourist or student visa. When my student visa expired, I went to the "Dorduncu Sube" — Fourth Section — of the police department that issued visas. This public building had a large rotunda over the first and second floors. The fourth section was on the far side of the rotunda, on the second floor.

In that office sat a police officer who displayed a very stern demeanor. He had a nose like the beak of a hawk, and sported a very long, groomed mustache. I placed my passport before him and requested a visa.

During my life I have had five passports; the first was issued to me January 5, 1960. Passports, at that time, also required the holder's occupation. The GC Travel Bureau arranged for my passport application and listed my occupation as "Teacher-Missionary." That designation — missionary — was the cause of my problem, that day when I placed my passport before the police officer. He issued a directive that my file be brought to him; upon receiving and reading it, he glanced again at my passport with that word — missionary — on it (shortly thereafter, in consultation with the American Consul, I was issued a new passport that did not ask for occupation).

He proceeded to shout at me, "You are in Turkey under false pretenses. You have claimed to be a tourist, you have claimed to be a student, but in reality, you are nothing more than a 'Cok pis domuz papaz' —a dirty pig priest." He then shouted, I was "persona non grata" and gave me forty-eight hours to leave Turkey.

"I have held on by my fingernails, these past two years; I love my work as a missionary, and I surely don't want to leave Turkey," I said to myself.

I consulted with Manuk and Kevork Yeshil, head elder of our Istanbul Church. Kevork's advice was, "Miller Berader, you need to see Osman Bey."

I thought Kevork had lost his senses. I had heard of Osman Bey; he was the Turkish Police commissar in charge of crushing out Christian missionaries in Turkey. "Why, oh why, Kevork, are you recommending I see the police commissar in charge of crushing Christianity?" I queried.

"It is time, Miller Berader, that you learned the story of Osman Bey," and Kevork proceeded to tell me that miraculous story. My predecessor, Ben Mondics, also had the audacity to apply for a visa as a missionary. The fourth section began an investigation, which included having Osman Bey come to our Mission House at 14 Saray Arkasi, Ayazpasha, Taksim, Istanbul. He rang the doorbell. It was the practice, in those days, for someone to peer out an upstairs window, to determine who rang the bell. Miss Yebraksi looked out, and recognizing Osman Bey, warned Ben Mondics, "Be very careful how you answer Osman Bey's questions. Don't give any more information than is absolutely necessary, and above all, do not say anything about our church behind the garden."

Mondics received Osman Bey and sat with him on the second floor of the building. Miss Yebraksi translated for Mondics. Osman Bey asked a number of questions, and Mondics even admitted he was a Christian missionary, then, suddenly Mondics asked, "Would you like to see our church?" Miss Yebraksi was shocked!

"Do you have a church? If you do, yes, I do want to see it."

Together, Mondics and Yebraksi showed Osman Bey around the church. He saw the children's classrooms, that had choruses in Turkish on the walls; he saw the mimeographed Sabbath School lesson quarterlies, that were in Turkish; he saw the numerous Bibles, Kitabi Mukkades — Holy Bibles — in the pews.

Finally, the three of them were standing in front of the rostrum, right below the pulpit, when Osman Bey asked Mondics, "Would you, as a Christian, pray for a Muslim?"

Mondics thought carefully, *If I say I would pray for a Muslim, Osman Bey might refuse me a visa. But if I say no, I would be both dishonest and in denial of my Christian duty.* Finally, Mondics said, "Yes, I would pray for a Muslim."

Osman Bey was quick to say, "Would you please pray for my son? He is five years old and has never spoken an intelligible word."

Then and there, standing below the pulpit of the Istanbul SDA Church, Mondics prayed for Osman Bey's son. The next day, Osman Bey gave the thrilling message, "My son speaks!"

That prayer, which wrought a miracle, was like a squirt of oil on the hinge of the door that opened for me to stay in Turkey.

On behalf of me, Kevork arranged for me to meet Osman Bey. He did not want to see me in any public place, for his security and mine, so he sent back word with Kevork that he would meet me at 9:00 p.m. that night, in the back office of a used furniture store located on a narrow side street in the business section of downtown Istanbul.

When I was ushered into that room, Osman Bey used a typical police tactic: he sat behind a desk on which was a bright light shining into my face; I could hear him, but I could not see him.

"Mr. Miller, you have led a very interesting life while you have been in Turkey the past two years." He proceeded to tell of several places, in both Istanbul and Izmir, where I had spoken; he even told what I had said in those places.

I began to fear Osman Bey, too, would declare me persona non grata, and order me out of the country; however, he sensed my concern, and was quick to say, "Mr. Miller, if there were 1,000 Adventist missionaries, instead of just one [I was the only SDA Missionary in Turkey, at that time], my country would be a better place."

What a wonderful testimony for the efficacy of SDA missions, I thought.

Osman Bey proceeded to have me describe the location and description of the police officer that had ordered me out of Turkey, which I did. "That man is very dangerous to you. You must go back to the fourth section, tomorrow. You must not let that man see you. Then you proceed by his office to the office at the very end of the corridor. Don't knock on that door. Just go into that office. There will be an officer behind the desk. Give him my business card and say 'I bring you greetings from Osman Bey.' He will give you a visa."

Having said that, Osman Bey proceeded to write a cryptic message on his card, in Turkish, but what he wrote made no grammatical sense — it was a secret code.

The next day, Manuk accompanied me when I returned to the fourth section. We climbed the stairs to the second floor, and I gestured to the open office where the man with the hawk nose and mustache sat behind the desk. "That's the man I must slip by without him seeing me," I informed Manuk, who replied, "Curtis, I will go to his office door, thus blocking his view, and I will ask him a question to distract him."

Adjusting his tie and coat, Manuk did just that, and as he blocked Hawk Nose's view I slipped by his door, and waited, just outside the door at the end of the corridor. There, we prayed for God to be with us, then, with the courage God gave me, without knocking we stepped into that office. There was a police officer seated behind the desk. Following Osman Bey's direction, I extended his business card, as I said, "I bring you greetings from Osman Bey."

As the man was reading the card, Manuk nudged me, then whispered, "Do you see that man's name on the placard on his desk?"

"Yes," I replied, "Who is Resat Bey?"

"If you were in the States, this man would be J. Edgar Hoover, head of your FBI."

"Wonderful," I said to God, "You have brought me to the office of the top man, and not some mere underling."

After reading the card I gave him, Resat Bey addressed me, "Mr. Miller, what is your request of me?"

"I would like a visa, to stay in Turkey, please," I replied.

"Very well, you shall have a visa," he said, as he rang a bell.

In response to that bell, Hawk Nose entered the room. Resat Bey said to him, "Please give Mr. Miller a visa," to which Hawk Nose replied, "Sir, I have declared him persona non grata, and ordered him to leave the country in forty-eight hours," and addressing me, Hawk Nose continued, "And you now have only twenty-four hours left."

To Hawk Nose, Resat Bey snapped, "Bring me his file." Shortly Hawk Nose returned with my file; it was not a small file, but at least an inch thick. Grabbing the file, Resat Bey placed it in the top right-hand drawer of his desk, then slamming his fist down on his desk, he bellowed at Hawk Nose, "Now, I direct you to give Mr. Miller a visa, immediately."

While Hawk Nose was out of the room, affixing a visa in my passport, Resat Bey said, "This visa will be good for two years, when it expires, come back to me and I will renew it." As far as I know, my file remained in Resat Bey's desk drawer for the next four years I was in Turkey.

Over time, Osman Bey came to know much about me, my mission work, my temperance work, and about the yearly youth camps. He sent his two girls to our youth camp at Lake Abant for several years. He also advised me that since my mission work took me out of Turkey several times a year, it would be well if I could arrange my travels outside Turkey to take place at least every three months, which I could easily accomplish. He said that he would arrange visas for Phyllis and our girls on the rationale that my work took me to several Middle East Countries, during the year, and I used Istanbul for my home base for where we lived; thus their visas were no longer a problem.

Again, God worked a series of miracles for me to stay in Turkey. I constantly remember the words of Cowper, who wrote, "God works in mysterious ways, His wonders to perform."

Valerie Ann Miller

The last of our daughters, Valerie, was born on a Friday, January 12, 1962, in the Amiral Bristol Hastahanesi — Admiral Bristol Hospital — in Istanbul. I registered her with the U.S. Consulate as an American citizen, by virtue of both her parents being U.S. citizens. For this I received documentation of her being an American citizen. When Valerie reached adulthood, I presented her with the document, which she still has. Turkish regulation allowed her to have American and Turkish, or dual, citizenship, until she reached age twenty-one, at which time she would have to choose which country would be her citizenship — and that was American, of course.

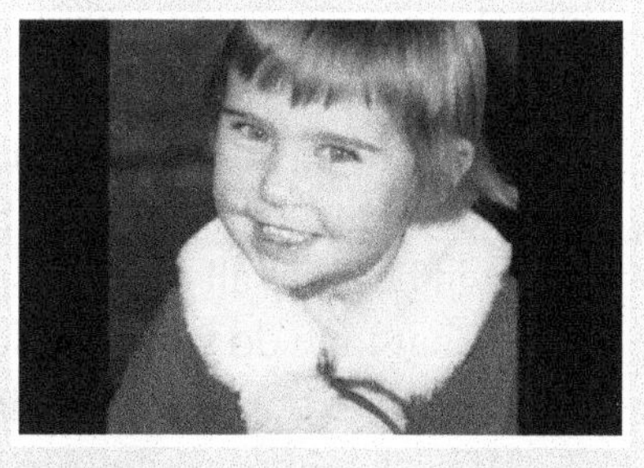

Life with Valerie followed a normal course until May 27, 1963; it was a holiday weekend in Turkey, Yirmi-yedi Mayis, the holiday commemorating the overthrow of the Turkish government under Adnan Menderes, two years previously. That particular Friday, I arrived home in the late afternoon, to find Phyllis sick in bed.

She informed me that she had heard Valerie choking, in the living room; she quickly held her up, gave her a hard blow to her mid-back, and a portion of a hazel nut flew out of her mouth. She wondered if Valerie still had a portion of the nut in her trachea?

Not wanting to take a chance on Valerie's well-being, I took her in the mission building, to seek Hermine, a registered nurse who had recently graduated from the Admiral Bristol School of Nursing. Hermine was a niece of Miss Yebraksi, and usually visited her aunt on Friday evenings. Finding Hermine there, I proceeded to tell her about our concern that a portion of a hazel nut may still be lodged in Valerie's trachea.

Hermine listened to Val's breathing, then said, "I don't hear her having difficulty breathing, but to be certain, let's have Dr. Ayan check her out." Dr, Ayan's wife was a faithful member of our Istanbul Church. Hermine held Valerie as we drove to his office, which was also in his home. Dr. Ayan listened to Val's breathing and heartbeat, then said, "I don't believe your daughter is in any danger; most likely the nut particle went into her stomach."

"But Dr, Ayan," I said, "I need to be certain, for tomorrow I am to drive to Izmit to hold Sabbath services at the NATO base and will be gone all day."

"What time do you need to leave for Izmit?" asked Dr. Ayan.

"I need to be at the ferry landing by 9:00 a.m.," I replied.

"If by the time you need to leave your house Valerie's breathing is normal, and her heartbeat is normal, it will be safe for you to go to Izmit."

The journey to Izmit meant that I would drive down the hill to the car and passenger ferry landing on the Bosporus, take the ferry to the Asiatic side of Istanbul, then drive around the Sea of Marmara to Izmit. In ancient times Izmit was known as Nicea, where in A.D. 325 a church council adopted Sunday to be the Sabbath, in place of the Biblical Sabbath being the seventh day of the week.

Sabbath morning Valerie seemed quite normal, as far as we could determine, so I drove to the ferry landing, arriving there just as one ferry was pulling away from the dock and another was pulling in. I drove to the short line of cars waiting for the next ferry; there were only four cars in line ahead of me,

Suddenly a dense fog settled over the Bosporus, causing the ferry boats to stay where they were, because they could not safely operate in heavy fog. I waited, and waited, and waited, until 11:00 a.m., then I pulled out of the line of waiting cars, for even if the ferries would shortly begin to operate, I knew I could not reach Izmit in time to hold Sabbath services. As I reached the crest of the hill above the Bosporus, I heard the toot of a ferry boat; glancing in my rear-view mirror, I saw the fog had cleared completely in just the time it took me to drive the half mile up the hill from the ferry boat landing. I wonder, "Did God cause the fog to descend over the Bosporus, to prevent me from traveling away from home that day?" I believe so, for when I reached home, Valerie was having difficulty breathing, and her heart was beating very fast.

Taking Valerie into the Chevy, I drove to the mission building, where I hoped Hermine would be visiting with her aunt Yebraksi. Hermine was not there. "She is on duty at the Admiral Bristol Hospital," said Miss Yebraksi. She offered to come with me, so that she could hold Valerie on the way to the hospital. Once at the hospital, I informed Hermine, "Valerie's having difficulty breathing, and her heart is racing." Hermine now decided that Valerie might need emergency surgery, but she said, in dismay, "It is a holiday weekend, and we don't even have a doctor on duty today." She knew of a prominent surgeon,

"Did God cause the fog to descend over the Bosporus, to prevent me from traveling away from home that day?" I believe so, for when I reached home, Valerie was having difficulty breathing, and her heart was beating very fast.

Dr. Suheyl Egilmez, and put through a call to find him. She found out that the surgeon was on vacation at a place about five hours away by train and ferry. Dr. Egilmez advised having an X-ray taken of Valerie's chest.

Once again Hermine was dismayed, saying, "Pastor Miller, there is no X-ray tech here at the hospital to take an X-ray, because it is a holiday." I will never forget that holiday, Yirmi-yedi Mayis. Getting back in the Chevy, Yebraksi holding Valerie, I began driving aimlessly around; I came to that historic Taksim Square, where the street made a circle about the statue of Musafa Kemal Ataturk, the man who overthrew the Sultan and formed the Republic of Turkey, after WWI. I circled Taksim Square a couple times, then, suddenly, I saw a sign over a building situated down a side-street; the sign read, "Rontgen," which is Turkish for X-ray. I drove quickly to that office building, which had a sign on the door, "Closed for the Holiday." I decided to knock on the door, anyway, which I did, as loudly as I could.

The door was opened by a man, who acknowledged he was an X-ray tech, who just happened to come by his office, "Because I needed a file."

"My daughter has choked on a hazel nut, and she may have a portion in her trachea. I have been directed to have her chest X-rayed," I rapidly said. The kind tech placed Valerie on the X-ray table, pressed the button, and held the X-ray up to a light. "She must have moved, as this X-ray was taken; I will have to take another one," which he quickly did. Holding it up to the light, he studied it, then said, "Mr. Miller, do you see this white spot in the right bronchial tube, leading to her lung?" I saw the spot to which he pointed, as he further explained, "I believe that bit of nut is wedged in such a way she can breathe in, but when she breathes out, the nut does not allow all the air to go out, so the lung is gradually expanding. The danger is that unless the nut is removed, her lung will eventually press on her heart and stop it. You need to have it surgically removed immediately."

"Where can I find a surgeon, who can perform such surgery?" I asked.

"I have a friend who is a pediatrician; she may be able to do it," he replied. He gave me the lady physician's address; I drove there as rapidly as possible, and rang the bell to her office, which was in her house. The doctor answered her door; I rapidly explained the situation, stating Valerie needed surgery as soon as possible. I will never forget the answer that lady doctor gave. "I am sorry," she said, "But it is a holiday and I am giving a party for some family and friends, and I don't have time."

Once more I drove rapidly to the hospital where Hermine was on duty and explained the most frustrating situation Valerie was faced. "I will phone Dr. Egilmez right away," said Hermine. The doctor listened to Hermine's plea, then said, "Have Mr. Miller take his daughter to the Gurabet Hastahanesi (a government hospital). You phone the hospital and have the staff there prepare a surgical room. I will come there as fast as possible."

Hermine assured me she would come to that hospital as soon as she got off duty, at 4:00 p.m. Miss Yebraksi, still holding Valerie, and I got into the Chevy, and I drove to the hospital, which was across the Golden Horn (a branch of the Bosporus, separating two sides of European Istanbul). We walked into the hospital, and I took Valerie into my arms, noting that she was having more difficulty breathing.

I prayed silently to God, in Jesus' name, for Valerie's life. Miss Yebraksi and I waited, apprehensively, for Dr. Egilmez and Hermine to arrive. Minutes dragged by. We waited, as even two hours went by. It was a great relief when Dr. Egilmez arrived, and shortly after Hermine joined us.

The surgical team and room were readied. I placed Valerie on the table, then started to leave the room. Taking a final glance at Valerie, who looked so small on that table, I saw Dr. Egilmez listening to Val's heart. He straightened up, and I heard him ask, "Who is the anesthetist on duty now?" Upon hearing who that was, he said, "I prefer another anesthetist. I will send a taxi to get her," which he did.

The new anesthetist, a lady, arrived shortly, surveyed the scene, then said, "This is going to be a complicated surgery, and I have only two hands; I want another anesthetist to assist me; I will call one who is my friend." That second anesthetist soon joined us, and once more I placed Valerie on the table, and turned to exit the room.

Suddenly a voice announced over the hospital speaker system, "There is an attempted coup taking place in Istanbul; martial law has been declared, and no one is to be on the streets between the hours of 8:00 p.m. and 8:00 a.m." That meant that no one could come to or leave the hospital; we were stuck there for the night.

As I was leaving the surgical room once more, I saw Dr. Egilmez checking Valerie with his stethoscope. He once more summoned me to him, saying, "Mr. Miller, your daughter's heart is racing, and she is struggling to breathe. I have only two hands, and I need another surgeon to assist me, or I cannot operate; it is too risky for me to attempt this surgery alone. I am sorry."

"Then call another surgeon," I pleaded.

"Mr. Miller, do you see that board on the wall? It lists just who is present in the hospital at this time. There are no other doctors here. Martial Law has been declared. We are under curfew now (it was past 8:00 p.m.) and there is no way I can summon another surgeon."

In despair, I paced the hall, praying for a loving God to do something to spare Val's life. As I paced, I heard a man speak to me, "Mr. Miller, what are you doing here at the hospital? Curfew has begun, and you can't leave the hospital until morning."

I glanced at the man but did not recognize him. "How do you know me, for I do not know you?" I queried.

He explained, saying, "Your wife is my English teacher at the Turkish-American Society, where I am studying English. I have seen you with her. That's how I know who you are. But what are you doing here at this hospital? You can't leave here until morning."

I shared with him my despair over Valerie, ending with, "My daughter is on that surgical table, in there, and Dr. Egilmez refuses to operate without another surgeon to assist him. I fear my daughter will die."

Upon hearing that, I was astounded as the man began washing his hands and gloving up, as though he was a surgeon. "Mr. Miller, I am a surgeon; I will be the surgeon to assist." He proceeded into the surgical room; the doors closed. Once more I paced the hall, praying silently. Miss Yebraksi prayed, also.

I do not know how much time went by, when suddenly Hermine came to the doorway of the surgery, exclaiming, "Valerie's heart has stopped. She is dead!"

I was stunned, on the one hand, but on the other, I had a sense of peace and acceptance, which to this day I cannot understand. Hermine disappeared back into the surgery.

Shortly Hermine came out, again, to declare, "The assistant surgeon is doing external heart massage, while Dr. Egilmez is doing a tracheotomy. Her heart is beating again," and once more she disappeared back into the surgery. I marvel, for Valerie was clinically dead for a short period while she received external heart massage by the assistant surgeon.

Again, I do not know how many more minutes passed by, but finally, Dr. Egilmez came out, holding a small portion of a hazel nut between his thumb and forefinger, as he said, "Mr. Miller, I took out the small bit of nut. Your daughter is breathing normally, and you can now understand why I insisted another

surgeon assist me, for while he did external heart massage, I was able to proceed to remove the piece of nut."

I rejoiced, thanking God for yet another miracle during my time in Turkey. I later learned that Dr. Egilmez took his surgical residency in the States, at Columbia University Hospital, and that he was one of the very few surgeons in Turkey at that time who was capable of performing such delicate surgery.

He had inserted a metal tube into the opening he made into Val's trachea, so that she could breathe during her recovery. When it was removed, several days later, I asked to have that tube, for which I paid a 100 lira fee, about ten dollars, which we kept as a reminder of that miracle Christ, the Great Physician, wrought for us. And Valerie still has the scar of her tracheotomy.

Valerie was placed in a children's ward in the hospital, where she could be watched through the night. There were thirty-five beds in that room, with only one nurse to watch over thirty-five young patients. Dr. Egilmez told me, "Mr. Miller, no nurse can adequately look after that many patients. Your daughter has that tracheal tube in her throat. That tube needs to be kept open. She will need to be aspirated by a small hand-held suction cup, whenever the tube is in danger of clogging. I advise you to hire a private nurse for her."

This I did, which coast me 59 lira, or roughly five dollars, which I consider well-spent. That nurse sat on one side of the bed where Val lay, while I was on the other. In the darkness, all through that dark night, whenever Val wheezed, the nurse aspirated her.

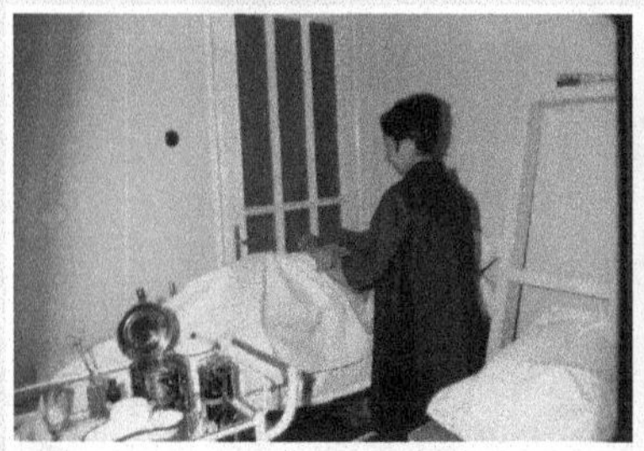

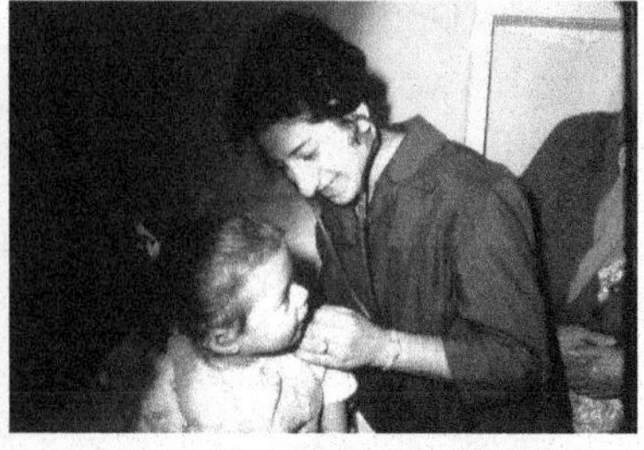

Pictures of Hermine Tulgar in the clinic in the church basement

As I sat by her bed, hearing Val wheeze, I felt her hand groping for mine. I held her hand; she calmed down. Through the night I held her tiny hand in mine. That experience we had together has bonded us in a special way, unto this very time.

I thank our Lord Jesus, that He is not only a prayer-hearing God, but also a prayer-answering God. He worked another miracle for me.

Care Food Distribution

In 1962 the General Conference arranged for the Turkish Mission to receive a very large shipment of CARE food for us to distribute to the poor of Istanbul. We received hundreds of large sacks of wheat flour, rice, and powdered milk. Manuk and I had the sacks trucked to our church, and we stored them in one of the basement rooms. Once a month we distributed this food to the poor.

The mission staff put these foods into small paper bags, which we gave out to persons whom we determined were genuinely in need. They were instructed to come to our church on the first Wednesday of the month, at 1:00 p.m., to receive their allotment. Well before we opened the gate to the church, people would be lining up in the small street leading to our church. It was a joy to be able to help about 200 persons or families a month.

Food distribution at our church

Our German Shepherd, Trixie

I often traveled to Ankara where I met a number of U.S. Airforce personnel who were stationed there in connection with NATO. One of these families had a six-month old German Shepherd they were not going to be able to take back to the states when their tour of duty was up. I was happy to acquire her, so on my next trip to Ankara I drove my '53 Chevy instead of flying, and brought the dog, named Trixie, home to Istanbul with me.

Trixie was one of the most intelligent dogs I have ever had as a pet. When we acquired her, the Miller family lived in Etiler, a suburb of Istanbul. Right behind our house was a large open field that led to a bluff that overlooked the Bosporus. I took Trixie there for exercise. She quickly learned everything taught to her: she would retrieve objects thrown for her; she learned to sit, stay, and come when called. In time I would tell her to sit and stay; I would then walk a long way from her and call her to come to me. She would come running. I could hold up my hand, palm towards her, and she would immediately drop to the ground to await the next command.

Soon after adopting Trixie, I learned she immediately sensed who was an American and who was a Turk. For some reason she had a strong dislike for strange Turks; I do not know why this was, but suspect she may have been mistreated by a Turk. Next door to us lived a Turkish family that had a teen-age boy as a servant. Early in the morning he could be seen going to the nearby bakery for fresh bread. This took him by our front yard where I sometimes would have Trixie tethered. One morning I heard Trixie yelp; I went to the front door to observe the boy throwing rocks at her; she began snarling at him. I warned him that he had best not throw rocks at her, but I caught him doing it again.

The next morning, I did not tether her, but let her out of the house, telling her to stay in the yard, then I watched out the window. Shortly the boy came walking by and started to throw a rock at Trixie. She leaped towards him, nipping him on his behind. He screeched and tried to shinny up a very small nearby tree. It had a trunk only a few inches in diameter, and he would slowly slide down to the ground, only to be nipped again by Trixie. He would shriek again and try to shinny up the tree. Each time he hit the ground he would be nipped again. I went to the door, watched it happen several times again, before I called Trixie to come. She nipped him again, then came trotting up to me, tail wagging, head high, with a grin on her face! That boy never tormented Trixie again; in fact he walked on the other side of the street, as far from our house as possible.

Trixie traveled to Lake Abant with us when we had youth camp. She was very popular with the kids and served as a good watch dog.

Our last home in Istanbul was still further from the city center, in an area called the Fourth Levant. Our address was 53 Meseli Sokak, Dorduncu Levant, Istanbul (Oak Street, Fourth Levant). The years we lived in Istanbul, there were night watchmen, called Bekchi, assigned to an area they were to guard. They carried a whistle which they were required to blow periodically, giving a signal they were on duty. When we first moved to Fourth Levant there were a series of mysterious burglaries in the area. It later was determined that the local Bekchis were the guilty ones.

The house we lived in had a set of large windows in the living room, overlooking the street. There were large wooden shutters for the window that I closed and bolted each night, about 10:00 p.m. One night, as I started into the living room to close the shutters, I saw Trixie crouched before the window, sounding a warning growl towards the windows I intended to shutter. The living room lights were off. I spotted our local Bekchi peering in through the un-shuttered windows.

I softly called Trixie to me, snapped on her leash, the opened our front door, which was just a few feet from where the Bekchi was peering through the windows. I called to him as Trixie lunged towards him. I let her snarl at him for a few moments, then told her to "sit," which command she readily obeyed. I proceeded to tell the Bekchi, "This dog is a better watchman than you will ever be. She knows who you are. I warn you to never again come on our property, for she will quickly attack you."

The Bekchi followed my advice and stayed away from our home, which was one of the few in the area not burglarized. Trixie was truly a great watchdog!

When we left Turkey, May of 1966, for our year's furlough in the states, we gave her to the family that owned a tea garden behind our Istanbul SDA Church. They were very happy to have her, and she and the family readily bonded. It was sad to say goodbye to her. A year later we passed through Istanbul on our way to our new mission station in Beirut. I preached in the Istanbul Church that Sabbath. The family that now had Trixie learned I was there, so they brought her to see me. I wondered if she would remember me, after a whole year. It was a very heartwarming experience when we met again: Trixie reared up on her hind legs, placing a forepaw on each of my shoulders, then proceeded to happily whine and lick my face. She remembered me. That was the last time I saw Trixie, one of the best dogs I have ever had. I am of a sentimental belief that in heaven God will restore my loved pets to me—many dogs and cats I have had through the years, plus several horses. I can hardly wait to be reunited with them again! Heaven will be a wonderful place, indeed.

Brenda Lee Benzatyan

In contrast to Valerie's miracle, something else happened to Brenda Lee, Manuk and Anahid's first-born daughter, born after Valerie. Anahid doted on Brenda Lee, but I still wonder if Manuk was ready to be a father. Brenda grew to toddlerhood, and she and Valerie played together.

One spring Manuk, Nurredin Bey, and I took a long trip into the interior of Turkey, planning to go as far east as Sivas, about 450 miles away. On the way, we planned to visit some other towns and villages.

Prior to leaving on this trip, we had our regular Monday staff meeting. I wanted those who lived in the Mission building to have a greater part in maintaining the small garden area to the side and back of the building. In the middle of the garden was a small pond, which had no drain; to clean it, it had to be emptied by hand, using a bucket. This had not been done for a considerable time, and the water was green with scum.

Speaking to Manuk, Anahid, and Miss Yebraksi, I said, "If I lived here, I would fill in this scummy pond," then looking at Anahid, I continued, "This pond could even be a place of danger for Brenda Lee."

Anahid quickly replied, "Oh, Brenda Lee is afraid of water; she would never go near the pond." I left it, at that.

Manuk and I drove to Ankara, where Nurredin Bey joined us. The small town of Konya, the biblical Iconium, visited by Paul during his missionary journeys, was the first place we intended to show our temperance films. We were traveling in a small German-made Opel sedan, that I had purchased in Beirut; it was licensed there, and I could keep it in Turkey, as long as I took it out of Turkey at least every three months; this was no problem, for I usually had to travel to Beirut several times a year to attend Middle East Division Executive Committee meetings.

It was this journey previously mentioned where my car failed, and we had to stop to have the timing belt replaced. The next day, after my Opel was repaired, we continued our journey to Sivas, which was fraught with another challenge: the mechanic had put the distributor wire upside down, which reduced engine power, especially when climbing hills. We were able to get that corrected in Sivas.

In Sivas, we not only planned to lecture and show our temperance films, but we were also looking for some very specific people: our maid, Araksi, was from Sivas, and she wanted us to find them and tell them about the SDA Church she had joined.

Together Manuk and I began the lecture and temperance movie show, then Manuk set out to find Araksi's relatives, which was, indeed, a challenge — Araksi was unable to supply an address for them!

Manuk left the school, which was located by a river. Once outside he prayed for God to guide him in his search. He felt impressed to cross over the bridge to the other side of the river; once on the other side, he prayed again, and was impressed to turn to the left on the first street, which he did.

Strolling along that river-front street, he prayed again, asking God to now guide him to the right house. As he strolled, he felt impressed to knock on a certain door, which he did.

And, miraculously, that was the very house of Araksi's relatives! Manuk identified himself, gave them Araksi's greetings, and made arrangements for both of us to return to their home later that evening.

We were eating supper in the hotel restaurant, when a man entered, announcing in a loud voice, "The American has a long-distance phone call." Knowing I was only American around, I asked Manuk to go with me, in case the phone call was from someone who spoke Turkish; he would be able to translate for me, if needed.

I asked Manuk to answer the phone; it was from Miss Yebraksi, at the mission house in Istanbul. "Manuk, you and Curtis must return to Istanbul immediately," she informed Manuk, who relayed the message to me.

"Ask her why we need to return immediately, because we still have more appointments in Sivas," I requested. Manuk proceeded to ask Miss Yebraksi for more information, which she refused to do; she simply insisted we return immediately.

We informed Nurredin of our change of plans, checked out of the hotel, and began the long drive home. We pondered, "What is the emergency that caused Miss Yebraksi to tell us to return home immediately?"

Our rationale was that there must be a crisis in my family, and Miss Yebraksi, knowing I was the only one of the three of us that could drive, did not want to stress me and impair my ability to drive safely.

As we drove as rapidly as possible — I calculated that it would take us at least ten hours to drive 450 miles, over two mountain ranges — we alternately prayed and sang hymns. The hymn we sang most was "Rab Kerim Bir Dostur" — "What A Friend We Have in Jesus." These words, from that hymn, were especially comforting to us as we traveled through the night:

Blessed Savior, Thou hast promised
Thou wilt all our burdens bear;
May we ever, Lord, be bringing
All to Thee in earnest prayer.

As we traveled, we monitored the car radio; around midnight we heard a special announcement that an Istanbul hospital was asking for donations of a specific blood type. "Was that hospital needing blood for one of our loved ones?" we wondered. We kept on singing and praying.

It was about 8:00 a.m. when we arrived at the mission. The kapaci — doorkeeper — of the building next to our mission, was standing near our doorway, "What's happened?" we asked him. He did not reply, but just looked upward, avoiding our eyes.

We entered the mission building, where we encountered our own kapici, Hayk. "What's happened?" we asked him. Hayk, too, avoided our eyes, by looking down at the floor.

Hearing our voices, Madam Pilkin, who lived in the first-floor apartment, opened her door. "What's happened?" we asked her. Madam Pilkin replied, "Manuk, you should go upstairs to your apartment."

Manuk ran up the stairs. I asked Madam Pilkin, again, "What has happened?" She sadly informed me, "Brenda Lee has drowned in the fishpond." I slowly ascended the stairs to the second floor, relieved to know the tragedy was not in my family, but sorrowing for Manuk and Anahid. I proceeded up the stairs. I could hear loud sobbing, coming from Manuk's apartment.

I entered Manuk and Anahid's parlor. Miss Yebraksi was there; Hermine, our nurse, and her husband, Hirant, were there; Phyllis was there. Anahid was sobbing broken-heartedly, as the others sought to comfort her. Hermine had given Anahid a mild sedative, but it was insufficient to assuage her grief.

Hirant quietly informed me, "Yesterday morning, Anahid was talking with a visitor just inside the hallway of the first floor. Brenda Lee was playing on the floor, but Anahid was so engrossed with her conversation, that she did not notice her daughter go out the door into the garden. After she was done talking, she looked around for Brenda. She called for her but heard no answer. Seeing the door to the garden open, Anahid began searching and calling Brenda. There was no answer."

Shortly I learned that as Anahid walked by that murky pond, she saw what looked like a bit of cloth on the surface of the pond. She paused, to pluck it out of the water; as she did so, she was shocked to pull Brenda Lee's arm towards her. Recognizing it was Brenda, she screamed. Others came running and seeing Anahid holding the limp body of her daughter, an ambulance was summoned. Brenda Lee was pronounced dead upon arrival at the hospital.

Anahid, now twenty-four hours later, refused to believe her daughter was dead. "Curtis," she sobbed to me, "Brenda was taken to the hospital; they are still trying to revive her."

Brenda was never revived, and the next day I conducted the most challenging funeral I have ever performed. Manuk and Anahid, along with many members of the Istanbul Church, were there, for the service, held in the local Protestant cemetery.

As we gathered around Brenda Lee's casket, our church's head elder, Kevork, translated for me. Anahid was sobbing, her whole bodying shaking. I positioned myself on the far side of the casket from Anahid and Manuk, for I found it hard to look into Anahid's face as I read the words of committal, from the SDA Ministers Manual:

> Forasmuch as God in His infinite love and wisdom
> Has permitted our dear Brenda Lee to fall asleep in Christ...

Anahid's family lived near Beirut, and I believed she would benefit from being with her family during the initial time of her grief, so we flew her to Beirut to be with her family for a few weeks.

After she returned to Istanbul, Anahid came to my office, saying, "Curtis, I have learned what you and Manuk were doing in Sivas, when you were called to come home because of Brenda Lee's death. I want you to send both Manuk and I to Sivas so that he can finish his interrupted visit with Araksi's family."

I sent them to Sivas, and we were all thrilled and praised God for what happened during that visit. Here is what happened in Sivas:

Manuk and Anahid began Bible studies with Araksi's family. During the course of the studies, when Manuk presented the truth that the Sabbath was the seventh day of the week, a lady related that many years ago, shortly after WWI, she and her family were having worship in their home, when a little old lady came sobbing into their home."

She related that she was a seventh-day Sabbath keeper, working as a maid in a Muslim household. The Muslims knew she kept the Sabbath, but that morning they had ordered her to "go to the bazaar and buy food for them." She endeavored to tell them she could not do so, on the holy Sabbath. She did want to keep the Sabbath, but was afraid she would be beaten, and possibly dismissed from the Muslim home.

Araksi's family kept that lady in their home, taking care of her for several years. She was likely a convert to Adventism by the itinerant ministry of Zedour Baharian, the first SDA pastor, around WWI. Now, a half-century later, Araksi learned that her own family had learned the seventh day is the Sabbath, some of them keeping Sabbath for many years, and Araksi did not know that.

Madam Sophia Pilkin

Madam Sophia Pilkin's father was a colonel in the Czar of Russia's guard prior to the Bolshevik Revolution after WWI. When the Czar was overthrown, Sophia Pilkin escaped from Russia, fleeing to Istanbul, Turkey, where she married a Russian engineer, who had also fled Russia. They both became Turkish citizens.

When her husband passed away, she opened a small dairy store in the shopping area near Taksim Square, not far from our Turkish Mission, where she barely eked out a living. In the early years of WWII our Turkish Mission was facing a very tight budget, so our resident missionary of the time decided to rent out the first-floor apartment, charging fifty Turkish lira — around five dollars — per month. Madam Pilkin, as she became known to us, gratefully rented the apartment.

During wartime, rents could not be raised, and with post-war inflation, fifty lira per month, which included all utilities — heat, water, electricity — would not keep up with the expense of the apartment. And the mission could not raise her rent. She was still paying fifty lira a month when I arrived in Istanbul as president of the Turkish Mission. Madam Pilkin took a shine to the Miller family. She made the most delicious Russian borsch I have ever eaten, and she often invited us to eat borsch and pierogi — a small dough dumpling stuffed with a filling such as potato or cheese. We loved her cooking!

Madam Pilkin belonged to the Russian Orthodox Church, of which there were none in the nearby area. As she aged, she was challenged to walk the distance to her church, and her income was very meager, so she could not take a bus or trolley. I invited her to attend our church, which was right in her backyard.

Madam Pilkin would say to me, "Mr. Miller, you know I am not a Seventh-day Adventist."

"But Madam Pilkin, you do believe the seventh-day is the Sabbath, don't you?"

"Yes," was her reply.

"And you also believe in the second advent of Christ?"

"Yes," again, was her reply.

Then, because you believe the seventh-day is the Sabbath, and because you believe in Christ's second advent, you are a Seventh-day Adventist."

I invited her to join our church, but she demurred, for if the Russian Orthodox Bishop learned she was a baptized SDA, she would not be allowed to be buried in the Orthodox cemetery.

The first of each month, Madam Pilkin promptly paid me her fifty-lira rent, and she was very thankful that was all she had to pay. I knew she was in deep poverty, for every now and then I would see a painting, or a small rug, or some other item, was missing, and I knew she sold them in order to pay her meager living expenses.

One month she came to me to pay her rent; she handed me a fifty-lira gold piece. fifty liras were its face value, but with the inflated price of gold, it was actually worth ten times that amount. "Mr. Miller, will you accept this gold coin in lieu of my rent, until I have an actual fifty lira currency I can give you, to redeem the gold?" I agreed to hold the gold until she could redeem it. Over many months I was holding many gold coins for her. I was ignorant about the gold market, not realizing the small fortune in gold coins that I was keeping for her.

Many was the time when, around lunch, she would come to my office to invite me to have a bowl of borsch, which I was happy to have. When she was not looking, I would hide fifty lira in a book, or behind a picture on the wall, knowing that sooner or later she would find it. I hid the money, for she was too proud to take charity.

Now, and again, I would hear her say, "I just don't remember placing any money in that book." But as she continued to come upon the money I sequestered in her apartment, she became suspicious of me. "Mr. Miller," she would say, "Are you leaving money in these places where I keep finding it?"

And I would also always reply, "Ask me no questions, and I will tell you no lies."

When I left Turkey, in 1966, for a year's furlough in the U.S., I made Manuk responsible for Madam Pilkin's care. I explained to him the gold coins accumulating in the mission safe, hidden in the basement. My mission office was hidden in that basement, behind the coal bin. I also explained to him how I would secrete money in her apartment, where she would find it. Manuk dutifully cared for Madam Pilkin, until he was transferred to Beirut in 1970. Prior to leaving Istanbul, he arranged for Miss Yebraksi to care for Madam Pilkin.

Madam Pilkin had only one known relative left in the world, an older sister who had fled Russia and settled in Paris. After learning of her sister, who also was poverty-stricken, had suicided by over-dosing on sleep medication, Madam Pilkin descended into depression.

Manuk gave me the news of Madam Pilkin's demise. With no resident pastor left in Istanbul, after Manuk was transferred to Beirut, the MED periodically would send someone to preach to the few members we had left in Istanbul. Dr. Kenneth Vine, president of our Middle East College, in Beirut, was scheduled to hold some meetings in Istanbul. Madam Pilkin showed great interest in Vin's coming, and learned he was scheduled to fly to Beirut on a Tuesday morning; Miss Yebraksi would meet his plane and escort him to the mission building. Every time Madam Pilkin would see Miss Yebraksi, as the time for Vine to come drew near, she would ask, "Are you certain Dr. Vine will be coming?" Miss Yebraksi would assure her he was coming.

As Miss Yebraksi was leaving the building the morning Vine was expected, Madam Pilkin stuck her head out her door, and once more asked, "Are you going to bring Dr. Vine to the mission building?" Miss Yebraksi assured her she was going to the airport to meet Vine.

Miss Yebraksi surmised that Madam Pilkin wanted to see Dr. Vine, herself. About two hours later, around noon, Miss Yebraksi and Vine arrived at the Mission. She knocked on Madam Pilkin's door, but Madam Pilkin did not answer the knock. She knocked again, mid-afternoon, and still no one answered the door.

Miss Yebraksi knocked again, at early evening, and still Madam Pilkin did not answer the door. Now, very concerned, Miss Yebraksi entered the apartment, to find Madam Pilkin on her bed, near which was an empty water glass and empty pill bottle. Madam Pilkin had evidently decided to follow her sister by taking an overdose of sleep medication. She was still alive when Yebraksi found her, but she was barely breathing.

Very shortly, Madam Sophia Pilkin breathed her last. She exited this life, likely because her funds were gone, and she did not want to be a burden to anyone.

I still miss Madam Pilkin, and hope to meet her again, in heaven.

Guiding Elders Figuhr and Beach Around the Seven Churches of Revelation

The seven churches of the book of Revelation have long been of great interest to me. During my tours giving temperance lectures and showing films in the greater area of modern Izmir (biblical Smyrna—the second of the seven churches) it was convenient to tour all those ancient sites. Throughout my years in the Middle East Division, I toured them several times: with my parents when they came to visit us in Beirut; with classmates of mine, from Walla Walla College years; and with Elders Reuben Figuhr and Walter Beach, president and secretary of the General Conference of Seventh-day Adventists. During those years, I probably toured the seven churches more than any other SDA.

Reuben Figuhr, President of the General Conference during my years in Turkey

Elder Figuhr, GC President 1954–66, is one of the godliest men I have ever worked with during my ministry. He came to the MED for our autumn council. Many GC leaders, enroute to Beirut, often passed through Istanbul on their way, and I was privileged to meet many of them. Elder Figuhr, in my opinion, took a liking to me, and mentored me. The first time he came to Istanbul, I was holding evangelistic meetings in the Istanbul Church, and he attended a meeting the evening before we flew together to Beirut. After hearing my sermon, he kindly suggested to me that several of my illustrations were taken from the U.S., and he believed I would improve my sermons by using illustrations from Middle East countries.

Manuk and I were delegates to the General Conference session of 1966, held in Detroit, Michigan. During the first pre-session ministerial meeting, Figuhr was the keynote speaker. Manuk and I were seated in the very front row. When Figuhr stepped to the podium, he looked directly at us, and his opening remark was, "I see our brethren from Turkey, pastors Miller and Benzatyan, are with us this evening."

I greatly appreciated Figuhr aiding me in my ministerial career. Elder Roger Wilcox, president of the MED during my six years in Turkey, was very determined that the Miller family return to Turkey after our one year furlough in the U.S. 1966–67. We were willing to do so, but requested that another SDA missionary family, with school-aged children, join us so that we could provide a church school education for our girls. During his second trip to the MED fall meetings, Figuhr learned of my request, and at a MED executive meeting, he said, very firmly, to the committee, "Grant Pastor Miller his request." I am forever grateful for his support.

At that 1966 GC session, as a delegate from the MED, I stayed in the same hotel with many world delegates. Figuhr was staying in that same hotel. The GC Nominating Committee (NC) was meeting; this committee was, and is, one of the most important of all the committees, for it puts in place all the key leaders of the SDA world field. In '66, early on the NC was in process of nominating the presidents of the world divisions. After the closing of one evening's meeting, I walked into the hotel lobby where I was staying. Figuhr was standing in the lobby, waiting for me. He beckoned me to come to him, and said, "Brother Miller, I notice the NC has not nominated Roger Wilcox to be MED President. I think you are in position to influence the NC to nominate him."

"Elder Figuhr, in all sincerity, I cannot consciously do that," I replied,

"Why not," he queried?

"Because Elder Wilcox does not listen to his Executive Committee members or take their counsel. He just stubbornly plows ahead with his own ideas," was my reply.

"Perhaps Roger could be counseled," he responded.

I agreed with him, that counsel might be worthwhile; but in my opinion, I doubted if counsel would be successful. I also knew that MED treasurer, Elder Vincent Fenn, had the same opinion, and I believe he had already voiced his opinion to the NC.

To the amazement of many at that GC session, the NC nominated Roger Wilcox to be president of the very large South American Division; thus, Wilcox went from being president of the smallest division, the MED, to one of the largest, in terms of total membership!

I was quite surprised and expressed that to an acquaintance of mine who was a missionary in South America; his response was very interesting, "In South America, we could care less as to who might be our division president. As long as we have strong union presidents—the ones who, in fact, have the most influence — we are satisfied."

Elder Beach, who participated in my ordination in Istanbul, as a minister of the SDA Church, was GC Secretary from 1954–70. I also considered him to be one of my close friends among our world leaders. When the Millers were on furlough in 1966–67, Beach sold me his slightly used, low-mileage Chevrolet Impala, at a good price. On one occasion I served as Beach's translator when he preached in Istanbul. He was known as "Shorty Beach," shorter even than I. He was also roly-poly—rotund, if you will. On one occasion, he and Figuhr were staying in the Opera

"In South America, we could care less as to who might be our division president. As long as we have strong union presidents — the ones who, in fact, have the most influence — we are satisfied."

Hotel located between Taksim Square and our church. I stopped by the hotel, prior to the afternoon meeting Figuhr and Beach were both to speak, to see if they wanted a ride to the church. Figuhr indicated he needed exercise and would walk to the church. Beach preferred to accept my invitation to ride. As I drove him to the church, I asked him, "Don't you think you could use some exercise, also?"

"No," he replied, "I get plenty of exercise being a pall bearer at the funeral of all these exercise nuts!"

Then came the day when both Figuhr and Beach came through Istanbul, on their way to Beirut, and requested me to guide them around the seven churches; MED President Roger Wilcox joined us on the trip. We flew on Turkish Airlines to Izmir, the biblical Smyrna, where I hired someone to drive around the church sites.

The Book of Revelation was written by the apostle John, who was known as the Apostle of Love, and was in a reciprocal love relationship between Christ and John, Master and disciple. John was the spiritual leader of the churches of western Asia Minor (modern Turkey). John was the only apostle to die a natural death; the other eleven were all martyrs. He was possibly the youngest of all the apostles. In his senior years he was exiled to the lonely isle of Patmos, a small island in the Aegean Sea off the southwestern coast of Turkey.

He wrote the Revelation of Jesus Christ around A.D. 95 while on Patmos, from whence he sent the letters to the seven churches. It is interesting to note the geographic location of these churches, which are in cities located in a fifty-mile radius circle. If the letters to these churches were to be delivered by a postal service, they are laid out in the order a postman would follow, beginning with Ephesus, which is the first church, followed by Smyrna, Pergamum, Thyatira, Sardis, Philadelphia, and Laodicea.

I guided my group of leaders around the seven churches. Elder Figuhr was a photographer, interested in taking many pictures of each site. Beach, on the other hand, carried no camera with him, saying, "I can always obtain any copies I may want from all the pictures Reuben takes." I still chuckle about Beach; as we approached each church site, he would begin giving us detailed information about the history of each church; he rattled it off as though he were reading from a guidebook, or an encyclopedia. He was a very intellectual man.

We came to Laodicea last. As we approached the site, Beach indicated he was looking forward to swimming in the lukewarm pool, for I had told the gentlemen that we would be staying in a motel with rooms opening right on the patio surrounding the pool. Beach kept saying he was going to swim in the pool, and each time he said it, Figuhr would say, "But Walter, you don't have a swimming suit!"

Arriving at the motel, just before dusk, we each had a small room right by the pool. The motel had its own generator to produce lights in the rooms. Notice was posted that the generator would run from dusk to 10:00 p.m. each evening. About 8:00 p.m., the generator suddenly stopped, leaving all in darkness. I was sitting in the doorway of my room, overlooking the pool. I saw two shadows approach the pool, then I heard Beach and Wilcox splashing around in the pool. I called out, "Is that you, Walter and Roger?"

Beach replied, "Yes, it's us."

"But Walter, how can you be swimming when you do not have a bathing suit?" I mimicked Figuhr.

"Never mind that," Beach replied, "Come on in, the water's great."

"But I don't have a swimming suit," I declared.

"Neither do we, but its dark, no one will know if you don't have a suit. C'mon in."

I doffed my clothes, and shortly joined the two men. Beach was right, the water was great.

Shortly Figuhr heard us splashing and talking; he came onto the patio, saying, "Walter, is that you out there in the pool?"

"Yes, it sure is, and Roger and Curtis are here with me."

Middle East Division President Roger Wilcox standing in baptistry at church in Ephesus from the time the apostle John was the pastor of the church

Home of Mary, Mother of Jesus, on hill above Ephesus

For the last time I heard Figuhr's classic statement, that I will never forget, and remember with a chuckle, "But Walter, you don't have a swimming suit!"

Weeks of Prayer I Conducted

During my tenure in Turkey, I was asked to conduct a Week of Prayer for both Middle East College (MEC), in Beirut, and Tehran Academy (TA) in Iran. For each of these series I would need a translator, for Arabic at Middle East College, and Farsi (Persian) in Tehran.

The students at MEC were from several nations, ethnicity, and language including Arabic speaking countries—Egypt, Libya, Sudan, Saudi Arabia, Jordan, Syria, and Lebanon, and Greeks, from Cyprus, speaking Greek. MEC classes were taught in English, but the predominant language at the college was Arabic, so when I held the Week of Prayer meetings there, I had an Arabic translator, When preaching through a translator, I had to plan a sermon that allowed time for me to speak English and the time the translator would need to speak into the other language—this meant my sermons would need be about half as long as I would use if the sermon were in only one language; in other words, I learned "to speak less, but say more."

I here digress from my topic, to explain a dynamic I faced at MEC, during that Week of Prayer. The MEC president at that time was Ed Gammon; prior to going to MEC, he was principal of Laurelwood Academy. Gammon was a very dictatorial man, both to his wife and to the MEC faculty (it was later learned that Gammon verbally and physically abused his wife). He used a "divide and conquer" technique of administration. He even forbade the faculty to fraternize with each other. He was so overbearing in his dealings with faculty, that some faculty did not return from furlough to MEC, choosing to resign and request a permanent return to America. Others simply resigned from being on the faculty and went back to their homeland. The MED Executive Committee, of which I was a member, finally told Gammon, the next time a faculty member departs from MEC, you will be terminated as MEC president, and returned to America. And that happened, when a key faculty member resigned, Gammon was fired!

It was Gammon who officially invited me to conduct the MEC Week of Prayer. He met me at the Beirut Airport, and as he drove me to MEC, he firmly informed me as to how I would conduct the Week of Prayer, and was very specific in stating, "I don't want you to have any 'altar calls' during your meetings."

This was quite contrary to what I had planned; I intended, at the conclusion of my second Friday evening sermon, to make several calls: for those who wanted to accept Christ as their Savior; those who wanted to become a baptized SDA; and I intended to also appeal to students who would become SDA ministers or teachers. This I stated to Gammon, and he was not pleased with my plans. I conferred with the MED president, who said, "Curtis, you have the right to preach your sermons according to your God-given convictions, and I will stand with you in making altar calls."

At MEC there were two young ladies, Samia Abou Ali and ... I can't recall the other lady's name, who were Druze. The Druze are an Arabic-speaking esoteric ethno- religious group originating in the Middle East who self-identify as Unitarians. Jethro of Midian is considered an ancestor of all Druze and revered as their spiritual founder as well as chief prophet.

At the close of my last sermon, I made an altar call, as both Druze ladies came forward (I wish I could remember their names, but after fifty-eight years, I simply can't remember). I am, even as I write this story, very happy and thankful I made that altar call that resulted in their being baptized into the SDA Church.

It was Kenneth Oster who invited me to conduct the Week of Prayer at TA. Kenneth was the son of Frank and Florence Oster, first SDA missionaries to Iran, the current name for Persia. Kenneth, and his wife Dorothy, spent many years of mission of service in Iran; in 1980, he wrote his book *To Persia, With Love*—a book I highly recommend you read. Kenneth is probably as fluent in Farsi as he is in English, for he grew up in Iran, and ministered there for many years.

I flew via Pan Am, from Istanbul to Tehran, and stayed in the Oster home, on the TA campus. Kenneth translated my English into Farsi. Of note, the nephew of Shah Pahlavi, last Shah of Iran, attended TA. I had two memorable experiences while holding those meetings at TA.

The first was with the mother of a Muslim student who attended Tehran Academy. The meetings were in November, during the American tradition of Thanksgiving. She knew I would be away from home for that holiday, so she invited me to a Thanksgiving banquet she gave in my honor. Her husband was a very wealthy Iranian. His business firm built the highway from the Tehran airport into the city. They lived in a magnificent mansion. When I went to their home, a servant met me at the door, and escorted me to the salon where the rich man sat to receive me. As I was seated, I felt something hard beneath the chair's cushion. I reached down to see what it was and felt the handle of a pistol. Seeing the look of surprise on my face, my host said, "Yes, that is a pistol, and it is loaded. There is a pistol under every cushion in this room, for I have many enemies, and I am armed to keep myself safe."

The dining room was the largest I have ever been in. There was a mammoth Persian carpet on the floor. Persian carpets are hand-woven and very expensive. I once visited a Persian rug maker in the Iranian city of Isfahan, one of the main places Persian rugs are woven. Because the finest carpets woven are those that have the most threads per square inch, tying such tiny knots is best done by tiny fingers, therefore many of the finest rugs are woven by small children, around ages five or six years old. The rug weaving site I visited, in Isfahan, was in a large room with several rugs in process of being woven. I approached one rug and saw tiny fingers weaving. I peered inside the loom and saw a tiny girl. I reached my hand through the loom, to touch hers, and was surprised at how callused her fingers were from the hundreds and hundreds of hours she spent weaving. Above her head, as she worked diligently tying those tiny knots, was a drawing of the pattern of the section of the carpet she was weaving. She was required to exactly follow that pattern. For all her twelve to fourteen hours per day labors she was paid the magnificent sum of about ten cents per day. I wondered, "With that sum of ten cents per day, how could a Persian carpet cost so much?" Certainly, the amount paid the weavers did not make them expensive, so I conclude it is because of the number of threads per square inch, and the many, many months it takes to weave a carpet, is a large part of the value of a Persian carpet.

"Yes, that is a pistol, and it is loaded. There is a pistol under every cushion in this room, for I have many enemies, and I am armed to keep myself safe."

Back to that Thanksgiving feast, of which I was the guest of honor. In that dining room was a long table, with the Iranian lady's family and other guests. There must have been twenty persons at the table that night. I was seated at the place of honor, to the left side of the rich hostess. Shortly a servant appeared at my side, holding a large platter of the first course of the feast: rice pilaf, with delicious pine seeds. The servant held the platter, indicating I was to serve myself; I took a couple of large spoonsful of the pilaf, but my hostess did not think I had taken enough, so she signaled the servant to heap my plate full of pilaf.

Being raised in boyhood to "clean up my plate, because I shouldn't waste food because of the millions of poor children in China who don't have enough to eat," I proceeded to eat the very last grain of rice on my plate. Having done so, I was surprised to have the servant once more at my side, presenting me with the platter of pilaf. I tried to avoid taking a second helping, for I knew such meals would have several courses; therefore, I politely shook my head to indicate I did not want more pilaf. Again, the hostess signaled the servant to put more pilaf on my plate; I again cleaned my plate and was offered a third helping. By the time the meal of several courses was over, I was so stuffed I could hardly eat the pumpkin pie that was served at the end. I was honored again, for pumpkin pie is not a Persian dish, and my hostess told me she had asked the wife of the American consul to provide her with the recipe for pumpkin pie, American style. It was delicious. I later learned, from Ken Oster, that if a guest eats all on his plate, he wants another serving. The signal you want no more, is to leave some food on your plate!

Farid

One day during that Week of Prayer, I walked through the boys' dorm after the morning meeting and was surprised to see a boy asleep in a bunk bed. I thought that strange, for all the boys were to be in their classes. I inquired of Ken Oster about the boy and was informed that he had arrived at TA late the night before.

Farid lived in a small village in the south of Iran where his father was the village chief. Farid signed up for a Bible correspondence course in Farsi, under the auspices of our Iran Mission. Before he completed the course, he decided to become a Christian and announced that to his father at bedtime one night. His father became very angry, screaming at Farid, "No son of mine will become a Christian. Get out of my house now!"

Farid fled from the village, to the edge of a field, where he shivered through the frigid fall night. The next morning an uncle spotted Farid. Knowing he was likely cold, his uncle brought him a warm coat and said, "Farid, your father has vowed to kill you if you become a Christian; you must run away to keep yourself safe." The only place Farid could think to flee was the address of the Bible course in Tehran. He arrived there late at night and was lodged at the dorm at Tehran Academy.

After taking more Bible studies Farid was baptized into the SDA Church. After a time, he received word that his father had forgiven him and that it was safe for him to come to his home village. Upon arriving home, he was enjoying a supper prepared by his mother. As he was happily eating his father said, "Farid, rejoice!"

"I am rejoicing, Father, for I am now back home," replied Farid.

Then Farid was shocked by his father saying, "But you have a much more reason to rejoice, for tomorrow you are to be married." Farid was shocked, but the next day he was married and that night he went to the bridal chamber with his new wife. When they were alone she asked the traditional question, "Husband, to what men may I show my unveiled face?" When a bride asked her husband this question, the husband would then name the men to whom she could show her face, such as her new husband's father, or an uncle, brothers, or cousins.

Instead of answering his new bride, he put his finger to her lips, telling her to be silent as he told her his plan to escape out a window, which they did, after which he and his bride made their way to Tehran.

I saw Farid and his bride the next summer, at the Iran camp meeting. I will say one thing about his father's choice of a bride, for she is one of the most beautiful Iranian ladies I have ever seen. At camp meeting I asked Farid, "Are you giving your wife Bible studies?"

"Yes," He replied.

"Which set of Bible studies are you studying with her?" I asked, expecting him to say the series he himself studied in Farsi, or perhaps another one. I still chuckle at his answer that he simply began reading the Bible to her, beginning with Genesis.

His plan must have worked, for by the time he was well into the New Testament his beautiful wife was baptized to become a beautiful Seventh-day Adventist!

Encircled in a Rainbow

I traveled many miles in Turkey, by car, bus, train, horse, and ox-drawn cars, but very often by airplane.

While serving in the Montana Conference from '56–59 I met USAF Sgt. Al Halley who was serving at Malmstrom Airbase in Great Falls. While we were living in Istanbul, he was stationed in Ankara for a couple years. When Al contacted me that he was in Ankara, I visited him when I was in that city in connection with my mission work. Al introduced me to the Studdard Family. Mrs. Studdard was SDA; her husband was supervisor of the U.S. NATO motor pool in Ankara. Another SDA Air Force family also was stationed there. Mrs. Studdard implored me to hold a preaching service for these families in Ankara whenever I was in that city. I informed the MED officers of this request and was granted permission to fly to Ankara twice a month to hold services. Usually I stayed in the Studdard home when I traveled there.

After holding services one weekend I was flying on Turk Hava Yollari (THY—Turkish Airlines) back to Istanbul; the plane was a DC-3, known as Dakota during WWII, a veritable workhorse of a very safe plane; however, during those years there were a number of THY planes that crashed, often due to pilot error. The American community in Turkey came up with the questionable slogan about Turk Hava Yollari: "Fly and die with THY."

As the airplane approached Istanbul's Yesilkoy Airport's landing strip the plane, instead of landing, began to climb and circle the airport. I wondered why the delay in landing; finally, the pilot spoke over the intercom to state the only one landing gear had descended into place, with one still retracted. He continued saying he would circle the airport while crew attempted to put the landing gear down manually. The plane continued to circle; finally, the pilot spoke again over the intercom, stating the landing gear would still not go down and that he would continue to circle the airport until close to all the fuel was used, thus reducing the hazard of landing. The runway would be foamed to reduce the risk of fire, and he would land the plane on its fuselage, with no landing gear down.

While inflight I had been reading my Bible. Seated across the aisle from me was a Turkish movie actress who was curious as to what I was reading; I explained I was reading the Bible, Kitabi Mukaddes, in Turkish. She asked if I could read to her from the Bible; I was reading Isaiah 26, so I was sharing the following verses with her when the pilot first spoke over the intercom:

"In that day shall this song be sung in the land of Judah; We have a strong city; salvation will God appoint for walls and bulwarks. Open ye the gates, that the righteous nation which keepeth the truth may enter in. Thou wilt keep him in perfect peace, whose mind is stayed on Thee: because he trusteth in Thee."

As the plane continued to circle many on board were dismayed, to say the least. The actress addressed the passengers within hearing range: "This man is a 'holy man.' He is reading from his holy book." Then she asked me to read loudly from Isaiah, which I did.

About that time, I looked out the plane window. We had been circling at fifteen thousand feet. A rainstorm had moved in below us, with the sun shining brightly above us. In the picture below you will see what I saw outside the window of the plane:

Shortly the plane landed safely.

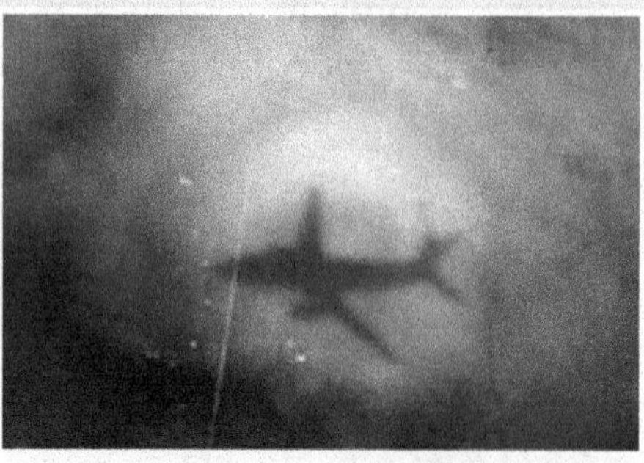

The shadow of the plane was completely encircled by a rainbow, which I took to be God's sign of promise that our plane would have a safe landing

Smuggling *Steps to Christ* into Turkey

I discovered that there was no literature in the Turkish language to promote Christianity in Turkey. After praying about this lack, I decided to have the small book *Steps to Christ* translated into Turkish and have it published at our Middle East Press in Beirut, for I would never be able to have this book printed in Turkey — it was against the law to do so.

For the initial printing, I decided to have one thousand copies printed. I drove my German Opel from Istanbul to Beirut, collected the books from the press, placed them in the trunk of the Opel, and covered them with my small amount of personal effects and a blanket. I was well aware that at the Turkish border it was very likely that customs inspectors would thoroughly search the car, looking for any items that were subject to a tax or forbidden to allow into Turkey. If inspectors looked carefully at the books, they would likely confiscate them; however, I was determined to bring those books into Turkey, and I fervently prayed God would intervene and somehow get those books into the country for the furtherance of promoting the Gospel of Christ there.

After loading the car, I drove further up Septia Mountain to where our Middle East College (MEC) was located. The college had a small grocery store, bakery, and gas pump where I filled up the gas tank on the car. As I was fueling the car, Herbert Faiman, our college baker, came out the bakery door and spotted me by my car. Herbert and I were good friends, and he called to me, "Brother Curtis, where are you going today?"

Herbert was born in Vienna and became a skilled bread and pastry chef, after which he was employed in a hotel in Baghdad during the 1950s. While working there he was stricken with polio and hospitalized at Dar Es Salam (House of Peace) SDA hospital. His illness became quite critical for which he was placed in an iron-lung to facilitate his breathing. While in the iron-lung he was cared for by a Jordanian nurse. After he recovered from polio he grew in love with that nurse and married her, which also resulted in Herbert becoming a Seventh-day Adventist. After they married, his wife became dean of women at MEC and Herbert became the college baker.

In reply to Herbert's question as to where I was going, I informed him I was ready to depart for Istanbul, with the *Steps to Christ* books. He asked me how long the trip would take. I replied, "It is one thousand miles. I will drive half-way today, stopping at Adana, Turkey, for the night, and reach Istanbul late tomorrow night."

Herbert disappeared into the bakery, shortly to return with ten packages of his most delicious cinnamon rolls — sixty rolls total — saying, "You will be hungry on that long trip, so take these cinnamon rolls to eat as you drive." I was most happy for his sweet and delicious gift. I placed them on the front passenger seat and set out on my journey.

By mid-afternoon I arrived at the remote Syrian-Turkish border post just south of Yayladagi (Meadow Village). As per usual the border gate was closed, so I came to a stop and turned off the engine. Shortly a customs office and a military border guard came to my car. The customs officer asked for my passport and asked me to step out of the car, while he looked under the front car seat and under the dash. He then asked me to open the hood of the car, where he checked to make certain nothing was stashed in an effort to hide anything. He then proceeded to the passenger side of the car, and I knew he would search the trunk next. I was silently praying God would somehow aid me in getting those books into Turkey.

As the customs official came by the front passenger door, he spotted the packages of cinnamon rolls and asked what they were. I grabbed a package, showed him the label on the package which stated, "Middle East College Where Students Earn to Learn." I quickly offered him one, and he smacked his lips as he began to devour it. "Cok lizzetli" (very delicious), he exclaimed. Then, seeing the other packages of cinnamon rolls he shouted to the other custom officers and military police, "Gel ve ye bunlari cok lizzetli pastalar!" (Come and eat these very delicious pastries). Shortly he was passing out my cinnamon rolls to everyone. Alas, I didn't even get a single bite of them.

I expected the inevitable search of the car trunk to come next, but to my amazement the military police signaled the guard at the gate to open the gate, and he waved me to drive through, and I very quickly did so and was on my way. I thanked God for once more working a miracle on my behalf, enabling me to bring one thousand copies of *Steps to Christ* to help spread the Gospel of Christ to a Muslim country that was, at that time, 98% Muslim.

Bibles to Bulgaria

A Muslim lady who lived in Bakirkoy (Copper Village) on the western outskirts of Istanbul, went on vacation to Varna, Bulgaria, on the Black Sea riviera.

Every morning she ate breakfast at an outdoor sidewalk café. Every morning the same waiter served her breakfast. For several mornings the lady thought, "This man looks very familiar to me." Finally, it dawned on her as to what was familiar about him, and the next morning she exclaimed, "Sir, you look enough like my next-door-neighbor to be his brother."

To this the waiter replied, "Madam, I am an Armenian, born half a century ago in eastern Turkey. During the genocide my parents and my siblings were tied hand and foot in our house then the Turks burned it down with them in it; I alone survived."

To this the lady replied, "But you still look like you could be my neighbor's brother."

"What is your neighbor's name?" asked the waiter.

"His name is Levon Benzatyan," said the lady.

At this the waiter exclaimed, "My older brother's name was Levon Benzatyan! But it is impossible that your neighbor is my brother, because I am the only one of my family to survive."

When the lady returned to her home in Bakirkoy, she did not immediately go into her own home, but immediately went to her neighbor Levon's house, and without knocking went right in to declare him, "Levon there is a man in Varna, Bulgaria, who looks enough like you to be your brother."

At that, Levon, who was sitting in a chair, reading the daily newspaper, looked up and said, "That is impossible, because fifty years ago when Muslim Turks were annihilating Armenians, all my family was killed; I alone survived."

Replied the lady, "Levon, I am certain that man in Varna is your brother."

"What is the man's name?" asked Levon, to which his neighbor lady replied, "His name is Vahan Benzatyan." At this Levon clapped his hand to his forehead and exclaimed, "My younger brother's name was Vahan, but he cannot be alive; I was the only one of my family to have survived the massacre."

"That is impossible, because fifty years ago when Muslim Turks were annihilating Armenians, all my family was killed; I alone survived."

Levon and Vahan then exchanged letters, and to their mutual amazement, they discovered they were indeed brothers, each thinking to other had been deceased for fifty years.

They wanted to meet each other, but Vahan, living in Bulgaria, the most Stalinist of the Iron-curtain countries, outside of Russia, could not obtain a passport to travel to Turkey. Levon passed away before he could arrange travel to Bulgaria. Levon and Vahan never had opportunity to meet, after all those years, but Levon, in Turkey, had a son by name of Manuk and Vahan had a son in Varna. When Manuk learned he had a cousin in Varna, he declared to his wife Anahid, "I have a cousin in Varna and I am going to visit him," and he arranged to fly early one week to Varna where his cousin met him at the airport and took him to his home.

As they became acquainted with each other, Manuk asked his cousin, "What is your occupation?" to which cousin responded, "I am the provincial chief of the Bulgarian Communist Government." Manuk was astounded by that information. Then his cousin asked, "And what is your occupation?" Manuk replied, "I am a Seventh-day Adventist pastor, and I believe there are some of our churches in Bulgaria." At this his cousin's face showed disgust as he retorted, "You mean there were some Seventh-day Adventist churches in my country, but the Bulgarian Government has closed them all down."

Then came Thursday morning during Manuk's visit, and as his cousin prepared to go to his office, Manuk made an appeal, "My cousin, I believe we still have churches meeting in Bulgaria, and I believe you can find them for me." That evening at supper his cousin was initially silent, but he finally looked frankly at Manuk then in astonishment declared, "Manuk, I believed my government had succeeded in closing all the Adventist churches in Bulgaria, but my investigation today revealed there are at least three of your congregations meeting secretly, in homes."

"Wonderful," responded Manuk, "and you can make it possible for me to preach to our Varna Church this Sabbath!"

And that Sabbath Manuk preached to the handful of SDA members in Varna (there were 232 members there in 2020). At the end of his sermon, he asked the congregation, "Is there anything

I can do for you?" to which the persons assembled, knowing that the Bulgarian government likely had a spy in their midst, quickly replied, "No, no, our government supplies everything we need, so we need nothing from you."

After shaking hands with the people as they filed out of their meeting place, Manuk began walking to his cousin's home. As he walked, an old man, who had been in the church service, caught up with him, and after looking carefully around to be certain no one was nearby, said to Manuk, "My brother, you asked if there is anything you can do for, and yes, maybe there is. Could you get us a Bible in our Bulgarian language? We do not have even one Bible among us." Manuk assured the old man that he would get Bibles in Bulgarian and visit those faithful SDA members in Varna, again.

Manuk returned to Istanbul where he then contacted the Bible Society in England and ordered not just one Bible in Bulgarian, but a whole large box of Bibles. It was against the law to import Bibles in Turkish into Turkey, but he could import Bibles in other languages. When the Bulgarian Bibles arrived, Manuk said to his wife Anahid, "We are taking these Bibles to Varna," and he quickly booked their airline flight and sent word to his cousin to please meet them at the Varna airport. They packed two suitcases, one with their personal items, and one they filled with Bibles.

When they arrived in Varna and collected their suitcases, the Benzatyans proceeded to the custom inspector, who asked, "Do you have anything in your suitcases that you should declare?" It was illegal by Bulgarian law to bring Bibles in Bulgarian into the country. Manuk and I often traveled to airports that required us to have a custom official to examine our suitcases. The usual question was, "Do you have anything to declare?" to which we would respond, "You are welcome to inspect our luggage." To this response, a customs inspector would often respond by lifting up one end of our suitcase to determine how heavy it was, for they could usually tell by that whether it felt like the usual things a traveler would have, or if there was something in the suitcase that needed to be examined. When Manuk told the inspector, "You are welcome to inspect my luggage," the inspector proceeded to lift up the suitcase full of Bibles. That suitcase felt abnormally heavy to the inspector who suspiciously ordered Manuk, "Open this suitcase!"

That suitcase was locked. Manuk had the key in one of his pockets. Manuk and I had suits sewed for us by one of our Istanbul Church members. We had him construct many pockets in our suit jackets, some of the pockets had pockets within pockets, where we could secrete items. Manuk proceeded to search his several pockets, as though to find the key, as he did so in came his cousin, who quickly assessed the situation that the inspector was ordering Manuk to open that suitcase. Manuk's cousin strode up to the inspector, shook his finger at him, and shouted, "How dare you try to inspect my cousin's luggage. I am responsible for him, and I order you to step away." Manuk's cousin proceeded to pick up that suitcase which was heavy with Bibles. As he carried it to his car, he called Manuk and Anahid to follow him.

The next day Manuk's cousin took those Bulgarian Bibles and gave them to our SDA Church in Varna. When God wants His Scriptures brought into a country, He can work a miracle to make it happen, and He did so when Manuk carried a suitcase of Bibles in the Bulgarian language to Varna!

God Saves the Cairo Seventh-day Adventist Church

The spring of 1964 found Manuk and I traveling in the area of Izmir, the biblical city of Smyrna. With us was Anees Haddad, a departmental director of the Middle East Division of SDA. It was a time of crisis for our SDA Church in Cairo, Egypt. The then-ruler of Egypt, Gamal Abdel Nasser, wanted to beautify an area of Cairo called Ramses Square.

1n 1955 Nasser had an ancient seventy-five-foot-tall statue of Ramses II erected in the square. (It is traditionally believed he was the ruler at the time Moses led Israel out of Egypt, but currently Pharaoh Menkaure is believed to be the Pharaoh of the Exodus. Thutmose I was possibly the ruler when Moses was born, about 1525 BC. It was likely his daughter Hatshepsut who took Moses out of the Nile River). It was in 1964 when Nasser stood in front of that statue of Ramses and declared, "I want to make Ramses Square the most beautiful place in Cairo. We will build new streets on either side of the square, and between them I want a large lawn, with trees, shrubs, and flowers planted." Shortly thereafter any structures within the square were leveled, until only one building was left, the Cairo SDA Church, which was next to be demolished.

So it was that on a weekend in April of '64 the Middle East Division declared a Sabbath of fasting and prayer, appealing to God to save our church in Cairo. Late that Friday, before sunset, Manuk, Anees, and I ate a simple meal and then began our Sabbath of fasting and prayer. I do not believe it was by mere chance that the following Monday Nasser once more stood with his city planners in front of that statue of Ramses and declared, "I have decided to leave the square as it now is and begin planting the gardens." Thus, the Cairo SDA Church was spared and the City of Cairo became gardeners to our church, planting trees, shrubs, and flowers on three sides of our church!

Ramses Square and the Cairo Seventh-day Adventist Church

1966 Furlough and GC Delegate

By spring of 1966, we had completed six years of mission service in Turkey, and the Millers were scheduled to have a whole year of furlough in our homeland.

Both Manuk and I were appointed as delegates to the General Conference session that was held that year in Cobo Hall, in Detroit, Michigan.

One privilege SDA missionaries had was traveling to and fro from their home country and their mission station. We had a choice of whether we wanted our MED to purchase our airline tickets, or we could take the money allowed and plan our own itinerary. We elected to take the amount allowed and plan our own itinerary.

During those years in Istanbul, I often flew via Pan Am, and developed a working friendship with a Turkish lady of Jewish ethnicity, who worked in the Pan Am Istanbul office. She was very helpful in helping me plan our trip back to the U.S. for our year's furlough.

I had always wanted to visit Vienna, Austria, the Scandinavian countries, and England, and the kind Pan Am agent helped me book my needed plane reservations. She advised me to attend a philharmonic concert in Vienna that featured David Oistrakh, the premier Soviet violinist. I had never even heard of him, which surprised the Pan Am lady, but she convinced me to attend his concert; she was even able to procure tickets for me. When we arrived in Vienna, I learned that even a Viennese had difficulty finding tickets for Oistrakh's concert, for seating was limited. Thanks to that wonderful Pan Am lady, the Millers had the privilege of enjoying that concert.

In Vienna was the famous Spanish Riding School for the white Lipizzaner horses, another site I keenly wanted to visit. The school is called "Spanish" because of the Spanish horses, which performed in the early days of the riding school. Today's Lipizzaner stallions are the descendants of this proud Spanish breed, a cross between Spanish, Arabian, and Berber horses. The slogan of the school is, "The old horses train the young riders, and the old riders train the young horses." The program begins with the grand entrance when a ranking officer leads a group of riders and horses into the arena, where they perform, often to the rhythm of music, dances and drills that are fantastic. After seeing the performance, we toured the stable where the horses are kept. Above each stallion's stall is his name and age; I was in my early thirties at the time I visited those horses, and some of them were older than I!

At the Vienna airport, as we were leaving, a tragedy happened. I had purchased a very fine Nikon F camera, with several interchangeable lenses. I had them in a custom-made leather Nikon kit. At the airport I had the camera around my neck and most of the lenses attached to my belt. I set the leather kit down, as we stood in the line to board the airplane, and walked away, forgetting the bag there. I had travel insurance on our luggage, and when I reached the States, I was able to use the insurance to replace the kit and the lenses that were lost.

In Copenhagen we rented a car, which we drove north through northern Denmark and southern Sweden and crossed into Norway. The highlight of this portion of our trip was driving from Oslo to the small village of Ulvik; the last leg of the journey was by a small car ferry, across and beautiful fjord. The water was as calm as glass, except for the wake of the ferry. Ulvik was a very picturesque village. We stayed in a motel right on the fjord where we could we sit on the small balcony and look right into the deep fjord. It was early June, a couple weeks prior to the longest day of the year. I was able to take a picture of the fjord at 11:00 p.m. that night.

Returning to Copenhagen, we flew to London, where we stayed in the home of an SDA couple. Staying there was very economical, costing around $20 for the five of us, including two meals per day. We toured London, saw the crown jewels, walked on a bridge over the Thames, saw Buckingham Palace and the colorful changing of the guard. The regiments stationed at Buckingham Palace and

St. James' Palace are under the direct command of the captain of the Queen's Guard. The guards' uniforms include red tunics and black bearskin hats.

At the air terminal outside London, I made another goof, like unto the one in Vienna with the camera bag. This time I took our passports and air tickets to the check-in desk. While the clerk gave me our boarding passes, I put our passports on the counter, where I forgot them and walked off to board the plane with the family. The airport person collecting boarding passes also wanted to see our passports, and I didn't have them! Fighting down panic, I remembered having them with me at the check-in desk. Leaving the family at the airline boarding gate, I raced back to the desk. Thankfully, the passports were still there!

We were elated to land at Dulles International Airport, Washington, D.C. Flying time from London Heathrow Airport to Dulles was eight hours, with a five-hour time change. We landed about 5:00 p.m., went to our hotel, hoping for a good night's sleep. We were in D.C., but our bodies were still on London time; consequently, the Millers all woke up in the middle of the night, not being able to go back to sleep. That was the first, but not last, time we experienced the phenomenon of jet lag.

The next day, we went to the General Conference Headquarters where Elder Walter Beach had the '64 Belair Chevy we had purchased from him, equipped with seat belts, which were a fairly new accessory in those years. We would later be very thankful for those seat belts.

We drove the 525 miles from D.C. to Detroit in two days, to attend the ten-day GC session in Cobo Hall. It was a thrilling experience, that first of three GC sessions I have attended. Each division of the SDA world fields had a display booth in a large side auditorium. It was interesting to visit each booth, meet fellow SDA workers and members from around the world, and see what they had to display about their division. I took my turns staffing the MED booth. During one of my shifts my great-uncle Winfred Hankins and his daughter Enid visited the MED booth. Uncle

Winfred and his wife Bess (my grandma Bonita's older sister) were among the earliest SDA missionaries to China, going there in 1906. They served in Kulangansu, a city deep in the interior of China, for nineteen years, returning to the States only one time during that time. When they left, they had brought more than 1,000 Chinese into the Seventh-day Adventist Church. It was great to meet Uncle Winfred again; I had last seen him in the early 1940s when he visited my family in Los Angeles.

One of the highlights of a GC session is the "Mission Pageant" when the 1,000 or so delegates parade across the stage, dressed in costumes portraying the dress of the countries in which they serve. The Miller family each had a costume of the traditional Turkish dress. We felt both honored and privileged to represent Turkey, in the mission pageant.

Manuk and Anahid were also delegates from Turkey. Manuk wore a costume representing Ephesus — very colorful. After the pageant, the Benzatyans and Millers went to enjoy a pizza, along with Duane and Annie Barnett, our longtime friends from Michigan. When the waitress served our pizza, Manuk, Duane, and I each wanted to give her a tip for her service and held our money out to her. She was flustered as to which of us she should accept the tip. Duane was closest to her, so she took the tip from him. I had already told Manuk, "You are a guest in our country, and should not be the one to give the tip," but he was determined to be the one who tipped. When the waitress took the tip from Duane, Manuk grabbed both her wrists with one of his hands. The poor waitress was terrified, for Manuk was very tall, with olive-colored skin, looking very menacing in his Ephesian costume. Manuk took

Picture of the '66 GC session in Cobo Hall, Detroit, Michigan

Duane's tip from her and pressed his into her hand. Grasping the money, she speedily fled from our table to the safety of the pizza kitchen.

After the GC session was over, Manuk and Anahid traveled with us across the U.S. The Millers were going to visit our parents in Oregon, and the Benzatyans were going to Loma Linda to visit some friends from the Middle East. Manuk was also going to see the best doctors that treated diabetics, at Loma Linda Hospital. He was a very brittle diabetic, and he surely needed to have his condition under better control, as the following incident demonstrates:

We traveled through the northern section of the States, showing Manuk and Anahid as many interesting tourist sites as possible. Driving through South Dakota, visiting Mt. Rushmore, we reached the Badlands, where the road had many curves. Exiting the Badlands and Dakota, we reached a straight stretch of highway leading to Newcastle, Wyoming. I was driving; Manuk sat in the front passenger seat. He was experiencing motion-sickness from the curves, and his blood sugar was very low; sensing this, Anahid began shoving a Snickers bar into his mouth. She was shoving too fast, and Manuk sensed he was choking on the candy. He was disoriented, choking, and decided he needed to get out of the car, so he opened the door to get out. Fortunately, his seat belt was still fastened, but he slumped over, with his head hanging dangerously out the door. Having just passed through all those curves, I was now accelerating to the speed limit of sixty miles per hour; I steered with my left hand and grabbed Manuk by his belt, with my right hand. Fortunately, I was able to safely bring the car to a stop, where we sat by the side of the road for Manuk to recover.

We wanted to have a meeting with the Choteau Church, to show slide pictures of our mission work in the MED, and to have Manuk and Anahid meet Millie and Max McCann (one of the famous Marlboro Men in cigarette ads).

Our families — Millers and Edwards — had arranged for us to have our first family reunion in six years, at a mountain cabin in the shadow of Mt. St. Helens. The families were to gather there on Friday evening, and we were hard-pressed to arrive there on time; it was dusk when we arrived, and the reunion was a great event. Not having seen each other for six years, we had a lot to talk about, and talked past midnight.

The next day, the group wanted to hear Manuk preach in Turkish, and me translating for him. It was a happy, happy Sabbath day.

Our Furlough Year, 1966–67

Because my planned year at the SDA seminary was cut short by taking the mission appointment to Turkey, I had not finished my graduate degree. I very keenly wanted to complete that degree during my furlough, so we proceeded to Andrews University (AU), arriving there in early September of '66.

We rented a seminary apartment, in the complex of Garland Apartments, within easy walking distance of AU. I enrolled in the School of Theology, and Phyllis in the education school. The girls attended the Ruth Murdoch Elementary School. It was a busy and full school year. Valerie, who was then five years old, became very ill and was hospitalized for a few days with an undiagnosed malady. Being so, she was upset being away from our home; Phyllis and I alternated visiting her in hospital, whenever our school classes, and caring for Melody and Cindy would permit. During our year at Andrews, the Millers often visited the Earl and Iva Hutchinson family, and the Duane and Annie Barnett family. Earl and Iva were youth leaders in the Junction City and Sutherlin, Oregon, churches, when I was young. They organized skiing, coastal, and other trips for those churches. Annie was the younger sister of Iva's, and while at Andrews we often fellowshipped with Annie and Duane, who lived near AU.

Because most of our furlough year was spent at AU, our families in Oregon wanted us to spend Christmas with them, so they supplied us with round-trip train tickets from Chicago to Portland. It was an adventure for us, because our girls had never ridden on a train; it was parts of three days, and two nights on the train. The main thing I remember of that train trip was that the train stopped at Dickinson, North Dakota, about 4:00 a.m. Two old geezers got on board and took seats in our train car. They were loud and boisterous, disturbing the sleep of everyone in that train car!

As the year progressed, I experienced growing concern about the GC fulfilling a commitment made to me: that during our year's furlough, another mission family, with school-aged children, would be recruited to service in Turkey with us, and we could have a small church school for our children.

I believed God still wanted me to be a missionary, and my hearts' desire was to return to the Middle East and continue my work there, carrying on the tradition of my family mission service starting with my Uncle Clarence and Aunt Kate being the first Seventh-day Adventist missionaries to Portugal in 1904. I continued to pray God would make it happen that I could continue in mission service.

CHAPTER XII

My Mission Work in the Middle East Division

1967 – 70

In November of 1965 I attended the Middle East Division Executive Committee meetings. In harmony with policy, I applied for a year's furlough in the States, indicating I was willing to return for a second mission term in Turkey after furlough was over, with the condition that another family with elementary school-age children would be recruited too so that we could have a church school for our children. Elder Wilcox was resistant to my request, but GC President Reuben Fighur said to the MED committee and Wilcox, "Grant brother Miller his request."

During my year of furlough, the Millers were at Andrews University while I studied for my first master's degree in systematic theology and pastoral counseling. By January '67, no family had, as yet, been recruited. Victor Fullerton, who had been history teacher at Laurelwood Academy, was now principal of Auburn Academy in Washington. We met when he came to AU, searching for someone to teach Bible at Auburn, and he invited me to take that position, however, I was still technically attached to the MED, and would have to be officially released from there, before I could accept Fullerton's offer.

At the GC session of '66, Elder Ted Webster had been elected President of MED and I had met him at that GC and found him to be a very godly and good minister and administrator. In January '67, I wrote him a letter, asking to be released by the MED, so that I could accept the position at Auburn Academy, stating I had to know by February 15. I didn't receive an answer by February 15, and reluctantly lost my opportunity to teach at Auburn.

My credo, through many years, has been to pray God will open the one door He wants me to pass through, and slam all the others shut!

On Thursday, February 16, I came home from my seminary classes and checked the mail. Thursday was the day of the week I received the weekly edition of the *Review & Herald* (R&H)—the weekly SDA periodical. Normally the first thing I would read would be the back-page cover of the *Review*, for it had the latest news of important events, death notices of important Seventh-day Adventists, and appointees to new or higher levels of leadership positions. I relegated the *Review* to be read secondly, for I spotted an airmail letter from Elder Ted Webster, MED President, postmarked "Beirut." I immediately opened the letter, which began, "By now you probably have been notified of your appointment to a new position. I want to congratulate you, and look forward to working with you."

I was mystified! I had no idea to what I had been appointed, for his letter didn't say!

Then, I glanced at the back cover of the *Review and Herald*, and there, in bold-faced type I read, "Miller Appointed Ministerial Director of Middle East Division." I was flabbergasted, to say the least! I was also very thrilled to be appointed to that new position. I would also be Sabbath School director for the MED.

Here is a copy of that *Review and Herald* back-page article:

The Millers immediately commenced to make plans to relocate at the MED headquarters in Beirut, Lebanon.

During that year at AU, I requested the GC to introduce to the committee that appointed missionaries a young family that I recommended to take our place in Turkey. The family was approved by the committee, but the young man was unable to satisfactorily pass a physical examination. I also met with GC president Robert Pierson, and vice-president Theodore Carcich, who were slated to visit the Middle Eastern Division Fall Council in November of 1967. Prior to the council meetings, as ministerial director, I was

News of Note

No Damage to Adventists Reported From Bogotá Quake

Gift Bible Program Spreads; One Conference Nears 2,500

Health Foods Witness in Australia and New Zealand

Miller Becomes Departmental Secretary in Middle East

L. C. Miller, president of the Turkey Section, has been elected ministerial and radio-TV secretary of the Middle East Division. Roger Coon, who was appointed to these departments and the educational department at Beirut, has resigned for health reasons.

At the same time Manuk Nasarian has become lay activities secretary, and D. L. Chappell has been given the leadership of the Sabbath school department in addition to his primary responsibilities as publishing secretary. The educational work will be under the supervision of R. L. Jacobs, division treasurer.

D. W. Hunter

Japan Union Gives Thanks as 426 Are Baptized in 1966

Book and Bible House Sets Record in Sales to SDA's

Pierson Has Audience With President of Finland

By T. A. LUUKKANEN
Departmental Secretary, Finland Union Conference

24 REVIEW AND HERALD, February 23, 1967

to conduct a Ministerial Institute for the many ministers who would be attending, so I requested Pierson and Carcich to be our primary speakers at the institute. Both men received me warmly, and it was a privilege to make plans with them. I had met Carcich many years before, when he was president of the Washington Conference in the North Pacific Union, and I was a pastor in Montana.

"Miller Appointed Ministerial Director of Middle East Division."

While at Andrews University, I completed the academic requirements for my first post-graduate degree, a master's degree in systematic theology and pastoral counseling. As graduation time drew on, there were ominous signs of renewed conflict in the Middle East.

Relations between Israel and its neighbors had never fully normalized following the 1948 Arab–Israeli War. In 1956 Israel invaded the Egyptian Sinai, with one of its objectives being the reopening of the Straits of Tiran which Egypt had blocked to Israeli shipping since 1950. Israel was subsequently forced to withdraw but won a guarantee that the Straits of Tiran would remain open. While the United Nations Emergency Force was deployed along the border, there was no demilitarization agreement.

In the period leading up to June 1967, tensions became dangerously heightened. Israel reiterated its post-1956 position that the closure of the straits of Tiran to its shipping would be a casus belli (an act used to justify war). In May Egyptian President Gamal Abdel Nasser announced that the straits would be closed to Israeli vessels and then mobilized Egyptian forces along its border with Israel. On June 5 Israel launched what it claimed were a series of preemptive airstrikes against Egyptian airfields.

The Egyptians were caught by surprise, and nearly the entire Egyptian air force was destroyed with few Israeli losses, giving the Israelis air supremacy. After some initial resistance, Egyptian leader Gamal Abdel Nasser ordered the evacuation of the Sinai. Nasser induced Syria and Jordan to begin attacks on Israel by using the initially confused situation to claim that Egypt had repelled the Israeli air strike. Israeli counterattacks resulted in the seizure of East Jerusalem as well as the West Bank from the Jordanians, while Israel's retaliation against Syria resulted in its occupation of the Golan Heights. On June 11, a ceasefire was signed. Israel's international standing greatly improved in the years after, for their victory humiliated Egypt.

Elder Carcich was one of the graduation speakers at AU. As faculty and graduates, in academic regalia, gathered to line up for the processional, I had opportunity to talk with Carcich about the potential Arab-Israeli conflict. I asked him, "Do you think all this 'saber-rattling' will torpedo our plans for meetings in Beirut?"

"I really don't know," he replied, "but we should both continue with our plans, amidst the uncertainty." Thus the Millers proceeded with our travel plans.

As our furlough time was ending, we prepared to drive to Washington, D.C., where we would depart from Dulles International Airport. Our plan was to fly to London, and from there to Hamburg, Germany, where we would take possession of a Volkswagen, which we would drive the approximate three-thousand miles to Beirut.

John and Viola Edwards, Phyllis' parents, journeyed by train to Chicago, and then journeyed on with us in our Chevrolet. Leaving AU, we drove into Canada and then eastward to Niagara Falls, then headed south towards D.C. We stopped at Gettysburg to visit the famous battle site of the U.S. Civil War and stayed a night in a motel, intending to leisurely drive on to D.C., however, we awoke early the morning of June 5, to hear on the TV news that the Arab-Israeli War had broken out. We immediately headed to GC Headquarters in D.C.

Upon arriving there, I proceeded to the GC to consult with SDA leaders about the Middle East situation, and how it would affect our travel plans. The men I consulted with informed me that due to the war, our overseas mission personnel in Beirut, Egypt, Jordan, and Iraq had been evacuated. They went over the list of missionaries in the war area, to identify where each one was. There were several which they could not locate. I went over the list with them, informing them which might still be on furlough, and finally we had accounted for each person.

I later learned that Dick Wilmot, MED assistant treasurer, anticipated the possible evacuation of overseas mission personnel, so he went to the Bank of Beirut where he withdrew funds which he issued to each family so that they would have sufficient money for any contingency. That was a very wise action on his part, and very appreciated by the families who received the emergency funds.

We were scheduled to fly from Dulles Airport to London Heathrow Airport, via Pan Am, early evening of Sunday, June 11.

A GC van provided transportation for the Millers and Edwards to the airport. We checked in at the Pan Am counter, checked our suitcases, which were overweight, so I paid a fifty-dollar fee and our luggage was sent out to the plane, which we could see on the runway. Our group sat waiting for the announcement that it was time to board the plane, when I heard my name announced over the public-address system, "Will Curtis Miller please come to the Pan Am desk."

They went over the list of missionaries in the war area, to identify where each one was. There were several which they could not locate.

I proceeded to the desk, where I took a phone call from GC under-treasurer, Bryce Pascoe, who was in charge of missionary travels. Pascoe informed me, "Curtis, after you left for the airport, we received a garbled cablegram from the MED leadership, which we thought was instructing us to stop you from departing for the Middle East. Even though we're fairly certain of the message, but because it was garbled, we decided to let you continue on your flight, however, a second cable was received, stating emphatically that with the evacuation from Beirut, they did not want to add you to the list of displaced persons and the additional expense of housing you in a hotel somewhere in Europe."

Pascoe directed us to return to the General Conference apartment reserved for missionaries during their stay in D.C. We returned to that apartment, to endure days and nights of humid D.C. heat. There was no air conditioning in that apartment, so we were thankful for the fans we could direct upon us, especially at night, for it eased our discomfort from the humid heat.

Elder Pascoe issued us meal passes we could use at cafeterias at Washington Sanitarium and Hospital, or at the Review and

Herald cafeteria. It was a boring routine — we would wake up and go to breakfast, fritter away time at the apartment until lunch, then deal with boredom until supper. Fortunately, the Chevrolet, which I had left with our transportation agency to be sold, was still unsold, so we had the use of a car, which we used to site see. We visited the White House, U.S. Capitol, Mt. Vernon, and Arlington Cemetery, where we witnessed the colorful changing of the guard at the Tomb of the Unknown Soldier. We also attended an evening performance of the famed Marine Corps Silent Drill Team at Watergate.

Boredom and more boredom went on for thirty days! One day I went to the office of Walter Beach, asking him if I could be assigned something to do that was productive, and I was thankful when he arranged for me to speak at some local churches and camp meetings, which was a most welcome break from the monotony.

Finally, the MED leaders sent word recommending we proceed to Istanbul, where we could stay inexpensively at the Turkish Mission building with the Benzatyans, until it was safe to proceed to Beirut.

Once more we went to Dulles airport, boarded the Pan Am flight and flew eight hours, overnight, to London. We arrived there 7:00 a.m. Monday morning, to struggle with a five-hour time change. Our flight to Hamburg did not leave until 11:00 a.m. and we were fighting jet lag. I struggled to keep awake, fearing I would not hear the announcement to board our flight. We finally boarded our flight, landed in Hamburg, picked up our VW, and headed to Istanbul, where I hoped to arrive by Friday, July 14.

We planned to travel by way of Munich, where we were to visit Phillip Harris, of our beloved Choteau, Montana, church. Phillip was a youth in the cabin I supervised at the 1956 Montana youth camp at Seely Lake. As we headed south, I grew sleepy, so I turned the driving over to Phyllis, warning her to watch for the sign directing to Munich, at a junction a few miles ahead.

I slept, only to be wakened by Phyllis saying, "I don't understand, the road sign says we are almost to the Swiss border, just a few miles from Basel." I checked the map, to discover that we were many miles south of the junction to Munich. I decided we had lost too much time, and would have to drive through Switzerland to Austria, and then head south. I was not happy, and berated Phyllis until I felt guilty for doing so. To make amends, I purchased an Omega watch for her as we drove through Zurich. We then proceeded to drive through the rest of Switzerland, Austria, Yugoslavia, Bulgaria, and into Turkey.

In Turkey Again

It was late Friday afternoon when we entered Turkey, at the small town of Edirne. We were excited to be back in Turkey, eager to speak Turkish again. After crossing the border, we picked up a Turkish soldier who was hitchhiking, so that we would have someone to talk Turkish with. It was great!

When we first arrived in Hamburg, I sent Manuk a letter, stating, "We will arrive in Istanbul late next Friday." Arriving at the mission, I rang the doorbell, and Manuk peered out the third-story window to see who was ringing the bell, and he was very surprised to see us. This is due to an idiosyncrasy in translating English/Turkish. I used the term next, meaning, literally the very next Friday from the Monday I wrote. Manuk, in translation, determined that next did not mean the following Friday (gelcek Friday), but the Friday a week later (sonraki Friday). Despite the mix up on days, the Benzatyans made us very welcome.

It was a thrill to preach again in the Istanbul Church, the following day. I would have attempted to preach in Turkish, with using a translator, but several visitors were there that Sabbath who spoke only English, so Manuk translated for me.

Another highlight of that day was meeting our German Shepherd Trixie, who I had given to the owner of the Cennet Cay Bachesi (Heavenly Tea Garden) that was located behind the church. Trixie's owner, hearing I was back, brought her to the church. I wondered if she would remember me, but when she saw me, she reared up on her hind legs, put her front paws on my shoulder, and licked my face. It was great to be remembered, and sorrowful that she could not come to live with us again.

The Lebanese border was still closed, so we could not continue our journey. It was time for the annual youth camp at Lake Abant, and it was great to be there for the 1967 camp which Manuk and I again conducted together.

Finally, the borders of Syria and Lebanon opened and we were able to drive to Beirut. It was wonderful to be there.

Arrival in Beirut

Upon arriving at the MED compound, we moved in — I should say, camped — in the vacant house assigned to us. A significant complication set in.

In those years, a mission station was designated "A," meaning household furniture and appliances were supplied, or "B," which mean the missionary was to bring his household goods with him. Beirut had a B rating. Because it would be both costly and difficult to have our household goods shipped from Istanbul to Beirut, the MED purchased our Turkish household for the next missionary to replace me and authorized us to purchase our household furniture in the States and have them shipped to Beirut.

This we did, but the complication was that shortly before our household goods arrived in the Port of Beirut, the Lebanese government changed their import tax on new furniture arriving in Lebanon, by putting a tax of 500% of value on new wooden furniture, which was done to protect the price of wooden furniture made in Lebanon. This meant that, for example, what we purchased in the States for $100 would be charged a $500 import tax. The total import tax Lebanon demanded was way more than the MED was willing to pay. It was decided to appeal the Department of Customs to reduce the amount of the tax.

The appeal process dragged on and on. Our missionary neighbors loaned us various articles of furniture, such as beds, table, chairs, a couch, and we camped for several months, praying that we would get our goods out of customs by Christmas.

The import problem became even more drastic because of an Arab named Nehme, who was employed by the MED to be our government liaison, meaning he would obtain travel visas for us from the various Middle East countries we would travel to, and work in our behalf with other government matters. Nehme was appointed to clear our household goods from Lebanese customs. He requested my passport for him to use on our behalf. Time dragged on, and Nehme seemingly made no progress. On one occasion he came to me to explain that he was appealing to the custom authorities to clear our goods on the basis that my employing organization had purchased our household goods and sent them as a "gift" to me. To do this, he had to make my passport show that I had not been in the States during the past year. My passport was full of visas, along with entry and exit stamps from many countries. I had so many stamps in my passport that periodically a U.S. Consul would have to attach a long fold-out sheet in my passport—in fact, my passport had two of those sheets. At the end of one of them was an entry stamp showing the date we entered the U.S. in the spring of 1966. Nehme cleverly cut off the end of that foldout, which was illegal, for no passport was to be altered by anyone, except by an authorized U.S. Consul.

I was completely disgusted with Nehme, and did not trust him. I went to his office and firmly stated, "Nehme, I want you to give my passport to me, right now. I will take charge of getting my household goods from customs, myself."

Nehme glared at me, then slammed my passport down in front of me, saying, "Here's your passport. If I can't get your goods from customs, no one else can, either."

Taking my passport, I sought the aid of Chaffic Srour, president of our Lebanese Mission. It so happened that Chaffic had a close relative who was connected with the Lebanese government. He was able to release our goods based on the MED writing a "Letter of Guarantee" that if I did not take my household goods with me, when I made my final departure with my family, from Lebanon, the MED would pay $15,000 to Lebanese customs authorities.

This arrangement would prove very beneficial to me, three years later.

Now, finally, the Millers were settled comfortably into our home on the MED compound which was situated a mile up Septia (Seventh-day) Hill. Middle East College (MEC) was still another mile further up the hill. Our home on the MED compound had a sturdy fence around it, topped with barbed wire, and a gate that was manned by a guard 24/7. We felt very safe and secure. There were five houses, two guest apartments, and a large apartment building on the compound, to house MED staff.

The sun appeared to disappear into the sea, and I could tell exactly when sunset was, when the last bit of sun vanished, bringing us another holy, blessed, and happy Sabbath.

Our home up on that hill had a beautiful view, looking west, of the Mediterranean Sea. We thoroughly enjoyed that view. I remember watching the setting sun on Friday evenings. The sun appeared to disappear into the sea, and I could tell exactly when sunset was, when the last bit of sun vanished, bringing us another holy, blessed, and happy Sabbath.

Performing My Duties as Med Ministerial and Sabbath School Director

As ministerial director I was responsible for the training and ordination of MED ministers. I approached this in several ways:

First, I started a quarterly journal, *Ministerial Advance* (MA), patterned after the GC Ministerial Department's *Ministry Magazine*. I solicited articles from key SDA ministers in the MED, and I wrote numerous articles myself. One article, researching how men decided to become ministers, was used by the editors of *Ministry Magazine*.

Second, I held Ministerial Institutes, either MED-wide, in Beirut, or in local missions, located in Turkey, Cyprus, Iran, Iraq, Jordan, Egypt, and Libya.

Third, I arranged for the SDA seminary, at Andrews University in Michigan, to hold a branch training seminar in Beirut. One of the seminary teachers, Arthur White, grandson of Ellen G. White, taught a course that gave MED ministers seminary class credits for the class "Spirit of Prophecy." I particularly wanted Arthur White to teach that class, for I had taken his class at AU, and consider it one of the best classes I have ever taken, both in under-grad and post-grad studies.

Fourth, in cooperation with Salim Japas, MED evangelist, we held an evangelism training class that qualified for SDA seminary credits in Beirut. We brought the youngest ministers from the MED missions to Beirut. Japas was the primary instructor.

Salim Japas was of Syrian heritage but had been born of Syrian parents who had emigrated to Argentina. He became an outstanding SDA evangelist, especially successful with Catholic audiences. He typically began each sermon, targeting Catholics, with these words, "Thou art Peter" (considered by the Catholic Church to be the first Pope) and then he would continue his sermon based on Catholic theology, and then very astutely he would continue teaching what the Bible truly taught about the subject he was preaching.

After taking the evangelism course, either Salim or I would go to the place where each young minister was posted, and conduct a model evangelistic series, assisted by the young pastor, then later each pastor would hold his own evangelistic meetings.

My Evangelistic Crusade in Upper Egypt

The Nile River is one of the world's great waterways, at 4,180 miles it is generally regarded as the longest river in the world and among the most culturally significant natural formations in human history. It is an "international" river as its drainage basin covers eleven countries, namely, Tanzania, Uganda, Rwanda, Burundi, the Democratic Republic of the Congo, Kenya, Ethiopia, Eritrea, South Sudan, Republic of the Sudan, and Egypt. The Nile is the primary water source of Egypt and Sudan. The Nile has been the lifeline of civilization in Egypt since the Stone Age, with most of the population and all of the cities of Egypt resting along those parts of the Nile valley lying north of Aswan.

Egypt is known as "The gift of the Nile," for prior to the construction of the Aswan Dam, during the 1960s, the Nile would annually flood most of Egypt, depositing alluvial rich soil which made it the "Bread Basket" of the ancient Middle East. In biblical times when there was a famine in Canaan, Jacob sent his sons to Egypt to obtain food.

While we Millers were still in Turkey, we visited Egypt. At that time Turkey was considered a "hardship" post, for which reason a MED policy allowed us a vacation-paid trip for rest and relaxation.

We flew to Cairo, then took a train by night to Aswan. The train car we were in was manufactured in Hungary and very comfortable. I wanted to see the area where the dam would be built, that would permanently alter the yearly flooding of the Nile. It was very hot that day, and I was suffering from a large boil on the calf of my left leg. After seeing the sights of that area, in the late afternoon we took a train to Luxor and the Valley of the Kings.

We thought it would be a first-class train such as we had taken to Aswan, but it turned out to be a very poor second-class train. The car we rode in was more like an open cattle car with seats. Our car was right behind the engine, and we were soon covered with coal soot.

We had been drinking only bottled water but had consumed it all. We were thirsty, but I warned the family not to drink from the lone faucet on the train, for it was polluted. I, however, was not concerned for myself, for I already had hepatitis A many years before, and was now immune to Hep A and B, so I took a drink from the faucet, not knowing that Cindy saw me do so. Shortly after I saw her take a drink from that faucet, before I could stop her. Cindy came down with hepatitis after we returned home to Istanbul.

We arrived at Luxor about 10:00 p.m. that night. When we checked into our hotel, I asked the desk clerk if we would have hot showers in our room, and he assured me we would. After settling into our room, I headed for the shower, but the water ran cold. I phoned the desk to enquire why there was no hot water, and the clerk assured me we would shortly have hot water. Finally, about midnight we had hot water. I concluded the clerk had likely turned the water heater on when we checked in, and it took a while to warm up. Once in the shower the water rinsed the soot off me, but it seemed to me the water cascaded off me with a sooty color, for a couple minutes!

Luxor, the ancient Egyptian city of Thebes, has frequently been characterized as the "world's greatest open-air museum," as the ruins of the temple complexes at Karnak and Luxor stand within the modern city. Immediately opposite, across the River Nile, lie the monuments, temples, and tombs of the West Bank Necropolis, which includes the Valley of the Kings and Valley of the Queens.

In modern times the valley has become famous for the discovery of the tomb of Tutankhamun, with its rumors of the Curse of the Pharaohs, and is one of the most famous archaeological sites in the world. We count our visit to the Valley of the Kings as privilege missionaries have.

Luxor has a hot desert climate and has the hottest summer days of any city in Egypt. The climate of Luxor has precipitation levels lower than even most other places in the Sahara, with less than 0.04 inches of average annual precipitation. The desert city is one of the driest ones in the world, and rainfall does not occur every year. When I was holding my evangelistic meetings in upper Egypt, it rained for a very few minutes. Some children were terrified, for they had never seen rain before!

When we returned to Cairo, we visited the several pyramids around Giza. I had long wanted to climb to the top of the Great

Pyramid. I climbed with an SDA minister from Ceylon, who had been a classmate of mine at AU. Melody, then about nine years old, wanted to climb the pyramid with me. She begged and begged, but I feared it would be hazardous for her to do so, for the great building blocks of the pyramid were chest high on me, so I declined letting her climb. (Melody, if you read this, I now regret not letting you climb that great pyramid with me. You were very athletic, and likely could have safely climbed. I ask your forgiveness.)

The view from the top of that 455-foot pyramid is awesome. Egypt is a very flat country in the area of the Nile, and from the top of the pyramid one can see the clear line of demarcation where the land is irrigated by the river, thus very green, and where the desert begins.

View from the top of the Great Pyrmid of Giza

Now, back to the evangelistic series I held in upper Egypt. A young Egyptian minister, Saad Khilla, asked me to hold a series of meetings in Upper Egypt, in Zowak, a mud-brick village with a population of two thousand, south of the medium-sized town of Sohag. Sohag is one of the warmest places in Egypt due to its place in the east side of the Sahara in North Africa. Sohag is ranked the fifth driest place in Egypt and the ninth globally.

On a Friday I arrived in the late afternoon at Asyut, where I was to preach on Sabbath, then proceed to Sohag on Sunday. The pastor of the Asyut SDA Church was Fakry Neguib, to whom I had given the '53 Chevy that the Turkish government refused to let me import into Turkey. Fakry and I had forged a good working relationship.

The Neguib family was very hospitable, and when I had visited their home on previous occasions, Mrs. Neguib prepared meals that were massive, and kept heaping my plate full whenever she saw I was close to cleaning my plate. I arrived at Fakry's home late on a Friday and I just plain did not want to go to bed feeling stuffed, so I told Fakry, "I am tired from the long train ride, and wish to rest, so please tell your wife to not expect me for supper tonight."

Fakry said he would tell her, then he escorted me to the guestroom. Many of our missions and churches in the MED had a parsonage attached to the church, and also a guest room, and through my years in the MED I stayed in many of them.

I stashed my suitcase, then stretched out on the bed for a welcome rest. Later I heard a soft knock on the guestroom door, and not wanting to be disturbed decided to ignore the knock by feigning sleep. Shortly I heard the door open, then the sound of footsteps approaching my bed, followed by the voice of a girl softly calling "Azziz, Azziz." Azziz, in Arabic, literally mean "Holy," which is the term given to pastors — who are supposed to be holy persons.

Right then I knew I must open my eyes, for a "holy" person, a pastor such as I, should not feign sleep to deceive a small girl, or anyone else.

I opened my eyes to see Fakry's youngest daughter. With a shy smile she invited me to share a meal with her family. I did, and Mrs. Neguib filled my plate. I ate, and when I finally went to bed, did I ever feel stuffed!

Arriving on Sunday in Sohag, Saad met me and together we began finalizing our plans for the evangelistic meetings. One of the finest of our Egyptian ministers, Abadir Abdel-Messih, was the district pastor of that area of Egypt. Saad was his ministerial intern.

The mud-brick village where the meetings were to be conducted had no hotel, therefore Saad recommended I stay in a hotel in a small town about midway between Sohag and the mud village. There was only one hotel in that town. There was no heat or air conditioning. I was thankful that the room did have a shower, but it was without warm water. From previous travels in Egypt I knew it was not wise or safe for me to eat in local restaurants in these small towns, for dysentery was all too common and very discomforting result. I came prepared with some small packets of instant soup, oatmeal, puddings, powdered milk, and cans of Loma Linda or Worthington foods, which the Middle East College store stocked. I had a small military mess kit to use, and my cookstove was a small regular gas-burning stove made in Sweden, which was about six inches square and fun to cook on.

I boiled water for drinking, for there was no bottled water available. In the bazaar I searched for soda pop, but only found Coca Cola. I am amazed that Coca Cola has gone from the U.S. to so many countries around the world! I didn't want to drink Coca Cola, but it was a challenge to boil enough water on that small stove. So, I bought a few bottles of the cola, which I was not at all used to drinking. After drinking cola for several days, I found I was not sleeping at night, so I went back to the bazaar with Assad to inquire of the merchant if he could obtain another kind of soda. He said he could obtain orange soda, but only if I would purchase a crate of twenty-four bottles at a time. During the month I was in that village I consumed several crates of orange soda and was thankful I could sleep at night.

Street leading to our village church—sign advertises the evangelistic meetings

I had arrived at the evangelistic site several days before the meetings were to begin, to get the "feel" of the village and the small mud-brick church. It was bazaar and market day, and the center square of the village was crowded with vendors. The square appeared to be the lowest place in the village, with filth from the village flowing into it. On one side of the square I saw a small herd of hogs, which I learned belonged to a Christian resident of the village that was approximately 50/50 Christian and Muslim. Upon learning who owned the hogs, I declared to Saad, "God willing, we will make an SDA out of that man, and rid this village of hogs!"

Our small mud-brick church was down a side passage on the far side of the square. Saad proposed we place a large banner announcing our meetings over the narrow passage, for without any public ways to advertise — for there were no local newspapers, radio, or TV — and that banner and word of mouth would be our only means of advertising. Saad added, "Because you are an American, these meetings will make you a curiosity that will attract some to come just to hear an American preach."

Banner Village Church

Going inside the church, I found there was a wall, higher than a tall person's head, running the length of the church. "The wall partitions the room and men will sit on the right and women the left," explained Saad. While preaching I could see men and women on their respective sides of the partition.

Village ladies who attended meetings had to come heavily veiled

When I first stepped into the church, I noted that there were rough wooden benches on the men's side, but none on the women's. I was, from my western perspective, indignant that the women would be treated as second-class persons in an Adventist church, so I dragged several of the benches to the women's side. But, alas! At the opening meeting the women pushed the benches to the rear of their side and proceeded to sit on the dirt floor. I was learning to not buck some traditions of the eastern culture. As I preached I was a little amused to see mothers nursing their babes in arms. They were so close I could even hear babies smacking their lips as they nursed.

The interior of the church was divided by a wall, with men sitting on one side and women on the other—this is the ladies' side

Saad and I traveled from the hotel to the church by taxi. This was during the 1960s, and the taxi was a Model T Ford which were manufactured from 1909–17. I do not know the year of manufacture of the Model T taxi in upper Egypt, but I was amazed that it was still running. That was the first and last time I have ever ridden in a Model T, but when I was in my teens Dad and I owned a '29 Model A convertible with rumble seat in back.

The village church, at the time I held meetings there, had about thirty-five members. The evening of each meeting, Saad and I would stand at the church entry to welcome the people. I now encountered another local custom, that women would not be seen outside their own home without wearing a scarf that covered their heads and faces. A woman was accompanied by a girl so young she was not required to wear a head-covering. Once inside the women's section of the church, the girl would take the headscarf and run back home with it so another woman could then wear it to the church. I never did learn why there seemed to be a shortage of headscarves in the households.

> *This was during the 1960s, and the taxi was a Model T Ford which were manufactured from 1909–17. I do not know the year of manufacture of the Model T taxi in upper Egypt, but I was amazed that it was still running.*

Opening night of the meetings found the church fairly full, and the second night it was completely full, and I had children sitting on the floor around me as I preached, so I had to be careful to not step on them. The mud church had a very dedicated deacon by name of Showgi, who faithfully came early to each meeting to fill and trim the several lamps that lighted the church for each meeting. I will always remember Showgi as an exemplary deacon.

A few days after the meetings commenced Saad recommended that we pay a "courtesy visit" to the local Coptic priest. Proudly, the Coptic Christians acknowledge and herald John Mark, author of the Gospel of Mark, as their founder and first bishop sometime between A.D. 42 and A.D. 62. The Coptic Church was actually involved in the very first major split in the early Christian Church, well before there was such a thing as "Roman" Catholicism, and it was also well before the East/

West split. The local Coptic priest was a young man who was pleased to receive us, clad in his colorful white and gold robe and mitre on his head. Here is a picture of the priest.

There was a most memorable event that occurred during these evangelistic meetings. I cooked my own food in my hotel room, on that primus stove, but on Sabbath the local church elder felt obliged to invite me to Sabbath dinner. His godly wife cooked a concoction in a pot over a buffalo dung fire. When it was cooked, we sat on the floor of the "front" room of her two-story mud-brick hut. The front room was also the only room on the first floor. During the day it was a multipurpose room, serving as a sitting room, kitchen, and dining room, while at night the family livestock — buffalo, goats, chickens — were quartered in that room, and the family slept in the lone upstairs room.

At the Sabbath dinner we sat on the floor with the pot in the middle. Each person was given a small loaf of bread and we would break off a portion, dip it into the pot and eat it. Not wanting to disrespect the local elder's hospitality, I broke bread, dipped, and ate, to my later regret!

That evening, after I preached, I returned to my hotel, and became very sick with dysentery. I vomited and vomited. The next couple days were a challenge, but I was able to preach each evening, then return to the hotel and strive to get better, but my efforts were in vain, for then diarrhea hit me, and I reeled from a double punch of vomiting and diarrhea. I grew weak and unable to eat for fear of making my condition worse.

Being very concerned for my welfare, Pastor Abadir took me to his own home and gave me his bed, while he and his wife slept with their children. Abadir's bed consisted of a very thin pad over boards, but I was too miserable to care. Across the narrow hall was their bathroom and toilet. I crept to that room, which had a faucet on one side and a hole in the floor for the toilet, on the other side. All night I crawled back and forth from faucet to hole in the floor. That dysentery in Upper Egypt, to this day, is one of the sickest experiences I have ever had. I went through stages;

first I feared I would die, and second, I feared I wouldn't die. I thanked God that by morning I was feeling much better, and that night I preached with renewed vigor.

The following Sabbath the local elder again invited me to Sabbath dinner. Pastor Abadir and his eldest daughter were present for the meal. Not wanting to risk another bout with dysentery, I broke off a bit of bread and pretended to dip it into the common pot. I glanced at Abadir's daughter, to see she was keenly watching me, having figured out what I was doing. I covertly gestured to her to not betray what I was doing, thankful that she understood, for she was very aware of the ordeal I had a few days before, when I was in her home.

On the third Sabbath of the meetings were celebrated the Lord's Supper in the mud church. The local elder and I washed each other's feet. His feet were rough and calloused, for he wore only the simplest of open sandals, and his feet were very dirty, as evidenced by the dirty water in the pan after I washed his feet. I overlooked the dirty water, for my foot-washing experience was very humbling, yet precious, as I contemplated the Last Supper, when Christ washed His disciples' feet.

The grape juice for the Communion service was not from bottled juice, for Saad purchased raisins from the local bazaar, which he soaked in water, which then became our Communion "grape juice."

Toward the end of the evangelistic meetings I made an altar call for those who desired to be baptized on the last Sabbath afternoon. The man who owned the lone herd of pigs in the village had attended the meetings and came forward for baptism, thus fulfilling my vow to rid the village of pigs!

Baptism of one of the men who attended the meetings

There were thirty-five persons to baptize — the largest baptism I have ever conducted, thus doubling the size of the congregation. The mud church even had a baptistery, but it leaked. The water was chest high when I began baptizing, but by the time I immersed the last person, a teenaged boy, the water was so low in the baptistery that he had to lie down for the water to cover him.

Men and boys who were baptized

Ladies who were baptized

After the very last meeting of the series, a Saturday night, I was scheduled to leave by train immediately after preaching. Just before leaving the village, Saad came to me, saying, "The granddaughter of the local elder, a babe in arms, was accidently dropped on her head by her mother, and is unconscious. The elder requests that you anoint the baby in special prayer," which I did. Saad later told me that by the next morning the baby wakened and was normal. The family attributed the healing to the anointing prayer.

The Miller Family Learns to Ski in Lebanon

Coastal Lebanon goes from the whole of the country's sea-level coastline up to the Lebanese mountains that average 2,500 feet elevation. In the wintertime those mountains often are snow-covered to a depth that makes skiing possible.

Downtown Beirut had a shop where snow skies could be rented or purchased. The Miller family decided to tryout skiing, so we rented skies and drove to the nearest ski resort called

Faraya, where there was a rope tow. Further away, to the north, was Les Cedres du Liban, Cedars of Lebanon, where the famous cedar trees have grown for thousands of years. Hiram, king of Tyre, supplied Solomon, king of ancient Israel, with cedar wood used in the construction of the holy temple in Jerusalem. Of the two ski areas, the Cedars of Lebanon site was the best, and the Miller family thoroughly enjoyed learning to ski.

I have a fond memory of skiing the Cedars. Grabbing the rope tow to be pulled to the top of the ski area was challenging for Valerie, the youngest of my daughters, therefore, she usually stood on her skies in front of me, by the rope tow, which I would grasp so that both of us could be pulled to the top of the ski run. On one occasion I had reached the bottom of the run before Valerie and proceeded to grab the rope tow. Valerie, from a distance, saw me being pulled on the tow and was dismayed that I was going up without her. I shouted to her to traverse the ski slope to the rope and be by it when I reached where she was standing. This she did, and when I reached her, I was able to be towed with her up the mountain to the top of the ski slope.

On one occasion, at the Cedars, I took a spill that brought the shin of my right leg down on the sharp edge of my left ski. I sustained a deep cut through my ski-pants and into my shin. I bled profusely, but by putting cold snow on the cut I was able to staunch the flow. I still have the scar on my right shin, more than half a century later.

When the Miller family returned to the States, after ten years serving in the MED, we lived in the Boise, Idaho, area, and had access to the Bogus Basin ski area, which even had night skiing. One evening as we were skiing, I paused by the edge of the ski slope near a place where there was a large rock that skiers like to use as a place to be airborne. Suddenly a skier came flying through the air, aiming right where I was standing. I had no time to dodge, and he struck me with the flats of his skies, knocking me down. From the resulting pain, I feared I might have a broken leg, so I did not get up. Shortly a ski patrol person arrived by my side, prepared to summon a sled to transport me down to the ski lodge, if necessary.

About that time, I spotted Phyllis skiing with a beginner's class ski group. She was in a line of students that were slowly skiing behind the instructor. I told the ski patrol, "There's my wife who is a nurse. I will call her to come over to examine me." I called to Phyllis to come over to where I was, but she, very intent in following her ski instructor, and replied that she could not leave her ski class to come to me right then. When she declined to come, the ski patrolman said, in surprise, "Are you sure she is your wife?"

Through the years I, with various family members, have skied the eastern Oregon Anthony Lakes resort, Mont Hood Meadows, and the Wenatchee, Washington, ski area. While in Wenatchee Phyllis, Valerie, and I took up cross-country skiing, which we greatly enjoyed.

As I reminisce about skiing, I now remember an occasion while I was a Walla Walla College and skiing at a nearby ski area. My skis were ancient, not equipped with ready-release bindings, but with cable bindings that kept my ski boots locked into places. I was skiing down an intermediate level slope when a lady skied across my path. In order to avoid hitting her, I tried to cut sharply to the right, and in so doing found my right ski completely reversed, with my left ski pointing one way, and my right the exact opposite, thus painfully wrenching the ligaments in my right ankle and knee! I did, overtime, recuperate from that injury.

My Experience with the Benghazi SDA Hospital

Before relating my experience at this hospital, I will give you the history of this SDA medical institution.

Muhammad Idris bin Muhammad al-Mahdi as-Senussi, known simply as Idris, was born in the country now known as Libya sometime around 1890 — the precise date of his birth is a matter of dispute. Heir to leadership of a powerful Muslim Sufi order, Idris led a sustained and vigorous campaign to overthrow Italian rule in Libya. Ultimately successful in 1951, he was the primary architect of the termination of four decades of colonization by the European power and that year ascended to the kingship of a newly independent Libya. Idris would prove to be an exceptionally gracious and kind monarch to Seventh-day Adventists.

In February 1955, Dr. Roy S. Cornell, an Adventist physician, arrived in Libya to offer his much-needed skills as chief surgeon at the government hospital in Benghazi, Libya's second largest city after its capitol, Tripoli, a bustling commercial port city on the Northern Coast on the Mediterranean Sea. Prior to Cornell's arrival, the Adventist presence in Libya had been virtually non-existent, with only a few literature evangelists selling Adventist publications in the Italian colony in the late 1920s.

Cornell, however, aimed to establish a Seventh-day Adventist presence in the newly independent nation, endeavoring to accomplish this feat by the time-honored Adventist method of gaining an entrance through health, which was his chosen profession.

So shortly after his arrival Cornell began supervising the remodeling of a war-damaged hotel building in Benghazi with the aim of renovating it for the site of an Adventist hospital. The versatile expatriate physician drew up papers, transacted fiscal deals, forged political connections, purchased equipment, and arranged for a staff, all while serving as surgeon and advisor to the Libyan government on medical matters.

The modest Adventist hospital was formally opened on May 21, 1956, with a patient capacity of approximately twenty-seven. Articles appeared in the *Adventist Review* heralding the missiological wonder with titles like "The Right Arm of the Gospel in Libya." Tragically though, a year later Dr. Cornell contracted acute paralytic poliomyelitis, which left him completely paralyzed and unable to continue directing the project he had pioneered.

The medical facility was operated by the Nile Union Mission, until, at the end of 1958, it came under the direct control of the

Middle East Division (MED). This by itself was a miracle, for even during the reign of Idris, the Libyan government did not permit foreign organizations to hold titles to property. This Seventh-day Adventist hospital was renowned for being the sole exception to this law.

Around this time, Libya was wildly prospering thanks to the discovery of what seemed to be unlimited oil reserves, propelling the North African state from one of the poorest nations in the world to the wealthiest. This oil revolution would be a boon and bane for Adventism — a boon because the oil money largely financed a new hospital plant, and a bane because it was this turn of fortune that would spell Idris' downfall and the end of royal patronage.

By 1963 minor construction at the Adventist hospital provided for an expanded laboratory and kitchen facilities and increased the patient capacity from twenty-seven to thirty-two. However, by late 1961, because of the need for expanded medical services, the MED decided to relocate the hospital to a more advantageous location in the port city.

Providentially, the "Black Prince," a member of the royal family, made available for purchase ten acres of choice property. Community support was enlisted, and oil companies operating in the area contributed $750,000. Construction on the project began in 1964.

In its New Year's edition in 1969, *The Middle East Messenger*, the official magazine of the Middle East Division, proudly reported on the cover, "It's Open."

The brand-new Benghazi Adventist Hospital was a sixty-bed facility, valued at $1.4 million U.S. dollars. On January 17, 1968, it was dedicated, with Adventist dignitaries attending the joyous event, including F.L. Bland, vice president of the General Conference, who was a towering figure in black Adventist history, and MED president, Frederick C. Webster. Webster was the wonderful MED president I served with for the last four years of my service in the Middle East Division.

The human interest behind this landmark episode in the history of Seventh-day Adventism, and specifically African Adventism and Middle East/Arab Adventism, is touching. Benghazi Adventist Hospital's one-hundred-five employees, an expatriate staff, consisting of forty-eight families and single workers hailing from all parts of the globe, were the picture of the Adventist sacrificial mission ethos that marked the 1950s and 60s.

A couple of these pioneers are worth mentioning. Two women from Seoul, Korea, Oh Hey Jah, 26, and Jo Chung Jah, 25, were nursing graduates from what is today Sahmyook University, and were the first Korean Adventists to be assigned to an overseas hospital. Hey Jah specialized in surgical nursing, while Chung Jah was a general duty nurse.

Only months after the grand opening, the hospital was graced by King Idris, who stopped by to check on close relatives being treated there. The ruler could not praise the facility enough. Soon Benghazi Adventist Hospital had the reputation for not only being the best hospital in Libya, but all of North Africa. However, this golden opportunity to plant Adventism in a strategic locale would be tragically interrupted by political upheavals.

King Idris, so accommodating to Seventh-day Adventists, was falling in general popularity in Libya. Because it was believed that he was shamelessly hording the dizzying profits from the oil boom, maintaining friendly relations with the United States and England, being lax in enforcing Islamic laws, and not propounding the Arab nationalism popular during the era, he was castigated by the growing anti-West, radical Islamic factions in the region, most loudly by a charismatic twenty-seven-year-old soldier named Muammar Gaddafi.

Political unrest percolated in Libya, birthing the so-called "Libyan Revolution" on September 1, 1969, in which the strongman Gaddafi staged a successful and bloodless coup, grasping leadership of the nation easily from the hands of Idris, who at the time was away in Turkey for medical treatment.

Gaddafi, notorious for bursting into discotheques and nightclubs with machine guns, scattering the revelers and closing the venue, saw fit to quench the light that was Benghazi Adventist Hospital. On November 23, 1969, the new Revolutionary Command Council, whose policy required that all medical services be owned and administered by the government, nationalized the Benghazi Adventist Hospital.

The *Adventist Review* of January 15, 1970, disconsolately reported that the staff of Benghazi Hospital would be assigned to other posts in the Middle East Division, and Gaddafi, who vowed to remunerate Adventists for the seized hospital, would negotiate with SDA administrators for a fair price. In 1977 the General Conference of Seventh-day Adventists received a settlement from the Libyan government for $1,290,963, for the Benghazi Hospital.

With the nationalization of the hospital and the departure of the medical missionaries, the short-lived Adventist presence in Libya departed. At present, more than five decades later, there is not a Seventh-day Adventist church in Libya, or a known Seventh-day Adventist.

Prior to my visit to Benghazi, a small group of hospital staff were uncrating the household goods of a newly arrived medical staff family. Nearby they kindled a fire to burn the packing crates, not knowing that right under that burn site was an unexploded WWII bomb. The heat of the fire ignited that bomb, causing the group to back away from the blast. The twelve-year-old daughter of a staff medical doctor sank to the ground. Two hospital staff nurses were present, rushed to the girl, who was unconscious, and examined her, but found no evidence of a wound. They rushed the girl to the emergency room in the Benghazi Hospital. The doctor on duty, Dr. Fahrbak, the girl's own father, was challenged to examine his own daughter. He found only a small nick in her chest and decided to have his daughter X-rayed. The X-ray showed a piece of metal, about the size of a nickel coin, in the tissue between two chambers of her heart. The doctor-father did not believe he, or any other staff doctors, were capable to do open-heart surgery, so it was arranged for the girl to be air-lifted to Loma Linda Hospital in California, where the highly competent heart-team repaired the wound, but decided it was too risky to remove the small piece of shrapnel which is still in that girl's heart to this day! I wonder if that piece of metal sets of metal detectors should she seek to board a plane?

The spring of '68 I was invited to hold a Week of Spiritual Emphasis, aka "Week of Prayer," at our Benghazi Hospital. These meetings were scheduled to begin on a Friday night. The day prior, Thursday, Dr. Clifford Ludington, a distant cousin of mine who was chief-of-staff of the hospital, agreed to perform a minor surgery to remove a large polyp deep in my nose. He initially wanted to do the surgery using a local anesthetic, but I told him, "You can amputate my arm or leg using a local, but when you operate on my head, I want to be completely sedated." Therefore, a nurse-anesthetist, Rae Anna Brown, of Oregon, administered the anesthetic, and I went to sleep about noon on that Thursday. The surgery was considered "minor," and I was expected to wake up shortly after the Ludington's surgery, but that was not to be!

As Clifford later related to me, when he used a wire snare to remove the polyp, I began to hemorrhage profusely, and the surgical team were challenged to control the hemorrhage. At one-point Clifford thought they might have to contact a nearby U.S. airbase at Tripoli to request blood to transfuse me. Finally, they were able to control the hemorrhage, then Clifford proceeded to pack my nose with gauze to absorb any subsequent flow of blood.

The surgery was considered "minor," and I was expected to wake up shortly after the Ludington's surgery, but that was not to be!

Clifford decided to keep me sedated for a few

more hours. The hospital beds were all full, so I was placed on stretcher in the room where they kept patients in isolation so they would not contaminate anyone. Clifford, still concerned for my well-being, slept through the night on a stretcher near me. The next morning, when I wakened, he explained to me about my hemorrhage, then he proceeded to remove the gauze. I was amazed! He pulled and pulled gauze until I began to think he must have packed my whole cranium full of gauze.

Clifford departed from the isolation room, then directed a nurse to give me an intravenous injection. Into the room came Oh Hey Jah, one of the two nurses who were the first Koreans to go from Korea into mission service. Oh Hey Jah, who was a very diminutive young lady, found it challenging to give me that intravenous injection, for the stretcher was only about four inches tall, causing her to squat down, place my arm across her knees, and then try to inject me. Poor Oh Hey Jah found it a very uncomfortable position for her. To complicate her effort, my vein kept rolling from side to side. She tried several times to pin it down, then fearing she was hurting me, she began to weep. Thank God, she was persistent, and finally succeeded in injecting me in the vein.

I will always remember Oh Hey Jah!

Unfortunately, my nasal surgery and its complications resulted in my not conducting that Week of Prayer for the Benghazi Hospital, and it was rescheduled for the late summer of 1969. Prior to heading via airplane to Benghazi for that rescheduled Week of Prayer, I traveled to Cyprus to hold weekend services, August 29–30, and was then to fly to Benghazi via Cairo, Egypt. I reached Cairo on schedule, then sat in the passenger area for my connecting flight to Benghazi. I sat and sat, and finally the scheduled flight time came, but the call to board the flight was not made. I went to the ticket counter to enquire about the delay but found no agent at the counter. Finally, over the loudspeaker came the announcement, "The flight to Benghazi has been cancelled due to a coup that has just taken place in Libya."

Muammar Gaddafi had overthrown kind Idris. To my sorrow, I never did travel to Benghazi again or hold that Week of Prayer.

On November 23, 1969, the new Revolutionary Command Council, whose policy required that all medical services be owned and administered by the government, nationalized the Benghazi Adventist Hospital. That evening an army officer under Gaddafi came with a group of soldiers to our hospital grounds. A hospital staff member was walking on the hospital grounds about that time. The officer had him seized, then demanded, "Take me to your arsenal." The officer and troops had come to take over the hospital and was under the opinion that the hospital likely had a stash of arms somewhere around the hospital. I do not remember the name of that hospital staff, but I later learned that the man endeavored to tell the officer that the hospital had no arsenal. The officer persisted in ordering the man to take him to the arsenal. Finally, the staff person took the officer and his troops into the hospital, down a hallway, and into the hospital library. Taking a Bible off the desk, he handed it to the officer, saying, "This is the only weapon we have in this hospital." The officer was finally convinced our hospital's only weapon was the Bible.

Gaddafi took possession of our hospital but did not immediately have anyone to staff the hospital so he had our hospital workers charged with continuing to supply staffing. Months later Gaddafi succeeded in bringing in staff from Pakistan, and our staff was evacuated to Cyprus. I was holding meetings in Cyprus when they arrived. One of our nurses told me that as the Pakistani nurses took over, she watched a Pakistani nurse picking lice out of another nurse's hair! So much for competent staff taking over our Benghazi Hospital!

My Experience Near the Sea of Galilee

As Sabbath School (SS) Director of the MED I held workshops to train local church members to conduct worthwhile SS programs for children. On one occasion I was holding such a training session in our SDA Jordan Mission, where Bill Clemons was mission president.

One day Bill asked me to travel with him around Jordan, to pay the monthly salaries to our SDA pastors. On that day we traveled towards Irbid, a small city in northern Jordan, near the Sea of Galilee. This was during the time after the June '67 Arab-Israeli War, and tension between Israel and the Arab countries was still very high. As we neared Irbid we were stopped by a blockade manned by Jordanian troops and the ranking officer came to our car, informing us, "The Israelis are strafing Irbid right now. You cannot proceed to Irbid until the attack is over."

We waited about half an hour until the Israeli planes left the area, then proceeded into Irbid. We arrived at our church just as the local pastor and his family exited the shelter they used for safety during the Israeli gunfire. We noted a shell hole in the side of the church and when we went inside the sanctuary we found a 50 mm shell that had penetrated the wall, went through the sanctuary where it struck the opposite wall, and fell to the church floor. That was one of the closest times I came to being under fire while in the MED.

Lyle and Cora Lynn Miller Visit the MED

Early in 1969 my parents truly surprised me, announcing they wanted to fly to Beirut to visit us. They began making travel arrangements, and I offered tips on travel that I had learned through my years of ministerial work. They planned their trip with a travel agent, but when I learned what that agent had arranged for airline tickets, I told Mom and Dad, "I can get you a much better rate on Pan Am from the travel agent the MED uses in Beirut." Using that agent, I was able to save them several hundred dollars. This was to be my dad's first experience flying in a plane, and he was apprehensive, saying, "I feel much safer on the ground," nonetheless he wanted to please Mom by taking the trip. When they arrived back home in Junction City, friends asked him how he liked flying. Like a very experienced traveler, which he was not, Dad told his friends, "Flying? It's the only way to travel if you are going a long distance." Mom and Dad traveled by air several times after that.

I had planned for my folks to fly via Istanbul, where I would be holding the annual youth camp at Lake Abant, but for some reason Mom had made Pan Am reservations for a few days earlier, and she was loath to change them; consequently, they arrived in Beirut a few days before camp was over.

Mom and Dad thoroughly enjoyed their visit to the Middle East. Dad Miller had always been a very social person, making friends very easily. Dad would go to the gate of our division compound to sit and chat with the gatekeepers. I was puzzled by his visits with the gatemen, for they spoke hardly any English, and Dad knew no Arabic. One of the men also spoke Turkish, but Dad knew no Turkish, so I wondered how they were able to communicate, but communicate they did. Dad would come back to our house telling about all kinds of things he and the gatekeepers talked about. I never did really figure out how they communicated across the language barriers, but they somehow managed!

My parents enjoyed attending church at Middle East College, and at some of the other SDA churches in Lebanon where I would preach. We took them to visit the Cedars of Lebanon and the Bekah Valley on the other side of the Lebanese mountains. They wanted to visit Turkey, but at that time the Syrian border was closed due to a recent attempted coup. Finally the Syrian borders were open, so we hurriedly put our baggage in our VW, which was crowded with luggage and seven passengers, but we all squeezed in and headed for Turkey. The folks were thrilled to see ancient Antioch, where early followers of Christ were first called "Christians," Ankara with Ataturk's mausoleum, Lake Abant where we held youth camp, and other places in between.

They were especially pleased to visit the Istanbul SDA Church, where I preached in Turkish on Sabbath, and Manuk translated into English so my folks could understand.

Mom wanted to buy a Turkish carpet, so Manuk and I took the folks to the "Buyuk Bazaar" (Grand Bazaar) which is probably the ancient equivalent of a modern shopping mall. The saying was, "You can enter one gate of the bazaar and leave through another, along with several suits of clothes and furniture for your whole house!" We took Mom to several carpet dealers, and when she indicated a carpet she wanted, we would leave that shop, then Manuk would later return alone to bargain for the price of the carpet because merchants would always sell at a lower price to a local Turk than to a foreigner, and especially to an American — merchants surely thought all Americans were rich!

The high point of the trip to Turkey, for my parents, was visiting the seven churches. Guiding them, at that time, was my last tour of the seven churches — a tour I have made many times. Yes, I still miss Istanbul and I miss Beirut. It has been over sixty years ago, now.

My Happy Experiences in Iran

I traveled to Iran several times during my years in the MED, before the Shah was overthrown. Usually, I flew there via Pan Am, with the flight arriving in Tehran late at night which meant that by the time I would go through passport control and customs it would be after midnight before I collapsed in a hotel bed. Flying into Tehran was a pleasant experience, for the usual landing took the plane over the city with the beautiful view of the lights of the city.

On one flight to Tehran, I left my seat to go to the restroom. While I was in there the plane hit bumpy air and the pilot announced passengers should fasten their seat belts. I exited the restroom, expecting to return to my seat and buckle down. About then the plane hit very rough air, causing the plane to rapidly loose about 500 feet altitude. I lurched against the cabin wall, right by a stewardess who was strapped in her seat. She immediately grabbed me, plunking me down on her lap to hold me safe.

When I exited the plane in the Tehran airport I was surprised by her asking me if I had a ride from the airport into the city, and if I didn't she invited me to share a cab and a hotel room with her. Imagine that — being propositioned by an attractive Pan Am stewardess! Needless to say, I was thankful our Iran Mission president, Harold Gray, was at the airport to meet me.

Evangelistic Meetings for Muslims in Tehran

In the Beirut MED headquarters building, where I served as ministerial director, my office was on the first floor at the right end of the main hallway. To the left of my office was that of the MED medical director, Hershel Lamp, MD. Herschel and I became good friends and colleagues.

One day I read in the Ellen White book *Evangelism* that ministers and doctors should become a team to do evangelism. As I thought and prayed about this, I was impressed to approach Herschel to form a team together to hold a series of evangelistic meetings for Muslims in Tehran. He agreed to this plan and the spring of 1968 we held meetings in the auditorium of our Iran Mission headquarters.

The format for the meetings was for us to dialog together, with each of us having our own translator. Mohammed Morovati, a Muslim who had converted to become an SDA, served as translator for Herschel, while John Minassian translated for me.

Morovati, Herschel, me, and John, taken during the evangelistic meetings

We were very thankful that our advertising for these meetings was very successful, for the auditorium was filled with Muslims the opening night of our meetings, and attendance continued that way for many evenings.

Our initial meetings were health-oriented, then we slowly introduced Christianity-oriented topics. As we did this, we wondered if the attendance would continue, and for the next several evenings those Muslims listened carefully to what we had to say. Herschel and I both knew that the critical topic would center on the divinity of Christ.

Muslims and Jews are monotheistic, as are most Christian denominations, including SDAs. However, Muslims challenge Christians on this, citing that Christians worship Allah (God) but then they also worship Jesus, saying He is the Son of God, so Muslims will say, "If Jesus has a Father, then who is His mother? If Mary is His Mother, then she must be a god also."

Muslims heed a call to prayer, the "Adhan," which is called out by a muezzin from the minaret of the mosque five times a day, summoning Muslims for mandatory worship (salat). A second call, known as iqama (set up), then summons Muslims to line up for the beginning of the prayers. The words to the Adhan are as follows: Allahu Akbar, Allahu Akbar. Allah is the Greatest, Allah is the Greatest. Allahu Akbar, Allahu Akbar. Allah is the Greatest, Allah is the Greatest. Ash-hadu alla ilaha illa-llah. By this they mean that Allah—God—is greater than any other god.

As Herschel and I talked over how to present to our Muslim audience the Godhead as monotheistic, with God the Father, Jesus as the Son of God, and the Holy Spirit as a part of the Godhead, we wondered how we could explain the concept of God the Father and Jesus the Son of God. Herschel and I had a very strong difference of opinion. Herschel wanted to use the Biblical concept that when a man and a woman unite in marriage, they become one, as cited in Genesis 2:24, "Therefore a man shall leave his father and his mother and be joined to his wife, and she shall become one flesh" (NKJV). In the same way, Herschel wanted to maintain that God the Father and Jesus the Son are one.

I disagreed with this approach, but initially could not adequately explain to Herschel the basis of my disagreement. Herschel was determined to present his illustration of a man and wife becoming one, so I said, "Then during that part of our dialogue, I will remain silent and you can present the topic your own way." Thus, we agreed to disagree.

That night, as we presented Christ as the Son of God, when Herschel proceeded with his illustration, I was shocked to see about half of our Muslim audience stand up and leave the meeting. As they did so, it suddenly dawned on me how they would reject the concept "a man shall be joined to his wife, and become one flesh." The founder of the Mohamedanism, Mohamed, maintained a man could have up to four wives, provided he "treated them all equally." As Islam — meaning "surrender" — as his religion is called, grew and spread far beyond Arabia, Islamists took many, many more wives. The founder of Saudi Arabia, Abdulaziz ibn Abdul Rahman ibn Faisal ibn Turki ibn Abdullah ibn Muhammad Al Saud, had as many as twenty-two wives, by a conservative estimate. Many have had as many as forty to sixty wives. From these facts I asked Hershel, "How can a Muslim, with many wives, become 'one flesh' with each of them? He can't I maintain, therefore our audience, when you presented your 'one-flesh' concept, left in protest."

Our meetings continued on to our planned end, but to a much smaller audience. Nonetheless, I still believe those meetings were a success, and those meetings were the first targeting Muslims in the history of SDA mission work in Iran from the time SDAs entered Iran in 1911.

There is a sad footnote to Herschel Lamp. The Lamps left the Middle East a couple years before the Millers did. Herschel took a position with the Arizona Conference of Seventh-day Adventists, and when I returned to the States I became a district pastor in the Idaho Conference, near Boise, Idaho. Because Herschel and I had held both Five-Day Plan to Stop Smoking clinics and evangelistic meetings, I invited him to do the same with me in Nampa, Idaho. Both were a success. After that Herschel took a position with the Adventist St. Helena Hospital, in California. While there he became connected with an apostate movement and left the SDA Church, where he was both a medical doctor and minister. When he apostatized, he declared "That sect" —meaning the SDA

Church — "deceived me for twenty-five years." He later became a pastor of a Pentecostal Sunday-keeping church.

My Unkept Promise

Frank Oster was the first SDA missionary to Iran, arriving in Rezaiyeh (aka Urmia) in 1911. The location was in the northwest corner of Iran, where it joins Turkey, to the west, and the old Russian Azerbaijan province to the north. Rezaiyeh is called the "Paris of Iran." Forty percent of the population were Christian minorities.

Here Pastor Oster began his many years of mission service. The population was 60% Shiite Muslims and 40% Christians, primarily Armenians and Assyrians. "Doubting" Thomas, one of Christ's twelve disciples, first took the Gospel of Christ to these ancient populations. The Armenians were the first nation to become Christian in the Apostolic Age.

In 1914, Oster baptized his first converts to Adventism. Shortly after WWI broke out, he made a preaching tour of the region. Most of the Christians had fled by 1918 as a result of the Persian Campaign during World War I and the Armenian and Assyrian Genocides. During the war, when all Christians had to flee the marauding Kurdish tribesmen, the Osters retired to Tabriz.

An SDA school in Urmia was established there. During my second term in the Middle East Division, I was ministerial director. I trained ministers, and I held evangelistic meetings in several places, such as Istanbul, Beirut, Upper Egypt, and Iran. My good friend, Pastor Harold Gray, directed our mission in Iran, and he invited me to hold a series of evangelistic meetings in Rezaiyeh, which we set the date for the spring of 1970. I flew Pan Am from Beirut to Tehran, arriving there around 10:00 p.m. By the time I collected my suitcase, cleared customs and immigration check, and arrived at a hotel, it would be at least midnight. On this trip I had to rise at 5:00 a.m. to catch a flight to Tabriz. Harold and Kevork Terzibashian, who was to be my translator for the meetings, flew with me.

Kevork was an Armenian, whose ancestors had settled in Palestine. On November 29, 1947, a United Nations decree partitioned Palestine between Arabs and Israel. Kevork's family land was in the Israeli sector, so they were dispossessed of their properties and lived for years in an Arab refugee camp. Kevork was fluent in Arabic, Armenian, English, and Hebrew. When he was sent to Tehran to pastor our Armenian Church there, he became fluent in Farsi — as Persian is now called. As we boarded our flight, Kevork began to complain of pain in his jaws. I glanced at him, saw the typical swelling and declared, "Kevork, you are coming down with mumps." Harold confirmed my diagnosis, counseling, "Kevork, take the most rear seat in the plane. Curtis and I will sit between you and the rest of the passengers, so you will not contaminate them."

What about me, I wondered to myself. I had never had mumps. Would I come down with them, from traveling with Kevork? I did not catch the mumps then, or ever. Amazingly, shortly after we arrived in Tabriz, Kevork's swollen jaws began to recede, and the swelling went down. Because we had no other interpreter, Harold and I decided we would keep Kevork with us.

We arrived in Tabriz, and I was to preach Friday evening and two times on Sabbath, in our church there. Upon arriving at our church, an old, white-haired lady, dressed all in black, the garb widows wore for one year after their husbands were deceased, came running up to me. Sobbing, she threw her arms around me, hugging me tightly. Her tears were those of joy. From previous contacts she knew Harold, and she knew Kevork. Seeing me, she assumed I was the pastor promised for the past ten years to our Tabiz Church. Upon Harold gently telling her I was not to be her longed-for pastor, and that I was only going to preach to them this one weekend, her tears turned to sorrow.

In years past, our Tabriz Church had around fifty members, but with wars, persecutions, and banishments, when I preached that weekend there were only ten members. The elder of the church was Sister Nectar, a tall, slender, and completely blind lady. No male members were left, so of necessity Nectar was the lone elder. She was led everywhere she went by Shushan, the deaconess of the church, who had only one leg and a crutch. Can you picture that, a one-legged lady with a crutch, leading a blind lady all around Tabriz, a city of 200,000, at that time?

Very early Sunday morning, the three of us boarded a village bus—a ramshackle bucket of bolts—traveling between Tabiz and Rezaiyeh. It was common for these village busses to carry all sorts of baggage, including chickens, sheep, and goats.

I remember on one such bus Harold and I traveled in, there was a man who had an ancient metal water container on his back, and he would scurry up and down the narrow aisle offering a drink of water, from a sole metal cup, to thirsty passengers, for the price equivalent of one cent. I finally thirsted enough to ask for a drink from that cup, and the man filled a cup and handed it to me. Before I could drink, an elderly man, in tribal robes, seated across the aisle, addressed me in accented English, "Let me have your cup, a moment, and I will show you something." I handed him the cup. "Do you have a handkerchief?" he queried. I handed him a clean handkerchief, which he folded over the cup, then handed it to me. "Turn it upside down." I was puzzled, thinking the water would gush out of the cup. "Turn it upside down," he urged again. I turned it upside down, and was utterly amazed, for not a drop leaked out of that upside-down cup with the handkerchief over it. "Now, take your hand away from the handkerchief." I did, and again, not a drop of water leaked. "How do you do that?" asked the man. He didn't answer my question, but instead he asked if I had a twenty-five riyal coin — an Iranian silver coin about the size of a quarter. When I produced one and gave it to him, he proceeded to put it in his mouth, then chewed on it vigorously. "Put out your hands," he directed me. I put out my hands and he spit out a double handful of whole twenty-five riyal coins. Utterly amazed — more like completely flabbergasted — I asked, "How did you do that?" His answer: "Don't believe everything you see." And he went silent.

Back to that village bus traveling from Tabriz to Rezaiyeh. The journey was only 150 miles, or around a two-and-a-half-hours journey for a car, but our bus stopped at every single village along the way, to let off passengers and take more on. It was bitter cold that morning. Although we did have heavy jackets to wear, we had nothing on our heads. The bus had a door that did not completely shut, and there were cracks in the floor. Some of the windows were cracked or broken. The bus had no heat. Cold drafts hit our ears, and our heads hurt from the cold. At the first village stop, vendors came aboard the bus, selling nuts, candy, and then there was one who was selling large angora wool caps. We each bought one, pulling that wool right down over our ears. That warm cap felt so good, and it was well worth the two riyals — fifty cents — that I paid for it.

> *Utterly amazed — more like completely flabbergasted — I asked, "How did you do that?" His answer: "Don't believe everything you see." And he went silent.*

It can be cold in mountainous Rezaiyeh in early April and there was snow on the ground when we arrived there. We were thankful for the guest room on the ground floor of our Rezaiyeh Church. The room was large with several smaller than twin-sized beds, with their very thin mattresses on board slats. Each had a warm hand-made quilt, for which we were thankful the two weeks we would be there.

In one corner was a shelf or two, and a small sink beside which was a bucket of water. In the center of the room was an old WWII GI stove, rather like a sheepherder's stove in the "Ol' West of the U.S." We cooked a large pot of vegetable soup on that stove. We lived on that soup while we were there. As I remember, the pot never came close to being empty; we just dumped in more veggies and water.

The evangelistic meetings began, with Kevork translating my English into Farsi. As I remember, the church chapel was two-thirds full the first night or two, but word soon spread that an American was preaching, and in a couple more nights the church was full.

Shaul — Assyrian for Saul — was in attendance from the very beginning of the series. He belonged to the ancient Assyrian Church founded by the apostle Thomas, two-thousand years ago. In his youth he converted to the Seventh-day Adventist faith. A very faithful member was Shaul.

One day, during the meetings, Shaul came to me, speaking Farsi, which Kevork translated for us, for Shaul spoke no English, and I, no Farsi. "Pastor Miller, about forty kilometers (twenty-five miles) is an ancient Assyrian village. There is a church there, that has not been preached in for forty years. They have had no pastor all these years. Would you go there with me? I know you would be welcomed to preach them a sermon."

I was intrigued. I was more than intrigued, I was amazed, even shocked, that for forty years no pastor had preached in that church. I quickly replied, "Shaul, I will gladly go with you to preach in that church."

There was a challenge. I had not the "Gift of Tongues." Kevork would translate my English to Farsi, and Shaul would translate Farsi to ancient Assyrian. Please know that in translation from one language to another, something can be missing in the translation process. And when you have to have two translations, even more loss can occur. That's why Scripture counsels that between speaker and his ultimate audience, there be no more than a two-step translation.

We arrived at the Assyrian village. "Little Mother, I have come to your village to preach about our Lord Jesus in your church," I said to the wizened old lady drawing water from the well in the center of an ancient Assyrian village. When she ran away from me, I wondered if I, a foreigner, had frightened her?

But no, she was not frightened. She was excited. She ran to the church, where she grasped the rope to the church bell. The ringing of the bell brought the whole populace of the village, from their mud homes, from small shops, and from the fields around the village. Shortly the church was filled until there was standing room only. Shaul stood by my right side, Kevork to my left. Shaul spoke a few words in ancient Assyrian to introduce me to the so-quickly-assembled congregation. I spoke on one of my favorite Biblical subjects, the second coming of Christ. No one stirred, as the Assyrians seemed to be drinking in the wonderful message of a Savior who has promised He would "Come again ... receive us ... and take us to where He has been preparing an eternal place for us" (John 14:1–3). When I made an altar call for any who wanted to be ready to meet Christ on that great day of His second coming, every hand was raised.

Shaul had told them about my meetings in Rezaiyeh. After my preaching, the village elders gathered around me. "Pastor Miller, will you please come to our village and preach Christ to us?" My meetings in Rezaiyeh would soon be over. It was mid-April 1970, and in May I was scheduled to furlough in my own homeland, to attend as a delegate from the Middle East Division, the 1970 World General Conference Session, held that year in Atlantic City, New Jersey. After a year's furlough, to be spent in visiting loved ones, and preaching in churches and camp meetings about the ongoing need for funds to support our world-wide mission program, I would return to my post in Beirut.

I explained all that to the Assyrian village elders, then promised them that the summer of 1971, after I returned to the MED after a year's furlough in the U.S., I would return and preach to them for three weeks. They were joyful, as was I. I hoped to turn that ancient church into a Seventh-day Adventist Church. But it was not to be.

I returned to Beirut, expecting to leave shortly for the States and furlough; however MED President Webster asked me to first go to Istanbul to meet with Manuk and the Turkish Mission staff to make plans for the coming year. Harold Sheffield, the new MED medical director who replaced Herschel Lamp, and Melvin West, of Middle East College, asked if I would make that trip by car so that I could guide them around the seven churches after the worker's meeting in Istanbul were completed.

We traveled in the medical director's car. After we passed through the Syrian-Turkish border, I warned the men that on our return trip we should definitely plan to re-cross that boarder well before dark, for the road south of the border was very narrow, with bandits often stopping cars at night and robbing those in the cars.

While I was conducting the meetings with the Turkish Mission staff, I received a cable from Elder Webster telling me that the General Conference of SDA was directing me to return to the States ASAP, for both of my parents were in the hospital, and as their only child they needed me. I aborted the staff meetings, carefully outlined a Turkish roadmap for Melvin West and Harold Sheffield to follow to see the seven churches, and I flew to Beirut to prepare the Miller family to return to the States. Melvin and Harold toured the seven churches, then proceeded back to Beirut, arriving at the Syrian boarder late at night. With little boarder traffic they quickly cleared passport and custom checks and proceeded south into Syria. They had to slow down to negotiate a hairpin curve, and in the very center of that curve were several bandits that stopped them at gunpoint. One bandit rested his gun on the window of the car and demanded, "Give us all your money."

Sheffield opened his billfold and slowly handed the bandit his money. He would pause after giving each bill, hoping the bandit would not ask for more, but the bandit always gestured for more. West had his billfold out, anticipating that shortly it would be his turn to give up his money.

Suddenly Melvin shouted, "Look up on the mountain at the bright light!" The bandits and Harold all looked up to where a bright light was coming down the mountain. The bandits fled in terror, leaving Sheffield and West to continue their journey in peace and safety.

I still remember that Assyrian village. I still remember my promise to the villagers, made in April of 1970, that I would return in 1971 and hold meetings in their church — a promise still unkept, and one I probably will never be able to keep, for which I still sorrow.

In the very center of that curve were several bandits that stopped them at gunpoint. One bandit rested his gun on the window of the car and demanded, "Give us all your money."

The years I spent in the MED are among the happiest and fulfilling years of my life.

I flew Pan Am back to Beirut where I would prepare for my permanent return from mission service, a life I still keenly miss.

Arriving home in Beirut, the Miller family hurriedly prepared to return to the States. Because of the arrangements made with the Lebanese customs authority when our household goods were finally cleared, we now had to ship all our goods back to the States. We packed, packed, and packed, placing all our belongings into a giant metal shipping container. I also completed all my departmental affairs to the best of my ability.

The MED staff gave us a farewell function. I remember R.L. Jacobs, MED secretary, in his farewell address, giving a resume of my years with the MED. As he recounted my career I began to weep, for I was full of sorrow over leaving the MED. Initially the MED officers suggested I not request a permanent return until after I assessed the needs of my parents, thus leaving a door open for me to possibly return to the mission field. At the 1970 GC session some world divisions and unions were reorganized, and the

MED and certain African countries were combined into the new Afro-Mideast Division. About a year later I received a letter from Elder Jacobs, inviting me to return to Beirut to be a departmental director of this new division. I declined the invitation, for by that time we were well-settled in the Idaho Conference, with Melody enrolled in Gem State Academy and Cindy and Valerie in our church school in Boise.

Within a few weeks we were ready to fly from Beirut to our homeland, but one important item remained: we still needed to sell our VW Wagon; it was three years old, with only 28,000 miles on it. Probably many of those miles were racked up taking me to and from the Beirut airport. There were several potential buyers for the VW, but each one ended in a no-sale, and I resigned myself to the possibility I would have to leave the car on the division compound, with the hope it would sell by the time we reached the States and needed the money to purchase a car. Finally, the day came for our departure and the VW was not sold. The Millers got into the car that was to take us to the airport when Edmund Haddad, who was the new president of Middle East College, came to see me. A few weeks earlier while he was in Amman, Jordan, his VW, same make, model, and color, was stolen. He had just received his insurance reimbursement for his stolen car and decided he would buy mine. God was good! He arranged for the sale of my VW right at the last moment I was leaving our MED compound for the airport.

In 1970 the Cold War between western nations and those in the Soviet Bloc, those communist countries wanted the good "hard currency" of western nations and were willing to give good accommodations to gain that currency. Several of us returning missionaries learned that our Beirut travel agent would sell initial tickets on the East-German airline, which would fly nonstop from Beirut to East Berlin, which was surrounded by East Germany. After flying to East Berlin, the Millers could then take a special bus into West Berlin, which was under the control of West Germany, a democracy and not under the communist regime.

From West Berlin we could then travel by air to any other western European nation we might choose. By beginning our travel on the East German airline, we would save hundreds of dollars that we could then use to travel wherever we desired in Europe.

Came the day I went to Mills to request the travel funds he had indicated he would give me as we had agreed I would make my own travel arrangements, but Mills stated he had learned how much I could save via the East German airline and that he would now give me only the amount that would cost me, thus denying me the rest of the funds I could use to make my own arrangements.

I was not at all happy over this, so I went to MED president Ted Webster, with whom I had always had a very good working relationship. I told him what Mills had originally promised and that he was now refusing to give me that amount. Webster immediately phoned Mills to come to his office, and when Mills arrived, he asked "Bob, did you tell Curtis you would give him X amount of dollars to purchase his own air tickets?"

Mills then proceeded to say, "Yes, I told him X amount, but I have since learned he would save hundreds of dollars by purchasing his own tickets, so I am now declining to give it to him."

Webster proceeded to firmly tell Mills, "Bob, if you promised Curtis that amount, I am directing you to give it to him!"

Mills gave me the amount he had initially promised.

I was now at liberty to plan my own itinerary home and purchase my own tickets. The Millers had a pleasant site-seeing journey through parts of Europe that I still wanted to see, including East and West Berlin, Paris, and Portugal.

We flew into East Berlin. It was sunset when our East German plane flew along the Yugoslavian coast and we could see the lights of the city of Dubrovnik, a place I had wanted to see, but now probably never will. We landed in East Berlin at midnight. We were each traveling with suitcases, for which we usually received help from airport porters to carry from the terminal to the bus. I was amazed that in communist East Berlin there were no airport porters to assist, so we each wrestled to carry our suitcases to the bus which took us to the lone hotel in East Berlin where the communist government would let foreigners lodge.

The next morning, we boarded a special East Berlin bus that would travel from East Berlin to West Berlin. There were very few persons on the bus, for East Berliners had to have a bona fide reason, acceptable to the communist regime, to travel between those two cities. After we boarded, an East German "Vopo" (communist volkspolizi) came down the aisle, briskly asked for our passports, which he carefully scrutinized. He then proceeded to search the bus to determine there was no one hiding in effort to sneak out of East Berlin.

The bus driver then maneuvered the bus through the famous Brandenburg Gate into West Berlin, and in so doing he had to go through the maze of anti-tank barricades. When we reached West Berlin a police officer came aboard. I held out our passports to him, which he could readily see were U.S. passports, and with a friendly smile he said, "Welcome to the free city of Berlin," and he didn't even look at our passports. This event happened several years after our U.S. president John F. Kennedy visited West Berlin, where he spoke to a large group of West Germans gathered to hear him and he thrillingly declared "Ich bin ein Berliner" — "I too am a Berliner."

We had a brief tour of West Berlin, then went to Tempelhof airport to fly to Paris. In the airport we went to a booth were travel agents helped passengers in various ways. I had no experience with hotels in Paris, so I went to that booth where a kind travel agent would help me select a hotel. Assuming I was a well-to-do American she initially found a luxury hotel, but when she quoted the price I informed her it was "too expensive." She then found a vacancy in a moderately priced hotel, which I again deemed too expensive. The lady was shocked that I would consider a much lower class of hotel but she finally found the cheapest of the cheap for us. It was located in the heart of Paris, where we had a third-floor room. The hotel was very narrow, sandwiched in the middle of the block. I will say one thing good about that hotel — it had on its ground floor a small bakery that produced the best croissants I have ever tasted.

The location of the hotel enabled us to easily walk to the sites we wanted to see: Champs-Elysées Avenue, the Eiffel Tower, Place 'd Invalids, and a delightful small sidewalk café where we had a delicious lunch.

From Paris we flew to Lisbon, Portugal. I had long wanted to visit that country, for in 1904 my great-uncle Clarence Rentfro went to Lisbon as the first SDA minister to take the advent message to that country. Before going to Lisbon, I contacted our SDA office there, which enabled us to be met at the airport by the Portuguese Union of SDA treasurer who arranged hotel accommodations and kindly guided us around Lisbon and a few other places in that country. We arrived on a Friday, and the day, Sabbath, I preached in our Lisbon Church. When I told the congregation, "My great-uncle, Clarence Rentfro, had been the first SDA minister to Portugal," an elderly lady stood up saying, "I am so glad to meet you, for Pastor Rentfro's wife, Mary, delivered me when I was born." It was heart-warming to meet that lady, who was the wife of the Portuguese Union Conference president.

The Miller's then flew from Lisbon to Washington, D.C.

But I still have that unkept promise, which I will never forget … that I would return to the Assyrian Village in Iran and preach to those still-waiting villagers.

But I still have that unkept promise, which I will never forget … that I would return to the Assyrian Village in Iran and preach to those still-waiting villagers.

TEACH Services, Inc.
PUBLISHING

CPSIA information can be obtained
at www.ICGtesting.com
Printed in the USA
JSHW030007060722
27594JS00005B/55

9 781479 614356